102905

North Yorkshire C

WILD WRITING

CW00346313

WILD WRITING GRANNY

A Memoir

MARY SHEEPSHANKS

STONE TROUGH BOOKS

To my parents
Geoffrey and Janet Nickson
and my husband Charles Sheepshanks
with great love and gratitude
for so much happiness

Reprinted February 2013

Published by Stone Trough Books
The Old Rectory, Settrington, York YO17 8NP
Printed by Joshua Horgan, Oxford

⟩

CONTENTS

ILLUSTRATIONS

Geoffrey Nickson
Janet Nickson
Granny Dobie, David, Mary, Janet Nickson, Sweetsong

David, Geoffrey, Mary
Mary and David
'Aladdin', Windsor Castle, 1943

David
An Eton wedding
Susannah, Nanny Featherstone, Belinda, William

Aunt Evelyn and Uncle Charles Sheepshanks
Charlie
Arthington

The house from the River Wharfe
The flying staircase

Mary and Charlie with his Arthington Tapestry (incomplete)

The Arthington Tapestry

Mary, publicity photograph in *The Times*, 1995, by Joan Russell
Mary's 80th birthday, Corfu

FOREWORD
by Bamber Gascoigne

'THE PAST is a foreign country: they do things differently there', as L. P. Hartley famously observed in the opening words of his novel *The Go-Between*. Similarly an autobiography written by anyone in their seventies, and therefore probably concentrating on the periods either side of half a century ago, will be like a travel book in time. And as time moves steadily onwards into another foreign country, the future, the journey back becomes ever more fascinating for new readers. Think of Flora Thompson and *Lark Rise to Candleford* or Laurie Lee and *Cider with Rosie*.

A good autobiography such as these requires a mix of several very different talents. They are a sharp eye for detail, whether relating to people, places or things; a well-stocked memory, reaching as far back as possible into childhood and recalling not so much the dry facts of experience as the impressions that then struck the writer; and, of course, a good way with words.

Mary has these qualities in abundance, and as both novelist and poet she even has two voices when it comes to the words. I discovered her skilful mix of poetry and prose as soon as I began *Wild Writing Granny*. I started as many of us do if there is a chance we might be in a book. There is no index, so I was spared the embarrassment suffered by Norman Mailer after he had been given a book by Gore Vidal—having reached the right page in the index he found in biro beside his name 'Hi Norm!' But I soon found my way to the moment I was looking for, the first occasion I had met Mary after knowing and loving her husband Charlie ever since he had been my Maths teacher at prep school. He was staying with us in Scotland and was going to give Mary, a guest in a nearby house, a lift back to London in an old banger of his. But the banger expired during his visit and my parents asked Mary to stay with us for the several days until it was mended. And it has always been a cherished conviction in our own family's autobiography that it was with us that Charlie suddenly proposed and was accepted.

That was the happy moment I was looking for, but it turns out that the family's collective memory is inaccurate. It wasn't Charlie's one and only proposal. It was his second. And under our very roof—our own romantic roof!—this new proposal suffered the same fate as the first (potential for tragedy, but it was to be third time lucky).

Turning the page, I then came across a beautiful example of Mary's ability to make an entirely convincing and appropriate gear change between prose and poetry. Page 172 ends with a simple sentence: 'A few weeks later Charlie proposed to me for the third time—and I said yes.'

Page 173 begins with a beautiful short love poem—*The Bird of My Loving (For Charlie)*. I hope and believe that this skilful transition will touch people far into the foreign country of the future as much as it touched me today.

INTRODUCTION

SCHOOLS have played a hugely important part in my life. When I walked up the aisle of Eton College Chapel in 1953 to marry Charles Sheepshanks I couldn't help wondering if I would ever be finished with terms and holidays and the process of going back to school. I was about to exchange a childhood spent in a famous public school as the daughter of a housemaster for adult life in the much smaller world of a boys' prep school as the headmaster's wife. Despite my scholastic background I never had any ambition to enter the teaching profession myself. From the age of four I intended to be a writer—though it took me another fifty-six years before I fulfilled this aspiration in a professional sense. A late developer indeed.

The writing idea had taken root when my father first read me Walter de la Mare's magical poem 'Silver' and I was bowled over by the sibilant sound of those alliterative lines and the mysterious moonlit picture they evoked. I was instantly hooked on the music of words and went round chanting the poem for days—which must have been dreadfully tiresome for everyone else. All through my childhood and adolescence I wrote poetry—mostly awful would-be clones of Tennyson or Gray's *Elegy*—though I had an unexpectedly bright flash of encouragement when I was seventeen and the *Sunday Times* published the first poem I had ever submitted to an editor—real beginner's luck. I didn't tell anyone I'd sent it and my parents were astonished to read it in the paper. However I have always been a queen of procrastination and I soon got sidetracked into doing other delightful things such as marrying, helping to run a school, salvaging a crumbling family house and best of all having children. Early authorial aspirations went into cold storage, but perhaps my novels might never have materialized without these experiences, on all of which I have drawn for both my fiction and my poetry. It took widowhood and a promise to my husband that when I was left on my own—which, sadly, we both knew was going to happen—I would try to take my dormant writing ambitions seriously.

This promise, made just before he died, turned out to be a parting gift from him because without giving that pledge, I might not have had either the courage or the perseverance to make the attempt. When my first novel was accepted for publication a couple of years later, one of my small grandsons referred to me as his 'wild writing Granny', a description I treasure.

I once heard a judge lecture on 'The Value of Evidence'. He told a cautionary tale: he'd been witness to an accident and, thinking he might be subpoenaed to give evidence, had jotted down the details which he then shoved in the glove compartment of his car. Months later, not having been called for, he came across it, and decided to test his memory—confident that all his recollections would be accurate. When he compared the two accounts he was amazed to discover how many small inaccuracies had crept in.

Bearing that story in mind I was reassured to find how accurate my recollections were, on going round, for the first time since 1939, the house at Eton where I spent my early childhood before my father took over as a housemaster in a boarding-house. The trouble with writing anything about Eton—whether it be about its long history and traditions, its ancient buildings, or the stories of its many eccentric characters—is that you may unwittingly trespass on other people's territory and risk repeating stories that have been told before. I apologise in advance for any repetition and for anything I may get wrong.

The Second World War hung across my childhood like the proverbial green baize door, separating two very different ways of life. My generation has lived through a period of enormous change, sociological and technical, in manners, morals and outlook, and since there are not so many of us left now who can cross in memory that particular divide, I have an urge to open a window and try to paint what I see before the sun goes down and the view fades. Neither I nor the story of my life are of interest in themselves and these reminiscences lay no claim to be either a 'celebrity' or a 'misery' memoir; if there is any appeal in the picture I present it will come not from me but from the people and places I have encountered and the changes that have taken place over the years. Recently I was introduced to Mark Twain's advice on writing autobiography: to start the story at no particular time and wander freely over your life. Though I have aimed for some chronological order, this advice has given me the freedom to take occasional trips to and fro across time. Perhaps a book of reminiscences is more like a potter round a garden than a progress from one place to another.

Memory is unaccountably selective and trivial moments can be as sharply defined as those black and white silhouette portraits of ancestors, while seemingly more important incidents may be hazy. I shall paint the picture as honestly as I can but contemporaries might view the same landscape from another standpoint or use a different palette with which to colour in their canvas.

Reminiscing with my brother David and trying to recall not only the Eton of our childhood, but the homes of both sets of grandparents, we discovered that whereas I could go on a mental tour of the houses they lived in and describe every room in detail, David was a deep well of information about the outdoors—especially the countryside round Cefn, the house in North Wales which belonged to our paternal grandparents and where we spent a lot of time. He remembered every variation in the lie of land or water—the rabbit warrens where his ferrets got stuck, the pools in mountain streams where trout might lurk—but could recall much less detail of the same grandparents' other house and garden in Cheshire which I loved more than he did.

We sparked each other off to dredge for long-submerged memories. The content of my bucket was often different from his, but we drew our recollections up from the same source and enjoyed sharing them, as we have enjoyed so many things together over the years.

A pilgrimage is a chance to view two separate but complementary journeys—an inner and an outer voyage—so I will let my mind roam and go backwards in time to a childhood that was, I suppose—at any rate until the war—extremely sheltered. Perhaps recollections will trigger my imagination into weaving more fiction or expressing old emotions in new verse. Poetry has been described as emotional shorthand and because it sometimes expresses things more vividly in a few words than can be achieved in whole paragraphs of prose, I have decided to include a few poems in this book—some old, some new.

Perhaps I shall encounter surprises on my retrospective journey.

Childhood

Then expectation hung upon each day
like early dew
trembling with greyhound eagerness
upon the grass.

Then we could pace the wind
or be as one with breathless summer days,
and we could hear the singing in the sky
and read the changing patterns
on the river's face.

Strong magic came in simple things:
gnarled stones or moon-smooth pebbles
feathers, leaves.
Then sticks were swords
and every tree a castle.

But oh with age the third eye
starts to close.

Halcyon Memories

Once their sharp beaks,
threaded with jewel-coloured silks,
were the needles that stitched
together the days of my childhood

joining week to week and year to year
as they wove a repeating pattern; darting
through a supply of minutes that seemed, then,
as plentiful as our nursery bag of tiddlywinks.

They silvered the river's edge with minnows
and daydreams; embroidered willow wands
where the Thames mirrors the mystic whiteness of swans
and reflects a castle in its dungeon depths.

Sighting Kingfishers is a rare treat now
and those shiny minutes, once flipped into the pot
with such casual prodigality, are in short supply
– but I can still unroll my halcyon tapestry.

1

BEGINNINGS

I was born and brought up at Eton where my father, Geoffrey Nickson, later to become a much loved housemaster, arrived straight from university as a junior assistant master.

From my earliest days, my world was dominated by the streams of black-uniformed figures of beaks and boys pouring out of numerous doorways, milling about in the ancient, cobbled School Yard, striding down the street or strolling—always chatting—through the labyrinthine lanes and passageways which connect the various scholastic buildings to the boarding houses scattered randomly around. Etonians are great walkers and talkers. The taller boys would be wearing the Etonians' distinctive tailcoats and striped trousers, the smaller boys—those under five foot one—would be in 'bum-freezers', the short Eton jackets which have long since been abolished. King's Scholars, or 'tugs' wore gowns over their uniform. Member's of 'Pop', the Eton Society, a self-elected body of school prefects, swaggered about in checked, sponge-bag trousers and fancy waistcoats, as indeed they still do. In my pre-war childhood boys also wore top hats and carried umbrellas.

The Reverend Dr Cyril Alington, then headmaster of Eton, had also been my father's own boyhood headmaster at Shrewsbury. He subsequently 'headhunted' Pa from Cambridge, where he got a First, to join the staff at Eton to teach classics, together with Jack Peterson, another brilliant classicist and Pa's lifelong friend. C.A.A., as he was generally known, was an immensely distinguished charmer, equally famous for his looks, his books and the well-loved and elegantly worded hymns he had written. He was a noted man of letters and a spellbinding preacher whose allegorical sermons, published as *Fables and Fancies* and *More Eton Fables* are still used by discerning clergymen. My father, a hero-worshipper by nature, loved and revered him, as did many among his staff and pupils—but charismatic clergymen are prone to blisters on their Achilles' heels. When the ordinary selfishness and vanity to which all humans are prone prevent them from measuring up to the standards of their exhortations from the pulpit, congregations can feel critical. Cyril Alington was not without his detractors and to those irreverent Etonians who were not among his fans he was known as Creeping Christ or Slippery Jesus—but my father would never hear a word against him. His wife Hester, a Lyttelton before she married, was greatly beloved and the stories of her many imaginative kindnesses—and splendid eccentricities—were legion. My mother was especially fond of her and had been grateful for her support when she first came to Eton as a shy young wife in 1927. My parents often dined and then played bridge with the Alingtons, an ordeal which my mother found nerve-wracking as Cyril was neither patient nor a good loser. Hester Alington would look gloomily at an unpromising hand and say 'Oh Cyril! I've got that Yarmouth or Scarborough or whatever you call it, again.'

Both my parents came from Cheshire. My mother, Janet Dobie, belonged to a predominantly medical family who lived in Chester, where her father practised as both a surgeon and a GP, and my father's family lived ten miles away on the outskirts of what was then the small rural village of Neston, on the Wirral Peninsula, from where my Nickson grandfather commuted into Liverpool to run the family business, originally concerned with the importing and canning of ox tongues, which went under the trade name of Gold Dish.

The two families had first met when their sons went to prep school together—after which my father and his elder brother were sent to Shrewsbury while my mother's brother followed Dobie family tradition and went to Marlborough. A shared passion for sport, fishing in particular, kept the boys' friendship alive after they ceased to be at school together and at some stage my Nickson grandmother got up a party for the local Hunt Ball, invited my mother to join it, and my parents foxtrotted their way into a two year engagement—which was not apparently at all what my grandmother had had in mind. Though they were both in their mid-twenties at the time of their wedding in Chester Cathedral, my father was considered very young to be married and Cyril Alington firmly told him that he must continue to dine out 'bachelor' without my mother, if so invited, by any of the band of formidable bachelor housemasters, some of whom entertained on a lavish scale. I suppose I remember the Alingtons more from their subsequent visits to Eton after they had moved north when Cyril Alington became Dean of Durham, than when they ruled Eton from the Headmaster's Lodgings in the Cloisters. It was Claude and Gillian Elliott, who succeeded the Alingtons, who were there throughout most of my childhood.

My parents had started their married life in half a house—number 117 A—in Eton High Street, where both my older brother David and I were born, but with my arrival it had become too small for us and when David was three years old and I was eighteen months we moved to Baldwin's End Cottage. Although I was so young I have a vivid recollection of our arrival at our new home and my astonishment at how enormous the new upstairs nursery seemed as David and I pedalled along on our bottoms, shrieking with laughter and sitting on yellow dusters to help Mrs Merrydew, my mother's daily help, to polish the green linoleum floor.

Baldwin's End Cottage was a gabled, wisteria-covered, higgledy-piggledy house of great charm and as a junior master my father was fortunate to be allocated such a plum house. Perhaps this had something to do with the great affection and esteem in which Cyril Alington held him. The house had some unusual features. One of these was a narrow, half-timbered room with mullion windows on each side which was built across the top of an ancient stone archway. This room didn't lead anywhere itself but had, I think, originally been the link between the existing building and a boys' house, Baldwin's End, which was burnt down in 1903 and later demolished. Two boys were tragically killed in that awful fire, unable to leap to safety because they were trapped by the bars across the windows which had presumably been put there to prevent anyone climbing out at night. We called this archway room 'The Fishing-Room' because my father's fishing impedimenta was kept in it, the rods hung horizontally on pegs along one side. On one of the lead-surrounded windowpanes he once inscribed two verses of a poem with a glass engraver's diamond pen. They are still there, though I have been unable to trace their origin. I imagine they refer to a sundial but I wish I knew who the author was and why the words were significant to my father. They are written in his unmistakable, neat, forward-sloping hand and dated March 1936.

> Slow on your dial the shadows creep
> So many hours for food and sleep
> So many hours till study tire
> So many hours for heart's desire.
>
> These suns and moons shall memory save
> Mirrors bright for the magic cave
> Wherein may steadfast eyes behold
> A self that groweth never old.[1]

The views from our attic bedrooms in Baldwin's End Cottage could hardly have been more calculated to fire the imagination of a child. Out of one window we looked towards the River Thames across the big water meadow known as Fellows' Eyot, where my brother's godmother, Grizel Hartley, grazed her horses—swishing their tails, munching buttercups and demanding titbits—and where later we kept our own wicked, wall-eyed Shetland pony Mickey Mouse. From this window we could also see Windsor Castle which appeared to float romantically above the trees in all its imposing splendour. We could clearly see the flagpole on the Round Tower which told us if the King and Queen were in residence, depending on whether the Union Jack or the Royal Standard was flying. From the other window we could see the back of College Chapel and look down into the old Brewhouse Yard, where there is now a museum but which then housed the Choir School (which no longer exists) where choristers for College Chapel were taught. Beyond and through an archway lay School Yard, the very heart of Eton.

---

[1] From Robert Bridges's 'Founder's Day. A Secular Ode on the Ninth Jubilee of Eton College.' Many thanks to Google.

King Henry VIth's statue in bronze, made in 1720 by Francis Bird who studied under Grinling Gibbons and worked for Wren, stands in the middle of School Yard surrounded by Eton's oldest buildings and is one of Eton's many important treasures. There is something touching about the idea of the intellectually inclined, if unbalanced, young man founding this great school for seventy indigent scholars in 1440 when he was only nineteen years old himself. He would surely have been happier—and certainly safer—if he could have spent his own days in an academic institution instead of becoming a player in a political game and ending up murdered in the Tower of London. His statue depicts him in Garter robes, holding orb and sceptre, but in real life he must always have felt extremely uncertain of his sovereignty. I have a fondness for pious Henry—after his death he was regarded by many as a saint and various miracles were attributed to him, especially cures for migraine. Until the Reformation, his hat was apparently kept by his tomb at Windsor where headache sufferers could drop in and try it on to invoke Henry's healing powers, which must be one of the few remedies I haven't tried myself for this boring and incapacitating complaint. History does not relate what eventually happened to the hat.

I was once taken up on the roof of College Chapel during one of the pea soup fogs that were a hazard of living in the Thames Valley in those days; from this high viewpoint Henry's head popped up above the sulphurous low-lying cloud like the head of John the Baptist being presented by Salome on a vast gold platter.

On a recent visit to Eton I was struck by the King's immaculate appearance. In my childhood I remember him as rather scruffy, his robes dingy and his head daubed with white splodges—not anointed with oil by an Archbishop as befits a king, but by the pigeons which circled above him. Occasionally, as a special treat, my mother would take me to feed these pigeons from a yellow enamel dish, kept especially in the kitchen for this purpose. In my memory it is a summer morning before breakfast and shafts of sunlight slant across School Yard, silvering the Portland stone of the chapel and the flagstones of the paths which criss-cross the cobbled areas, and deepening the rose-coloured brick of the Tudor buildings which form a quadrangle round

King Henry. As I chucked stale bread about, there would be a thrilling whirr of wings overhead before the pigeons landed at my feet to strut about and peck up the crumbs I scattered. I fancied myself as a bird-charmer of rare ability—a sort of cross between Papageno from *The Magic Flute* and Dickon in *The Secret Garden* with a dash of St Francis of Assisi thrown in.

On such a morning, my brother would no doubt have been enjoying a treat too: fishing for chub with my father in a backwater of the Thames off Luxmoore's Garden, the island off Fellows' Eyot from which H. E. Luxmoore, a famous past Eton housemaster, created an enchanting garden from a wilderness. Pa and David were probably using a bag of cherries for bait, removing the stone and concealing a hook in the hollow. Chub apparently have a surprising penchant for cherries, giving a sinister truth to the expression if they were to be described as being hooked on cherries. It would have been a 'non dies'[2]—one of the days when my father had no 7.30 a.m. 'Early School', for boys and beaks[3] started the learning and teaching process on an empty stomach then. If a master were to be fifteen minutes late for any lesson the boys were allowed to leave and it was declared a 'run'. Hopes would start to rise after five minutes had gone by—any beak who turned up after ten minutes was very unpopular. I imagine my conscientious father must have been a disappointment in this respect as I doubt if his division ever got any 'runs' out of him.

Living as we did so close to the Thames, the river played an important part in our lives: we watched boys rowing on it; we paddled in its shingled shallows collecting minnows and tadpoles in jam jars of water and watched stately swans glide past us, their powerfully efficient webbed black paddles propelling them along, apparently effortlessly, but at considerable speed; kingfishers skimmed up river like electric darts, or perched motionless, minnow-spotting, on the willows which lined its banks while overhanging branches trailed their green fingers in darker green water.

---

[2] Whole holiday on major saints' days.
[3] Eton word for masters.

My Eton childhood has given me a 'thing' about kingfishers and they are my lucky omen to this day. When I see one I have an illuminated moment—but this is not, alas, such a common happening now. A good place for sighting them was off the furthest point in Luxmoore's Garden, beyond the orchard, where we could sometimes watch them flying in and out of the holes in the sandbank at the river's edge, feeding their young—as dedicated to fishing as my father and brother.

Baldwin's End Cottage had its own small garden across the lane from our back door, carved out of a bit of Fellows' Eyot. The previous occupant of the house, Michael Bland, had written a charming book called 'Birds in an Eton Garden' and from him we inherited lots of nesting boxes which delighted my ornithologically-minded mother and were a great source of interest to us all. One of the boxes was inside the tool-shed, and there were always blue tits nesting there in the spring, popping in and out of the little round hole in the shed wall that acted as their front door. The boxes had lids on top so we could stand on tiptoe to monitor the progress of eggs to babies, and babies to fledglings. Feeding fledgling blue tits was a delightful occupation to us though I doubt if the parent birds appreciated our efforts to help them—like watching some well-meaning neighbour stuff one's children with junk food perhaps.

In our garden was a huge mulberry tree. Its branches swept the ground and made wonderful steeds for us to ride on, heaving up and down in a most satisfactory way as we galloped off on imaginary adventures. It was our secret hideout, our headquarters, our wonderfully adaptable camp or castle. Its leaves, which hid us from prying eyes, were delectable to the silkworms David kept—dreary pets that shrouded themselves in cobwebs and never showed any response—and no silk either as far as I could see. The only snag about this favourite haunt was that the purple fruit could stain clothes indelibly, and this was not only far from popular, but provided cast-iron evidence of disobedience if, like Tom Kitten, we had been dressed in our best and told not to get into mischief. All the best fairy stories have elements of forbidden fruit in them, and this risk added to the enchantment of the tree.

Beside the mulberry was our sandpit. We once had a ceremonial funeral there, and tearfully buried our dead canary in a cardboard shoe box. Some weeks later, happily making pies and castles on my own, I accidentally dug it up and looked inside the soggy coffin. The horror of that moment is sharply imprinted on my mind—a reminder of how reality penetrates even the most protected childhood. I don't know if I told anyone about the incident—facts often being too painful for a child to put into words—but it must have had a bearing on the fear of death that haunted me throughout my childhood and cast dark uncertainties across an otherwise sunny existence.

This fear was mixed up in my mind with a terrifying physical feeling which sometimes overtook me as I was about to go to sleep at night. It started in my hands and rapidly spread all over. I felt as if I was swelling up like a balloon and was about to burst out of the shell of my body. As I seemed to expand, all the familiar things in the room grew smaller and more distant as I was rushed away from them at great speed; then I would 'come back'—in the nick of time as it were—and scream the house down. I called it 'feeling big' but I could never explain this nightmare sensation to grown-ups. I eventually grew out of it and indeed had almost forgotten about it until I became seriously ill, soon after I was married. At the height of my sickness this old affliction returned and continued to haunt me again whenever I was really unwell or very over-tired, though as an adult I could consciously control the feeling to some extent. I am still occasionally aware of it.

I was a timorous child. Terrible unknown creatures lived under my bed—as I knelt to say my prayers there was always the possibility of fingers groping towards my knees. Shadows menaced and it was a toss-up as to which was the more terrifying—total darkness or flickering half-light; heart-stopping silence or the creaking of floorboards. My mother had a brisk way with ogres under beds and could flush them out in a twink, though they had a way of returning the moment she had gone. My father, temperamentally better equipped to identify with imaginative terrors, was in practice not nearly such an effective operator. If called on to help he would try to reason with me and explain away my fears; but a small child's demons don't respond well to intellectual discussions: they just need banishing.

The terrors of childhood are a dark and fascinating territory which we do not really understand. Certainly I was afraid of falling asleep, fought to keep consciousness and often dreaded bed-time. I became convinced I would die young like Little Eva in Harriet Beecher Stowe's famous anti-slavery novel *Uncle Tom's Cabin*—whose story lent credence to my fear of early demise. Later there would be more justifiable panic caused by air-raids at night. No one could have been more surrounded with love and security than I was from my earliest childhood, but it still didn't save me from night terrors. Perhaps this helped set the pattern of a life-long battle with insomnia.

From an early age I adored my father. If my mother was the nourishing bread and butter of our lives, my father was certainly the cake. He had an off-beat sense of humour, and great wit and charm. He told us wonderful stories about two characters called Farmer David and Farmer Muddleduck. Farmer David was the hero who always got everything right and ultimately triumphed. He was of course meant to represent my brother who had agricultural leanings at the time and spent much time playing with the carved wooden animals of his toy farm; Farmer Muddleduck, on the other hand, tried to copy Farmer David but got everything wrong and chaos reigned round him. My father was horrified, years later, to discover, that I had identified myself with this inept bungler. I was equally surprised—and even slightly miffed—to learn that he had not intended me to feature in these gripping sagas at all. Anyway my supposed fool's role in no way detracted from my enjoyment of the stories at the time; I knew myself to be an impractical daydreamer so I had fellow feelings for Muddleduck; like him, I thought of my older brother David as something of a hero who was better than me at almost everything we did in our childhood, though I had one useful weapon: I possessed a quicker and a sharper tongue, which I could occasionally employ to deadly effect if I needed to defend myself. He won all competitive games and I was content for him to do so—it made him much more agreeable to live with—but my forked tongue provided an essential balance of power and we were boon companions: David was my protector; I was his camp follower. We were and are devoted to each other.

Although we had our own garden at Baldwin's End, we also spent a lot of time in Luxmoore's Garden. Sometimes my mother and Nanny would carry our Noah's Ark and the farmyard animals over there and we set them out in the summer house overlooking the lawn. The wooden bridge to Luxmoore's, which was only a stone's throw from our garden gate, was a steep, pointed affair considerably to the right of the present bridge and it brought you out in front of the arched rose pergola.

Turn right and you reached a plank across the stream which led to another island where there were two masters' gardens—one assigned to the Horton family, our next door neighbours at Baldwin's Shore. (The family were later to become Horton-Fawkes when George Horton inherited Farnley Hall, the house in Yorkshire where Turner stayed when he painted many of his Wharfedale watercolours.) It was perilous crossing the swaying planks high above the stream. I thought it exciting until Margaret Horton, my particular friend, fell off it into the water below and broke her arm. I was rather envious of the attention this brought her and longed for a greenstick fracture myself—it sounded so romantic—but it didn't make me so keen to brave the bridge and go to play in their garden any more.

Turn left after the rose arch and you came to a bronze statue of St Francis holding a dove, which I specially loved. Nanny said if you touched his foot you got a blessing, but my mother was sniffy about such a superstitious notion. I put it to the test many times but can't say the results were very noticeable.

The lord of Luxmoore's Garden in David's and my eyes was Stroud the gardener. He habitually wore a green baize apron and a tall brown trilby hat—I was shocked and felt uncomfortable to see him without his hat once: it seemed positively indecent. He had a luxuriantly bushy moustache, as carefully trained and tended as his shrub roses. He used to take us into his rustic style thatched garden shed with lattice windows—the perfect prototype for the witch's cottage in *Hansel and Gretel*—where he kept his tools and stored apples. The smell of the apples was intoxicating and he picked out the best ones to give us whenever he saw us, polishing them on his apron until they gleamed.

'That'll make your hair curl' he said to me—but it never did.

I had a problem with hair. David had a mop of curls, inherited from my mother who'd had equally riotous curls in her childhood and as a young woman had pretty, wavy, auburn hair cut in a fashionable shingle. After admiring David's crowning glory with due reverence Nanny's friends used to look at me sadly and shake their heads: 'Shame the little girl hasn't got THE HAIR,' they would say. Nanny had done her best to remedy this neglect on Nature's part and massaged my head from babyhood with a gooey product called Nestol. Practically guaranteed, according to its makers, to put a kink in the straightest locks, Nestol met its Waterloo with me. Until I had my first alarmingly frizzy perm aged sixteen my hair remained obdurately straight. I felt I had failed poor Nanny.

My father had stories about the great rivalry there had once been between H. E. Luxmoore, founder of the garden, and his contemporary beak, vast Mr Broadbent. Apparently they both prided themselves on their encyclopaedic knowledge of saints' days and the Church calendar and loved to try to catch each other out.

'Morning Luxmoore,' Mr Broadbent is supposed to have greeted his colleague one day.

'I suppose you're aware that today is St Crispin's Day?' 'Morning Broadbent. Yes, of course—naturally I'm aware of it.'

'Oh you are, are you?' said Mr Broadbent, 'Well, it isn't!'

I didn't know Mr Broadbent, but I can just remember statuesque Mrs Broadbent, a powerful old lady, who once stuck her alarming face inside the hood of my pram to inspect me at close quarters. I nearly died of shock.

Another highlight of those early years of living by the river was to watch the cavalcade of Household Cavalry that rode down from Windsor each summer in all their jingling glamour to swim their young horses across the Thames from Fellows' Eyot to the opposite bank. We would hear the exciting clip-clopping noise below the nursery window and look down enthralled as the gleaming horses trotted by, two by two, to turn into the meadow by the gate just up the lane. We would rush downstairs and out of our back door to follow them to the water's edge where thrilling tussles would ensue between riders and horses. Not surprisingly some of the horses were terrified of entering the wide, strongly-flowing river and reared up and pawed the air, plunging about on the bank and refusing to go in, though a few, presumably experienced old stagers brought along to encourage the novices, would go straight into the water and head for the far side. The minute the horses were out of their depth and well and truly swimming, the riders slid off their backs, put an arm over their necks and swam, fully clothed, beside them. I adored this event, which like so many other things stopped with the war.

During February there was the excitement of floods which would suddenly sweep across Fellows' Eyot from the swelling Thames to come ominously close to our back door. College Chapel itself was built thirteen feet above ground level to protect it from floods. David and I longed for the waters to sweep through our house and imagined ourselves escaping by boat. A line was carved quite high up on the wall of the house to mark the spot where the water had once reached in the last century. It was always a thrill if we heard that the planks for the flood walks were being attached to the special posts for this purpose along the Eton Wick road to make a footpath well above the pavement if water swirled across the road, and we would beg to go this way for our daily walk. The odour of rotting vegetation when the waters receded and the Thames sank back exhausted into its own bed, was not so pleasant: Rupert Brooke immortalized this smell in 'Granchester' as the *'thrilling-sweet and rotten, Unforgettable unforgotten / River smell'*. To us it foretold the first snowdrops and aconites, catkins, pussy willow and eventually the appearance of the fluffy grey cygnets which peered out from under the wings of their elegant white parents in nests by the river. While admiring the swans from a discreet distance, I was also wary of them. They could advance threateningly, necks stretched out like snakes and great wings spread. Nanny said a single beat of a swan's wing could break your arm, and I didn't doubt her.

In summer, on the evening of the famous Fourth of June, the great social event in the school calendar, the whole of Eton and its guests gathered on Fellows' Eyot (retrospectively partying for King George the Third's birthday) to watch fireworks let off on the opposite bank as darkness fell. I remember being taken from my bed, wrapped in a shawl, and carried through the cloisters—eerie with shadows—to the Headmaster's house so that I could watch these magic explosions in the sky from the drawing room windows of Claude and Gillian Elliott, successors to the Alingtons. Memories of the Fourth of June, pre-war, are a brilliant kaleidoscope of impressions: acres of newly mown-grass; immaculate white cricket flannels; flower barrows everywhere selling carnations—the only day that boys other than members of Pop were allowed to wear flowers in their buttonholes; the chatter of sophisticated small talk and the clink of champagne glasses from the lunch parties which were then held in the various boys' houses; the scent of expensive cigars wafting from Eton gardens; bands playing; Wet Bobs parading in fancy dress, their straw boaters rampant with flowers. There were strawberries and cream; glamorous clothes—and for me my best smocked dress and a wreath of daisies and forget-me-nots round my hat.

I sometimes wonder what my mother did all day during our early Eton years—once the war started and my father had become a housemaster and she suddenly had a household of fifty to cater for, it was a very different matter. No one could have worked harder or been more indomitable then.

Ideas of what constitutes wealth are relative: compared with many people we must have been affluent, but in the privileged setting in which we lived and by the standards of the time, my parents were considered to be hard-up compared to many of their friends—yet we had a cook, a nanny and part time daily help. For a short while, unbelievably, we even had a fourteen-year old nursery maid as well, who was referred to by the Dickensian sounding name of 'Tiny-Wee-Jess'.

My practical mother, domesticated and deeply involved with her family, was not sociable by nature so I can't think my parents entertained much; unlike some of her fellow Eton wives, my mother had no particular hobbies of her own. She was not artistic like Isla Gladstone nor a classical scholar like Gillian Wilkinson; did not converse in French with the VIth Form boys or get involved with the music of the school like Sylvia Horton; she did not entertain lavishly, ride, sail, and teach algebra at the Choir School like beloved Grizel Hartley, our near neighbour and a star in all our firmaments; nor, as far as I know, did she do any voluntary work. She may not have been academic, but my mother was bright and competent and all her life had an abundant supply of energy so it would have been totally out of character for her to be idle; she was a constantly warm and loving presence in our lives—but with so much help in a not very large house, what did she actually DO?

I can only think it was an extreme case of Parkinson's Law. Certainly after breakfast each day she went into the kitchen to see the cook and discuss our meals.

Our cook, Amy, had the red cheeks and black hair of a Russian Doll. She had much the same figure too—solid all the way down—so that one felt she might have a series of wooden replicas, ever diminishing in size, stored away inside her. I don't think she can have been a very good cook. My father liked to tell the story of the curious savoury Amy once served up for his dinner when my mother was away. Too courteous a man to risk hurting Amy's feelings by leaving unpalatable food on his plate, Pa had dutifully chomped his way through six extraordinarily tough and tasteless strips of black leather on toast. When questioned about this dish afterwards by my mother, Amy said: 'It was those hare's ears, Ma'am. I couldn't find it in the cook book so I just fried 'em up.' Always a passionate fisherman who tied his own flies, Pa used the fur from hare's ears for making the body—or 'dubbing'—of a particular kind of trout-fly and my mother had obligingly ordered three pairs for him from Mac Fisheries, the shop in Eton High Street which sold game as well as fish. My father also sometimes tied a fly known as a Tup's Indispensable (said to have been invented by an Anglican clergyman called The Reverend Canon Austin) for which the 'dubbing' was made from the hair off a ram's testicles. History does not relate whether Amy ever attempted to cook that particular delicacy for my father.

I narrowly escaped being named Olive Nymph after a trout fly, and Pa never lived down an entry—spotted by Grizel Hartley—in his meticulously kept fishing diary which read: 'Beautiful day. Experimented with a Nymph.'

'Oh darling,' said Grizel, 'how wonderfully exciting for you!'

Scents are notoriously evocative, and if I ever get a whiff of the clove-like smell of that variety of dianthus called Mrs Sinkins—which are actually white, though they are always mysteriously referred to as 'pinks'—it vividly brings back my childhood because they grew in abundance in many of the masters' gardens. I was told that the original Mrs Sinkins was the wife of the stationmaster at Slough, but I've been unable to discover if this is true. I can never smell newly mown grass without being transported back to afternoons spent under the chestnut trees in the Playing Fields. Circular iron seats surrounded the massive trunks, and there, on hot summer afternoons, uniformed nannies and their small charges congregated, like swallows on telegraph wires, to chitter-chatter to each other.

Once when I was very small, and deeply huffed about something, I decided to run away. That'll teach everyone, I thought: they'll be sorry when I've gone. I got as far as the next chestnut tree but two, behind which I lingered expectantly, waiting to watch the search parties set out to look for me. Alas for my ego! The nannies had more interesting things to discuss than my umbrage level. No one appeared to notice my absence at all, which not only put my importance in true perspective but switched my timorous view of life back into overdrive again so that eventually I had to make a pusillanimous return. At least the lack of interest allowed me to saunter sulkily back without loss of face, scuffing the dusty earth under the trees with the toe of my sandal and deliberately dirtying my white socks.

I can hear in memory the click of bat on ball in the summer half, and blood-curdling shouts reverberating through open windows of 'Boy---y-y-y-up!' as the elite yelled for fags to run errands for them; this would be followed by a thunderous pounding of feet on uncarpeted stairs as the lower boys rushed to the summons—the last to arrive got lumbered with the job. Fagging was abolished during the 1970s but it was taken for granted then. I can hear again the tremendous swell of male voices bellowing out the Eton Boating Song—surely one of the best quick waltzes ever written—at the school concert. And I hear bells. Always in my early childhood there was the ring of bells. We lived within sound of the school clock on Lupton's Tower, like a regular heartbeat of the school, always there but hardly noticed; we heard the bells of both College Chapel and Lower Chapel and at Baldwin's End we could also hear the bells of Windsor, their different notes and chimes floating down the hill and drifting over the river. It was a magic place for a small child to live— at any rate before the war

After war broke out bells were silenced throughout the country, only to be tolled as a signal of enemy invasion—though it still thrills me to remember the joyful peals which rang out after peace was declared. I remember less happy sounds too. The wailing of a siren gives me a lurch in the stomach to this day; the noise of anti-aircraft guns, and indeed of bombs falling, made for nights full of dread. I can still remember the dream I was having when I was woken by incendiary bombs falling all round our house—one landed in our garden and another a couple of yards outside my bedroom window.

When they were little, two of my grandsons were impressed to be told that I'd actually been *blitzed* as a child and it gave me great kudos in their eyes—though they were subsequently disappointed to discover I couldn't give them a first-hand account of the Great Fire and the Great Plague.

Moorland Song

For David, with love

Wind through the heather sings me a song
of mountains and moorland where freedom is strong
—where mists round the fir trees drape curtains of sleep
and tear-stained with water, rock faces weep.

Breeze in the bracken murmurs a rhyme
of city-free spaces uncloistered as time
where chimes from the harebells wild honey bees ring,
and crooning and droning, a cradle song sing.

Pipits are piping: they flute me a chant
of cloud patterned hill tops with sunlight aslant
on weathered grey boulders where lichens have grown
a rusty green tracery printed on stone.

The wind and the wildness tell me a tale
to heal me and help me if courage should fail;
oh blessing of beauty—my heart must belong
where the wind in the heather blows me a song.

Swing-Song

A chant for children

Bird-singing children chant to and fro
'Swing me over the apple tree, Joe'.
Buckets of laughter, pockets of hope
wonderland wings with a swing on a rope.

Straighten your legs, then bend your knees
Sail off with swallows over the trees:
to and fro, to and fro:
'Push me harder!' 'Over you go!'

Feet in the air and head in the grass
daisies and dandelions swishing past;
flowers for a hat and sky for a shoe
skim with the dragonflies into the blue.

'Don't stop pushing - I've just begun -
swing me higher into the sun!'
Over the branches - jump if you dare
into your daydreams and disappear.

2

NURSERY DAYS

IN all my earliest memories, in the background of our lives—but in sharp focus—is Nanny: diminutive, loving, brisk and totally secure. She had a lump on her left cheek the size of a walnut which in no way impaired her beauty in my eyes though no doubt nowadays it would have been whipped out for health or cosmetic reasons. Her hair was brownish, beginning to go grey, crimped into waves which ran across her head like corrugated cardboard, and ended in a roll at the back which required crinkly hairpins to keep it in order. These were called 'invisible pins' which was a misnomer.

Nanny had been a nursery maid to my mother and her elder brother John, before becoming nanny to their much younger sister, Ruth. Her real name was Helena Bailey.

Nanny's bedroom at Baldwin's End Cottage opened out of mine and the comforting knowledge of her presence held the terrors of darkness at bay. At night she tied up her hair under a brown net made of a shiny, silky kind of thread—such as might nowadays enclose a bag of lemons at the supermarket; she dressed and undressed beneath her nightdress with many contortions of elbow and knee which made curious bulges in the tent-like garment. Nanny's movements were always quick and darting so it was rather like watching someone taking part in a stationary sack race, except that the sack went up to her chin. The first glimpse we had of her in the morning, after emerging from this voluminous tent, was wearing a green Ceylonese petticoat before she donned her crackly uniform dress (also green) and a bibbed white apron.

On her day off she looked disconcertingly different in her going-out clothes—a floral dress, lace-up shoes with two inch heels to 'lend' her height and a dab of lavender water behind her ears in case she unexpectedly met Mr Right. She never did.

Nanny was full of those time-honoured sayings which have been repeated down generations like a nursery litany, often puzzling, but reassuring because of their familiarity. Nanny couldn't run because she had a bone in her leg; she was as old as her skin and a little bit older than her teeth—a good deal older than her teeth actually, which fascinatingly, she could take out.

If we hurt ourselves she would say: 'Nanny'll kiss it better, darling' and it frequently worked—a good example of faith healing and the soothing power of touch. She said: 'Eat up your nice porridge—it'll stick to your ribs,' though why this should have been an incentive, I can't imagine. On the other hand, over-enthusiastic gobbling might merit 'Leave the pattern on the plate, please.' She reminded us sharply, 'What's the magic word?' when we omitted our pleases and thank-yous and asked 'Where's Mr Manners gone this afternoon?' She often warned me: 'If you pull that silly face and the wind changes you'll stay like that for ever,' and sulks or tantrums were greeted disapprovingly with 'My word! Somebody got out of bed the wrong side this morning!' At the end of the day she said: 'Spit-spot up those stairs, then it's Shadrak, Meshak and To-Bed-You-Go!'

David and I mostly had our meals in the nursery with Nanny and though my mother quite often joined us for lunch, our parents usually ate in the tiny dining room downstairs. We sat at a gate-legged oak table by the window with the view of Windsor Castle. There was no easily wiped Formica in those days so spills were a disgrace which shamingly marked a clean white table cloth. David and I were great spillers. From whom we inherited the clumsiness which still afflicts us both I don't know—certainly not from either of our parents. Recently after some act of domestic disaster on my part someone said to me: 'It's not *really* that you're clumsy—you're just terribly over-optimistic.' Balm to my feelings! Our food had to be carried up the steep stairs on trays, and afterwards Nanny or Tiny-Wee-Jess washed up in a little cupboard-of-a-room with a sink in it, further along the passage which led past my parents' bedroom to the 'fishing-room' over the arch.

34

Sometimes we had dining room tea—a slice of thin cut white bread and butter first, then sponge fingers, or chocolate fingers and buff sugar biscuits with white animal pictures on them, called Playmate Biscuits; these were put face down on the plate, so that we could pick them up picture-side down, and hold them unseen against our eye, trace the animal shape with a finger and guess what it was. I was very good at this game, but often accused of cheating, a nursery injustice which bit deep into my soul.

Our social life was divided between other Eton children, offspring of my father's colleagues, and Nanny's personal friends. I found the latter far more interesting.

Top of the list in attraction were Mr and Mrs Butler who lived in Upper Club Lodge by the entrance to the Playing Fields off the Slough Road. Mr Butler, known as The Bluebottle on account of the uniform he wore of blue frock coat with silver buttons, matching trousers and a blue peaked cap like a chauffeur's, was the park-keeper of the Playing Fields—this was a separate, though possibly over-lapping, job from that of Mr Bowles who was the head groundsman. Mr Butler had lost an arm in the First World War—always referred to in my childhood as The Great War—and in the mornings as he bicycled round his domain, he was dressed in an ordinary tweed cap and old tweed jacket with the empty sleeve tucked into his left-hand pocket. In the afternoons he sported an artificial arm and therein lay his fascination for me. When not in use, the spare arm, complete with hand in a glossy brown leather glove, was kept on top of the row of boys' washbasins in the Upper Club cricket pavilion attached to his cottage. The stump of his left arm ended with a metal plate which had a hole in the middle and into this the false arm was fixed by something resembling the stopper of a hot water bottle. As a special treat I was sometimes allowed to screw the arm in for him before Mrs Butler, a gargantuan lady-in-waiting, eased him into his coat. He then strode off to parade round the Playing Fields on foot carrying a matching leather glove in his real hand. I doubt if other Eton children enjoyed this singular privilege for which we were indebted to Nanny's friendship with Mrs Butler.

I was deeply in love with The Bluebottle and thought him a figure of great glamour. My father's teaching uniform of black suit, white piqué bow-tie and stick-up collar seemed dingy by comparison, though mortar board and gown perked things up a bit and were good for dressing up.

The Butlers had a son called Our Alby about whom Nanny and Mrs Butler held discussions in lowered voices. 'What's wrong with Our Alby?' I asked Nanny, and she crimped her mouth up and said mysteriously that he was *unsatisfactory*. I didn't fully understand what that meant but I adored long words. An artificial arm and an unsatisfactory son—lucky Butlers!

Next on our list of favourites were the Merrydews. Mrs Merrydew— she of my floor-polishing memory—was a bright little winter apple of a woman who worked for my mother for years and whom we dearly loved. The Merrydews lived in a row of cottages down the Eton Wick Road and tea with them was a treat. Garden ornaments abounded: gnomes lurked everywhere and a metal one bobbed up and down in the most satisfactory way when the wind blew and caused him to fish, jerkily, in the small round pond in the back yard. Mr Merrydew who had been an odd-job man - the Odd Man in Eton parlance - to a previous housemaster, was now retired. My mother was disparaging about Merrydew as she called him. She thought him slovenly—another word I liked the sound of—but to us he was a figure of distinction. Nanny said his wife had a hard time with him; I think this was due to ill-health by the time we knew him, though Nanny said he'd been 'a bit of a one for the ladies' in his day—whatever that meant. He wore carpet slippers and an old cardigan over a vest, and his vast white moustache was stained yellow in the middle from nicotine. His greatest attraction to us came from his tame birds.

There was a handsome but vicious magpie who bounced athletically from perch to perch in his cage as though he was on a pogo stick, and sat on Mr Merrydew's shoulder if let out. We were warned not to go too near, and certainly his beak looked wickedly threatening. There were several small finches in cages and a dull pigeon called Percy who mostly lived on the roof but who would flop down and devour corn if Mr Merrydew whistled for him. Percy was much less glamorous than his whirling, wheeling relations in School Yard, and had the generally dowdy, moulting appearance of a bird that had gone down in its world—a bit like its owner. The star of the collection was undoubtedly Tocca, the jay, who could imitate his owner's whistle and bring the dim Percy down with false hopes of food. Mr Merrydew had rescued Tocca as a fledgling, and taught him to talk. We never tired of hearing him say 'ello, ello ello' and 'Noice boy Tocca, pretty boy, good *fellow*,' in Mr Merrydew's rich Berkshire accent. Tocca could apparently say other things too, but Nanny and Mrs Merrydew would exchange glances and a cover would be flung over his cage to shut him up if he really got going.

Amy and Tiny-Wee-Jess—who were in some way related—lived down Tangier Lane, a small road off the High Street. Tiny-Wee-Jess was an orphan—a title which greatly added to her interest—and on Nanny's day off she occasionally took me to visit the grandfather who had brought her up and with whom she lived. I wasn't keen on Jess's grandfather. He seemed extremely friendly but I never felt comfortable when he pressed me to sit on his knee which I never wanted to do. When discovered, these visits were disapproved of by my mother. Soon after this Jess departed from our lives and questions about her whereabouts went unanswered.

It strikes me now that my mother had probably given Jess temporary employment at Amy's request. Perhaps the poor girl—a child herself—became pregnant and was sent to some bleak home for what were then horrendously called 'fallen' girls.

Walks were a great feature of nursery life and there was a large choice of route. Sometimes we went up the High Street, over Windsor Bridge—not closed to through traffic in those days—turned left past the Southern Railway Station with Windsor Castle looming above us, to cross the Thames again over the Datchet Road Bridge.

'Hold onto the pram darling and don't *lag*.'

How that word brings my childhood back! I was a great lagger, always meandering along in my own daydream. Looking over the bridge, I was fascinated by the houseboats on the river below. Nanny said darkly that people who lived in houseboats were no better than they should be, which gave me a passionate desire to live in one, an ambition which I have not achieved—yet.

The Eton Wick Road was popular even when not flooded. There was always the chance we might drop in on the Merrydews but there was also a wattle fence which made a particularly satisfying noise if you ran a stick along it, and our coalman—another friend of Nanny's—stabled a pony called Bonny in one of the arches under the railway. Like many little girls I was pony mad and if Bonny was not out on deliveries, dragging her too-heavy cart with all the deliciously tarry-smelling sacks of coal on it, we could give her sugar lumps and carrots. The coalman was fascinating in himself because his occupation turned him black. If he came into the kitchen to have a cup of tea with Nanny and Amy, a newspaper had to be placed on the chair before he sat down. Once when we met him in the High Street with his wife, I didn't recognize him because he had changed colour. Most walks, however, were in the Playing Fields and usually started through the Cloisters. I loved the ancient pump opposite the steps which led up to College Hall. There was a silver cup, attached to the pump by a chain, from which one could drink ice-cold water—a magic draft which might cause almost any excitement to happen. The pump is still there but sadly one can no longer drink the water. I never tired of going through the Cloisters, which gave me a satisfyingly pious feeling like a visit to an empty church and I liked the contrast on a hot day as we emerged from the dark coolness into the light and openness of the Playing Fields: whiffs of newly mown grass in the summer, and the nutty scent of dead leaves in the autumn when we searched for conkers under the horse chestnut trees. David liked these as ammunition for his catapult, or pierced through and threaded with string for vicious games with other little boys; I liked them to make furniture for my dolls' house with glass-headed pins and wool and we both liked them for their satisfying gloss and satin smoothness to the touch.

Sometimes we cut across School Yard, past the Founder's statue and through the passage in the centre of College, thence into Weston's

Yard, and on past the sunken garden donated by the Old Etonian King Prajadhipok of Siam in 1929. The King of Siam's garden contained a statue of Perseus holding up the freshly severed head of the Gorgon. My father had read us the Greek myths and legends so we knew all about Perseus and Medusa. His statue has an expression of pleased nonchalance such as might be seen on the face of a boy who has just shot his first pheasant and is holding it up for a photograph, very much hoping that all the older guns have been watching. The Playing Fields had good bridges for playing on. First there was Sheep's Bridge, a pleasingly simple red brick structure dating from the sixteenth century, which crossed the stream called Jordan just before it flowed into the Thames. Turn right and there was a three-sided seat overlooking the river called Sixth Form Bench—a good place for kingfisher spotting; turn left and you could go for about a hundred yards between Fellows' Pond and the Jordan down a stretch of grass romantically known as Poet's Walk because Thomas Gray is said to have frequented it. My father read me his famous 'Elegy Written in a Country Churchyard'— by the time I was eight I knew all of it by heart—and I liked to imagine Gray pacing along with his head full of words. My head was always churning with words too—though not, alas, to such memorable effect.

In the Lent Half there was invariably a swan's nest at the end of Poet's Walk which added to its attraction.

My father had once been in trouble over Fellows' Pond. Early in his Eton career he had been detailed, as part of his duties, to become a scout master by The Reverend George Snow (later Bishop of Whitby), the earnest cleric who ran the scouts. A rope had been rigged up across the water so that the scouts could swing across it in 'Outward Bound' style. Thinking that a little surprise menace would make the enterprise more fun, Pa had borrowed two ferocious-looking stuffed alligators from the Natural History Museum down Keate's Lane, and had hidden them in the long grass on the bank. The Reverend Snow was not amused by this visual aid to adventure, and Pa was asked to resign as a scout master—a state of affairs which suited him well.

David adored going to the Natural History Museum, but to me the visits were ruined by my terror of the huge Grizzly Bear that stood at the top of the stone stairs. I had nightmares about that bear—but then I had nightmares about practically everything. The curious thing about this particular bear was that he was only menacing in prospect. Once I had tremulously scuttled past him—fingers crossed, counting to ten, holding my breath—to the comparative safety of a room full of skeletons (including a whole horse) which one would expect to have been more terrifying but were harmless compared to the Grizzly, his malign aura would have evaporated and the return trip would hold no terror: he would have metamorphosed into a veritable teddy bear: I could even *touch* him, albeit very cautiously.

'There now! Not so frightening after all,' the accompanying grown-up would say, hopefully, and I would agree—until the next time.

In Summer, if we crossed Sheep's Bridge, Nanny might want to settle with her knitting under a chestnut tree on the edge of Upper Club with other Nanny cronies, ostensibly to watch the cricket in which they none of them had the faintest interest. Click went bat on ball, click-clack went the Nannies' flying needles, yackety-yak went their tongues beneath the navy blue hats as they regaled each other with the perfections or peccadilloes of their charges and dissected the characters of their employers. Plodding Nanny Butterwick, in charge of David's friend Anthony, the youngest of the four Butterwick offspring, wore her hair in 'ear phones' on either side of her large placid face; ginger-haired Nanny Hills, who had a temper, was held up to me as a disciplinarian—'I 'll tell Nanny Hills about you!'; Nanny Kerry, in brown Norland Nursery Nurse's uniform, pushed Anthea in—shock sensation—a *white* pram and was considered rather grand; Nanny Hillard looked after a fat small boy whose name proved too much of a tongue twister for our Nanny, never too secure with her aitches, who always referred to him as 'that Hanthony Illhard'. His father was known to beaks and boys as Taxi Hillard because his swarthiness and square shape were reminiscent of a London cab. The Horton family who lived next door to us at Baldwin's Shore didn't have a Nanny, but they had Mrs Davies, the housekeeper, who also looked after the children. Mrs Davies had some nice turns of phrase: 'Don't you do that,' she would warn Margaret and me if we ventured to go up the carpeted front stairs in Baldwin's Shore rather than the lino-covered back ones, 'or your mother'll be vivid. Absolutely *vivid!*' It was a good adjective for the mercurial Sylvia Horton. With her distinguished bony face and her hair scraped up into a knot on top of her head, Sylvia bore a striking resemblance to the picture of Mrs Pots the Painter's Wife in our Happy Families pack of cards.

In chillier weather we could go beyond the chestnuts, past the football field known as The Triangle, to the little wooden bridge across the Willowbrook, where the fast-flowing stream scurries along beside the Datchet Road. David and I called this the Pooh Sticks Bridge and many happy times were spent racing our rival twigs, throwing them in one side and dashing to the other side to see which was winning. There were sometimes fierce arguments about where the agreed winning post actually was. David was a great one for changing the finishing line. On a recent visit to Eton I walked up here early one morning before anyone else was about, snapped off two leafy bits of elder and threw them over in memory of our childhood. I watched them whiz downstream and swirl out of sight—but I took care not to assign a particular twig to either David or myself—it might have seemed a portent and I have no desire to know which of us will go first. The bridge has been renewed since our childhood and though the new one is much smarter, it's still ideal for playing Winnie-the-Pooh's immortal game.

The Datchet road—or Pocock's Lane—divided the Playing Fields in half. If we crossed it and went through a small gate we came to the long gravel path bordered by trees, known as The Avenue, which reached to the outskirts of Slough. Halfway up on the left on the edge of 'Dutchman's' was an octagonal wooden building used for storing cricket impedimenta called The Beehive, round which David and I played thrilling games of cat and mouse. My heart thumped as I edged along one of its sides when it was my turn to be the mouse.

I loved to canter along the grass beside The Avenue on the stout Shetland pony, Mickey Mouse, which was passed on to us from the Lyttelton children. Mickey—a piebald as his name suggests—had menacing 'wall' eyes of a piercing blue. On the outward journey, my mother had to flog along on her bicycle tugging a reluctant Mickey on the leading rein, but once his nose was pointed towards home again, his thoughts would turn to the luscious grass on Fellows' Eyot and he would pound homewards at a thrilling pace, leaving my valiant mother pedalling away like mad, anxiously shouting unheard instructions, but quite unable to keep up. These homeward dashes were not without thrills and spills for me, because Mickey had once been a circus pony and learnt tricks which may have been delightful to watch in the ring, but were disconcerting to the rider. What cog in his brain would occasionally flip him back into Big Top mode I've no idea, but he could suddenly slam on his brakes, mid-gallop, as fast as any polo pony, and would then either spin round and round on the spot like a top, or stand on his hind legs punching the air like a boxer while I slithered backwards over his fat rump. More alarmingly, he might lie down with extreme suddenness and roll over several times: when he was in rolling mood I learnt to nip off extremely smartly in order to avoid being squashed beneath him. Eventually his antics became too much for my mother and despite my torrents of tears Mickey Mouse was sold. He must have been one of the few creatures who caused my mother to admit defeat. Mickey was as near as I ever came to having a pony of my own, though I went on nagging hopefully for years.

There was a more glamorous bridge across the Willowbrook opposite Agar's Plough, designed by Sir Edwin Lutyens. It had been put up in 1933 in memory of Denys Finch-Hatton, killed in a flying accident in Africa and made famous to modern generations by the romantic film based on Karen Blixen's book *Out of Africa*. The bridge had satisfying pointed niches on each side which were useful for playing houses in, and a pair of stone griffins at one end which I thought incredibly beautiful and romantic.

I remembered these heraldic creatures when I was writing my first novel, and placed some griffins on the pillars of the drive gates to an imaginary stately home. There was great excitement each summer when a bandstand was put up near the Finch-Hatton Bridge in preparation for the Fourth of June. Eton nannies and children would watch the progress of its construction with eager anticipation; bossed by the small boys amongst us, who far outnumbered the girls, we all immediately became soldiers and practised marching when the military band started to rehearse.

In May 1935 Britain celebrated the Silver Jubilee of King George the Fifth and Queen Mary. We were up at Cefn, our Nickson grandparents' enchanting holiday house above the Conwy Valley in North Wales at the time, so I suppose Eton must have had a special holiday to celebrate the event. David and I were given flags to wave and wore red white and blue paper hats. Hugh Hughes, the old gardener, put up a tall flag pole at the end of the lawn; beloved Katie Jones, my grandmother's cook, came out from the kitchen with the rest of the staff and as the Union Jack was hoisted, Hugh, my father and the uncles fired a salute—one shot for each year of the King's reign. David armed with a toy gun which fired 'caps' stood proudly to attention, revelling in the occasion but—oh the shame of it—I had to be ignominiously removed, howling, when the bangs started.

The following year the King died and we wore black crêpe arm-bands stitched on the sleeves of our outdoor coats. I loved the drama of this sign of mourning and made a fuss when we were deemed to have demonstrated our loyalty for long enough and my mother removed them. After the funeral at St George's Chapel Windsor we were taken up to the Castle to see the amazing display of floral tributes which were laid out on the grass in Lower Ward, between the Chapel and the houses of the Military Knights. In particular I remember a cushion of white flower heads against a yellow background depicting the King's favourite grey pony Jock. We had seen pictures of the bearded, bowler-hatted King riding Jock and this made a great impression on me. Always a sucker for animal sob stories—the tears I shed while reading *Black Beauty* would have filled a swimming pool—I felt the pony's loss of his master to be infinitely sadder than the nation's loss of a king. I think this was my first actual visit to the Castle which I had looked at so often through my nursery window.

I always thought the expression describing someone deep in thought as being 'in a brown study' was directly based on my father's study at Baldwin's End Cottage. His kneehole desk and breakfront bookcase were made of dark mahogany, there was an old oak chest of drawers in which he kept his fly-tying equipment, the chair covers were rust-coloured, the curtains were made of fawn velvet and the haircord carpet was brown too. The room smelt thrillingly of books and tobacco.

On Pa's desk stood a large yellow Easter chick dressed in mortar board and gown, the gift of a pupil. It had originally been in Pa's particular schoolroom opposite Lower Chapel, where he'd been in the habit of setting its head nodding if he thought any boy's attention had lapsed; the other boys would then stamp their feet until the wanderer's mind returned. Some humourless School Inspectors had taken exception to this gimmick as being too frivolous and so it had been banished to his study in our house. They had also been dubious about Pa's habit of lampooning those whose scholastic achievements he considered to have fallen below their own personal capability, by drawing a lightning caricature of them on the board: 'Could Mr Nickson be told that there are better uses for the blackboard than drawing on it?' read their report—though they acknowledged him as a brilliant teacher. His drawing style was very much modelled on Bateman's famous cartoons. Sometimes he would draw huge set-pieces on the board of classical scenes—Achilles sulking in his tent, for instance, or the battle of Thermopylae.

Despite the School Inspectors' jaundiced view, Pa's drawings were much prized by the boys and became collectors' pieces; after he died my mother received many Photostat copies of drawings he'd done on his pupils' 'fortnightly order cards'. No one was prepared to part with an original. He was also famous for his ability to flip these order cards, Frisbee-like, across the room to each boy with extreme accuracy. If someone had done especially badly in their work my father would aim for the open window and the order card would sail through it to land on Racquet's Court Field outside—from where the miscreant would have to retrieve it.

I have a collection of the 'Welcome Home' pictures Pa drew for me at the start of each holidays on my return from boarding school. In the early ones a huge beak with a large nose dressed in scholastic regalia is greeting a tiny pig-tailed schoolgirl. As the years go by the beak gets smaller and the girl gets larger, until in the last of the series a tiny, trembling little beak with a shaky drip on the end of his nose is reeling backwards with shock as a galumphing great harpy with long red nails and frizzy hair bears down on him with outstretched arms.

Though my father had his own schoolroom in Montague James' Schools down Keate's Lane, his classical pupils also came to our house for tutorials, according to the Eton tradition of having a tutor as well as a housemaster for each boy, and I remember a stream of black-clad boys trooping in and out of Baldwin's End Cottage.

Of my father's classical pupils, one I remember particularly was Daniel Pettiward, who later became a well-known contributor to *Punch*. In a review of one of his books of light verse he is described as 'The Homer of the home farm, the Wordsworth of the woodlouse', a bit of alliteration that I like. He sometimes came to Sunday breakfast with my parents—entertaining at breakfast was an Eton tradition—and occasionally came upstairs to nursery tea when he drew wonderful pictures for us. Once he rashly attempted to portray my brother's imaginary friend, Joey, and depicted him as a little boy with a mop of golden curls, a prototype of David himself, riding on a dappled rocking horse like the one we had inherited from my mother's childhood. David apparently looked at this work of art with withering disdain and said: 'But Joey's *black*,' which came as a surprise to my parents. However the reason I remember Daniel Pettiward so well is because he saved my life, so naturally I felt a proprietorial interest in him. The huge white-painted cupboard in the nursery, which housed on its upper shelves the china and glass used for Nanny's and our meals, and on its lower ones our toys, was unstable. Tugging at its doors one day when I was about three, I pulled the whole thing away from the wall, and had it not been for Daniel's quick action in snatching me out of the way, I would undoubtedly have been crushed beneath it. After this drama one of the carpenters from the School Works Department was called in to fix the cupboard to the wall, but I always felt mistrustful of it.

Not long after this I had another dice with death when I was knocked down by the car belonging to Henry Marten—later Sir Henry—the Vice-Provost. His chauffeur was driving sedately enough up the lane past our back door but as he rounded the corner of the house I hurtled out of the front door. This was during the Lent Half, and David and I had just been dressed up in our pale green tweed coats with stitched velvet collars—topped in his case by a matching tweed cap and in mine with a green velvet bonnet—all ready to be taken up to Agar's Plough in the Playing Fields to watch the School Sports, the athletics competition which took place in February. We were looking forward to this event as madly as racing fanatics might anticipate attendance at The Grand National. The front door was already open as we came downstairs, but I clearly remember Nanny instructing me on no account to go outside, but to walk down the passage to the back door where the pram was kept. I deliberately disobeyed and dashed straight out into the road. I can date the inconvenient arrival of a conscience to this incident. Nanny was distraught; whether or not my mother blamed her for the accident I don't know—knowing my mother, I suspect she did—but I was aware that Nanny blamed herself, while I knew without any doubt that it had been entirely my own fault. Though no bones were broken, I was badly bruised and concussed and for a short time unconscious. I remember coming to on the sofa in the drawing room being attended by the alarming Dr Amsler, the senior Eton doctor. Afterwards a terrific fuss was made of me, which I would normally have relished, but could in no way enjoy because of my agonized guilt about Nanny's misery. I doubt if I articulated this. David was taken to the Sports by someone else and though naturally I couldn't go too, the disappointment seemed fitting. Compensatory treats which I was offered later were like the proverbial coals of fire.

I was a weedy child, prone to splitting headaches and what were called 'bilious attacks'. These had a nasty habit of turning up at inopportune moments and ruining the treat to which I had been looking forward for weeks. In winter I was often laid low with tonsillitis. This brought the joy of a real fire in the bedroom giving light as well as warmth and keeping the dreaded darkness away.

Sometimes instead of a proper fire in the grate the extra heat was produced by a portable oil fire, a round, three-legged black stove with holes in the top which could be opened or closed by a lever, causing lovely patterns to flicker on the ceiling but easily tipped over and giving off awful fumes. It would be considered far too dangerous a contraption to put in a child's bedroom now and I'm also sure it would no longer be permissible to leave a small child unattended to inhale the steam from a basin of boiling water even if it did contain what my mother considered to be the life-saving properties of Friar's Balsam or Oil of Eucalyptus.

If I ailed in the winter, poor David's miseries started in the summer with hay fever. He had to wear special dark glasses with black shades at the side which enclosed his eyes completely like some sinister Mafioso type, in an attempt to prevent the pollen getting to them, but his nose and eyes were often streaming and itching despite all precautions. Flowers had to be banned from the house.

Of course there were no antibiotics in those days but there were some dreaded tonics and medicines to be endured. Scott's Emulsion— how I hated the picture of the jolly fisherman in a Sou'wester on the label—was a noxious form of cod liver oil which made me sick, as did Radio Malt which other children inexplicably loved; Syrup of Figs was a horrendous laxative, the taste and after effects being equally awful, and my mother had unbounded faith in Milk of Magnesia: she thought that a large spoonful from its blue glass bottle would fix anything from influenza to a sprained ankle. There was something disciplinarian about this last panacea: 'You need a dose of Milk of Mag' was a threat for crotchety behaviour. Aspirin was freely handed out, and there was a dreaded substance called Gregory Powder which was sprinkled on the tongue from a sinister little folded paper. I'm not sure what it was meant to do or whether it ever succeeded, but it tasted horrible and made one's tongue as dry as emery paper. On the other hand there were delectable Allen & Hanbury's Blackcurrant Lozenges in the blue and yellow tin, Glycothymolin gargle—pink and soothing, Vick's Vapour Rub to be massaged on one's throat and lovely Cherry Linctus to calm a cough. My mother once made an unfortunate error and rubbed the sticky Cherry Linctus on my brother's chest while forcing a spoonful of a fearsome liquid called Roach's Embrocation (for external use only) down my throat. I nearly exploded and the inside of my mouth was quite badly burned. Even Mum had to admit to being mistaken that time, but she recalled with pride that when David and I were seriously ill with measles Dr Attlee—cosier successor to Dr Amsler—had told her to call him without fail in the night if either of our temperatures climbed to 105 degrees. 'They both did—but I didn't call him,' she told me triumphantly when recounting this incident in later years. She sat up with us all night but even when David's temperature soared to over 106, Mum held firm.

This was typical of her, an example of her mix of selflessly passionate devotion and dangerous obstinacy. No one could have been more concerned or attentive in their nursing—but she did like to call the shots. For a doctor's daughter she had some very odd ideas about health.

We loved to watch the boys in the Corps, drilling on the Parade Ground. Their uniforms were a reddish brown colour like the earth of a newly ploughed field in a sandstone area, their legs were bound round with puttees to match and they wore peaked caps. The particular tune the Corps usually marched to had a refrain that went perfectly to the name of a retired housemaster which the boys used to chant; we used to parade round the nursery chanting it too: Chute, Chute, John Challoner Chute, we intoned, marching round the nursery and stamping our feet in the rhythm of the Corps.

The shoes we stamped about in were always handmade. Mr Long, a short stout man dressed in black jacket and pin-stripe trousers—I thought he was an Eton beak like my father—came down from Dowie & Marshall's in London to measure our feet. We had to stand on pristine white sheets of paper while Mr Long drew round our feet with an upright pencil—slant the pencil and the finished shoe might be too tight, he explained portentously. It was a tickly procedure but produced satisfyingly personalised outlines: Miss Mary Nickson's left foot, Miss Mary Nickson's right foot.

My mother had great faith in certain materials for our clothes which apparently had the same almost magically health-giving properties as 'Milk of Mag.' There was Deimal for instance, of which my nightdresses and summer vests were made. This boring fabric—like Aertex but thicker—had apparently been invented by a dismal sounding character called Dr Deimal with the sole purpose of preventing me from having the pretty underclothes which some of my friends wore. Not a fairy, a rabbit or a rosebud in sight on Dr Deimal's nightwear, a narrow band of green piping on the collar marked the boundary of his concession to frivolity. He pandered to my mother's Dobie dread of ostentation—and I have been in flamboyant reaction to him ever since. She had equal faith in Chilprufe for our unhygienic woollen 'combinations', all-in-one undergarments relying on too narrow a slit for the performance of bodily functions. 'That's not *genuine* Chilprufe' was a damning utterance from either Nanny or my mother. Similarly pure 'Viyella' was considered safer and more health-giving than its thinner relation Clydella—let alone any suspect substitute fabric. Little girls wore constricting garments erroneously called Liberty Bodices, which were covered in hideous white tape and had horrible rubber buttons from which a pleated skirt could hang. My best dresses were much nicer and came from 'The Bunny Shop' in Eton High Street, where the owner, Mrs Stubbs, did wonderful smocking for little Eton girls. All the dresses had knickers to match—very desirable for those like me who fancied their prowess at cartwheels. This lovely shop was still in existence when my own children were small and we lived at nearby Sunningdale. Mrs Stubbs made delightful party frocks for them too.

I dreaded parties, and was one of those awful clinging children who are the bane of any hostess. I twined myself like goose-grass round my mother or Nanny and usually only started to enjoy myself when it was time to go home and the dread of pulling crackers was over. I do remember loving my own fourth birthday party however: we went up the Thames in a motorboat to Queen's Eyot, the island in the Thames to which Wet Bobs could row, and where one could get 'strawberry messes'—the best ice-creams in the world. The one party to which

I looked forward without any dread was the party given at the end of the Michaelmas Half for the choir of Lower Chapel by Alfred Conybeare and known as The Lower Master's Party. Invitations were much prized. There were no terrifying competitive games, one was not expected to hide in dark cupboards—let alone be chased on being found; no social graces were required, one simply had to go to the Music Schools and be entertained by a wonderful conjurer. The boys stamped their feet in thunderous applause at the end, but my legs weren't long enough for that satisfactory form of accolade so I clapped until the palms of my hands were scarlet.

In our nursery days we attended Sunday services in Lower Chapel, Eton's second place of worship, College Chapel only seating the senior school. We sat in the 'hen coops'—the pews for visitors and masters' wives and children that ran along a gallery above those where the boys sat. It was irresistible to try and make any boy sitting opposite laugh by pulling funny faces. During Lent, we sang the Benedicite instead of the Te Deum and I relished the words of this great paean of praise. Before I could read well enough to follow it in the Psalter for myself I used to make up my own version: 'O all ye taps in the bathroom, bless ye The Lord' I warbled loudly to my own huge satisfaction, causing much frowning and shushing from my mother and a sharp dig in the ribs from Nanny. The tapestries opposite the hen coops depicted St George slaying the dragon—poor demoted St George was still a five-star saint then—and I made up my own gripping sagas about him to while away the tedium of the sermon.

We loved Mr Conybeare, the Lower Master, known as Coney by his friends, and he was always particularly kind to us. He was notorious as a fearless and terribly bad driver, and to all the Sheepshanks family into which I married, 'doing a Coney' meant driving straight across a major road from a minor one without looking, or backing the wrong way up a one-way street. Luckily Coney had a charmed life. Some Old Etonians might be surprised to learn that another of my childhood friends was an irascible bachelor housemaster called Charles Rowlatt. He had been badly wounded in the First World War, and was said to have a tin stomach and a head entirely held together by wire—legitimate grounds for irritability one would think. Charlie Rowlatt couldn't say his 'R's. He's supposed to have been overheard after a theatre outing in London saying 'Wefused my good woman—definitely *wefused*' when greeted by a lady in Piccadilly who was actually the mother of a boy in his house, but whom he failed to recognize—mistaking her for quite a different kind of lady. My mother once made the error of offering him hot milk—another substance endowed in her mind with magically health-giving properties—when he dropped in on my father after dinner one evening. '*Milk?*' he asked, thunder-struck, 'Dwink *milk*— wiv the port still wed-hot in me fwoat?'

There was no such chumminess with the terrifying Mr. H. K. Marsden however—known as Bloody Bill by beaks and boys. He was famous as a devoted housemaster, a brilliant mathematician—and a dedicated misogynist who never acknowledged women or children. He was said to know the whole of Bradshaw's rail guide off by heart. H.K.M. was immensely tall, with a drooping moustache, a squashy hat and incredibly long feet; he used to bicycle down the centre of Judy's passage (the longest of Eton's paved alleys which made a short cut from Common Lane to the Eton Wick Road), the knees of his spidery legs sticking out sideways. A risky form of Tom Tiddler's Ground, played by some Eton wives and children, was to keep on walking as long as one dared at the approach of Bloody Bill in the hope that he might feel impelled to give way. He never did: one always had to skip out of range at the very last second in order not to be run over while he pedalled on. If he was an alarming disciplinarian he was also a fiercely partisan champion of the boys in his house and was so desolate when he had to retire from being a housemaster that he was constantly to be seen pathetically lurking outside the Boys' Entrance of his successor, Prescott Hedley. Some wag sent a circular to all beaks, via the School Messenger, suggesting that funds should be raised for a sentry box to be put up so that he could find shelter in bad weather.

Another bachelor beak who was very good to me was Tom Cattley, who in my childhood was in charge of the School Library. He came to tea with my parents every Monday—in later years we all rather grew to dread this—but when I was little he was always giving or lending me books and cleverly suggesting what I might like to read next. Uncle Tom, as we called him, had been my husband Charlie's housemaster and I was considerably taken aback to discover from him when I was grown-up that Uncle Tom had been in the habit of kissing the boys in his house goodnight. A witty man, he had an unfortunate tendency to kill his own jokes stone dead by announcing their arrival beforehand: 'Feeble joke coming,' he would warn, which made it sadly difficult to laugh spontaneously when the punch line was delivered.

When I was four and a half nursery days as we had known them till then came to an end when Nanny left. It was a total shock. David and I had understood that she was on holiday and naturally assumed she would be returning as usual, so when my mother announced that she had left to look after a new baby I was shattered. Mum's explanation that this was because we had 'outgrown' Nanny was incomprehensible and seemed a terrible betrayal all round.

It was my first taste of bereavement.

Eucalyptus

A leaf crushed in my fingers
rolls the years away.

I'm wrapped and smothered,
trussed in panic.
'Don't move till I come back'
she says, 'or you'll get scalded.'
A safety-pin—so called—
closes the vent to air and light.
I wait and wait.

Trapped under a towel
with my cowardly obedience,
clogging cold and chronic fears
I sit, desperate to catch
clack of returning footsteps,
click of lifting latch
—the sounds of rescue.

Aeons later, she returns:
'Good heavens! *Silly child*—
are you still under there?
The water must have cooled down
long ago. You should have called.'
The odour of injustice
lingers on my fingers.

Accidental Design?

Frost ferns ice window panes.
Grown-ups in mellow mood
allow a messy ploy:
too cold to venture out again.

Fingers pleat pristine paper
thumb-pressed precise
then splash a random radiance
of paint across the crease.

Long minute's agony of waiting
while it dries! Open to
ghosts with trailing fingers
strange flowers, monsters' wreaths.

Abstract artists of the nursery
new avenues perceived
scream with delight:
'Oh look at *mine*!'

How did God feel
after releasing a rampage of greens
to fold a page of snow
and see revealed

His new design
cushioned miraculously
on this white expanse:
wild cyclamen leaves?

3

BALDWIN'S END COTTAGE

NANNY was replaced by calm, freckled Miss Hicks, a Froebel-trained Nursery Governess. We liked Hickie, as she chose to be called. She was patient, kind, fair and firm; she got on with my mother, read aloud well—though not as well as my mother—and had a penchant for wearing surprisingly jaunty hats, but she wasn't Nanny.

With the arrival of Hickie, walks continued to be part of nursery routine, but the tapestry of our lives no longer included the varied and richly coloured threads woven into it by our visits to Nanny's friends. We now had nature walks. We collected catkins and sticky chestnut buds, pressed wild flowers, grew mustard and cress on blotting paper, sprouted beans, listed birds and studied, in intimate detail, the lives of the newts which used the lead tank in Luxmoore's Garden as their swimming pool. All this was useful and interesting but could never compare for me with the thrill of fixing Mr Butler's arm.

On the other hand Hickie brought something called 'Music and Movement' into our lives which I adored. This would certainly not have been an occupation of choice for David and, with that Freudian-accredited ability to blot out unfortunate childish experiences, he claims to have no memory of this thrilling activity. I thundered happily round the lawn or nursery linoleum as a circus pony: 'Keep in time to the music and feel the plumes on your heads children.' I had no trouble with this at all as I rolled a wicked eye, neighing and pawing the ground to Schubert's Unfinished Symphony played on a portable wind-up gramophone. There are still certain passages of music which give me the feeling that I may at any moment toss my head, start snorting and break into a brisk canter—leading, naturally, with the appropriate leg—though I try to restrain myself.

My parents were not exactly unmusical, but it wasn't of great importance in their lives. They possessed a few rather scratchy records which included a jolly song about 'polishing up the sun', and a more mysterious one with the opening lines: 'When it's night-time in Italy it's Wednesday over here, When it's midday in Germany you can't get shaved in Massachusetts'; there was Beethoven's *Kreutzer Sonata* and some Gilbert and Sullivan—but I never remember my parents going to concerts or sitting down to listen to music together. I played all the records to death.

My father had some good songs—a hangover from his scouting days I think—which he sometimes sang in the bath. There was one about a Carrion Crow sitting in an oak (hey derry down derry dido) and a rousing one about Dives and Lazarus with some equally jingly words in the chorus which I loved:

> Oh Roger Rum! Oh Roger Rum!
> Skin-a-me linky doodleum
> Skin-a-me ling-a-me orium
> Glory allabelorium, Oh Roger Rum!

The verses of this were good too:

> Now the rich man he asked
> for some water down in Hellium
> Skin-a-me linky doodleum, oh Roger Rum,
> But the devil he answered
> 'This ain't the Ritz Hotelium -
> so shovelly on more coalium
> Oh Roger Rum!'

When we heard the sounds of this coming out of the bathroom in the mornings we knew my father was in buoyant mood.

Nineteen thirty-six not only brought the—to us—earth-shaking departure of Nanny, but on a national level saw the looming abdication crisis (fascinatingly disapproving chat among the grown-ups about someone called Mrs Simpson) and the following year the Coronation of King George the Sixth and Queen Elizabeth, events commemorated by our sets of Coronation mugs—the ones of glamorous King Edward the Eighth eventually became collectors' pieces—and our toy replicas of the Coronation coach. Without television, State occasions were far less memorable to us than they would be to children of today, though I remember being taken to the cinema (a rare treat) to see the Coronation on a flickery black and white film. *The Little Princesses*, as they were always referred to, aroused a good deal of nursery interest and a wealth of books were brought out with such titles as *Our Little Princesses and their Pets*, which I devoured avidly, the pets being far more interesting to me than the owners.

David, with various other Eton children, had previously attended a small class which took place in the Lytteltons' house—Mary Lyttelton, the youngest of George and Pamela Lyttelton's brood was my brother's twin and Pamela Lyttelton and my mother had vied for Dr Amsler's obstetric attention on the night of 27th November 1929 as he and his black bag shuttled between the two of them. Mary was Pamela's fifth child, David my mother's first, but Mum always vowed that it was the pecking order of their respective husbands' seniority rather than any medical consideration that was the factor in deciding their rival needs. Miss Scott who taught the children had died suddenly, so for a while David and I did lessons together with Hickie, run on the Parents' National Education Union guidelines. My Nickson grandmother, Neinie, had helped to found this organization, originally started as a sort of correspondence course for teaching children at home. The teaching manuals and exercise books all had the round PNEU logo—a bird, I think—surrounded by the words 'I am; I can; I ought; I will'. This inspirational text stood for 'I am going to learn, I can learn, I ought to learn and I will learn', which model PNEU children were supposed to chant at the beginning of the morning's lessons. Of course we changed it—as I imagine generations of children have done—to 'I aren't, I can't, I shan't, I won't' which had a much more pleasurable ring and seemed the acme of nursery wit. I remember being made to stand in the corner for laboriously altering the words on all the books. I felt extremely smug at my achievement and contemplated the meeting point of the two walls with satisfaction.

By the time Hickie came to us I could already read fluently, though my mother said she never knew quite how I learned. I suppose I must have picked it up from David's early lessons; fluent or not, I never mastered spelling which made many childhood lessons an agony and is still a problem. Years later my husband was to treasure one of my love letters, not for its touching sentiments or telling turn of phrase, but because he found it so funny that anyone could spell the same word in three different ways on one page.

When I was about five I conceived a passionate determination to read a childhood book which had belonged to my father and his brothers. It beckoned me from the shelves in the old schoolroom at Hinderton Lodge, my grandparents' Cheshire house near Neston. It was called *Jock of the Bushveld* and I was beguiled by the embossed gold dog on its blue cover. The line-drawing illustrations were all covered by a sheet of tissue paper, shrouding them in mystery, and the pages were edged with gold: irresistible. To make it even more enticing I was told it was too grown-up for me and anyway was not 'a girls' book'. Perhaps a little opposition would be a more effective teaching weapon than either persuasion or coercion for unwilling readers: anyway it had a strong effect on me, and soon I was deep in Jock's story—the first proper long book I remember reading entirely by myself. The only thing I recall about the actual story was that Jock, who had a brave way with a lion, would only eat meat from the hand of his rugged, pioneering master, something which greatly impressed me. Alas, I totally failed to instil this loyal behaviour into Peggy, the greedy Dandy Dinmont terrier who was a present for my fifth birthday, and was to become my inseparable companion.

Peggy arrived by train in a hamper, crawling with lice, and had been terribly sick on the journey. She smelt appalling. I was also busy being sick at the time, convalescing after our serious bout of measles which had swiftly been followed by whooping-cough and I was thin, pale, plain and weedy-looking. It was love at first sight for both of us.

Peggy proved to be a brilliant dribbler of a football, an incredibly skilled catcher of a tennis ball, an accurate nose-driver of a golf ball and a forbidden—usually undetected—sharer of my bed; she was incredibly long-suffering about my efforts at training her though the results were not very satisfactory. On one of the platforms of Slough station, there was a stuffed dog in a glass case called Station Jim who was a source of pilgrimage to us if we were taken up to London by train. Jim had once patrolled the station, a collecting box strapped round his mongrel's chest, and a brass plaque told us of the amazing sums he had raised for charity throughout years of devoted service to The Great Western Railway—and we could still put pennies in the slot to enable him to continue his good work after death. Neinie having sent me a postcard from Switzerland of a St Bernard dog harnessed to a small cart, I conceived the idea that Peggy should become a working dog too. Together we would set out on many charitable and life-saving expeditions—and possibly make a little pocket money on the side. I roped her, shivering and moaning, between the shafts of my toy wheelbarrow. Alas she did not share my vision of this life of service and bolted round the garden like a demented Ben Hur, screaming with panic and bashing down all my mother's irises. Hickie was rightly cross with me and sent me to bed—where the forgiving Peggy soon slunk up and joined me.

Peggy proved to have one major drawback for a dog in a boys' school as—apart from my father and David whom she tolerated—she detested the male sex. I think she must originally have been kicked by someone because she became a dedicated chaser of any bicycle ridden by a man and a ruthless attacker of trouser legs, especially those of the mackintosh-clad School Messengers who were a sort of human cross between carrier pigeons and email. Their job was to pedal round Eton from house to house picking up communications from beaks' 'out' trays and delivering them to other beaks' 'in' trays. Once when I was laid low with tonsillitis and the doctor was attempting to shove his dreaded spatula down my throat, my loyal defender leapt from beneath the eiderdown and seized him by the wrist. Neither the doctor nor my father were amused by this protective behaviour.

Peggy was under constant threat of banishment, and some years later, towards the end of the war, this threat was carried out: Peggy had taken a bite too far. It was the only time she ever snapped at a woman, but unfortunately she chose Daisy Glazebrook, a family friend of my parents and the mother of four boys in my father's house. My defence that the lady in question, a fervent Christian Scientist, should not have allowed herself to feel the bite through her mauve suede glove, bore no weight with my father. Peggy was sent to live at Hinderton Lodge to be cared for (and I thought neglected) by the nursing sister who by then looked after my grandfather. I was heartbroken. The boys in the house were convinced they had eaten her as stew.

Miss Hicks and Peggy were with us during a crisis in my parents' marriage. My father took a sabbatical half in 1937 and jaunted off to join my Uncle Jack on a fishing expedition to Canada on the River Romaine. Neinie decreed that we were not only to spend the time my father was away with her at Hinderton Lodge, but also the subsequent summer holidays after he was back. Faced with a disagreement between the two women in his life, my father backed his mother and Mum staged a strike. Grizel Hartley came to her rescue by lending us St Catherine's, the house she and Hubert leased for many years on the edge of Loch Fyne in Argyllshire. My mother, David, Hickie, Peggy and I spent most of the summer in Scotland. In my late teens I spent other blissful holidays at St Catherine's with Grizel and Hubert, but I have very happy memories of that first, long visit too. Grizel, who adored my father, must have been on my mother's side on this occasion—but then she knew a thing or two about overbearing parents herself and often took Mum along to act as a buffer between herself and her own mother who lived at Marlow. Grizel, the least timorous of characters, could be reduced to pulp by wicked old Lady Buchanan, her awesome parent.

We had no idea at the time that all was not well between our parents, and I only discovered this from talking to my mother after I was married myself. My aunt Ruth also told me that my mother's family were extremely concerned about the marriage at the time. There must have been more to it than a tiff about an overbearing mother in law, but as far as Neinie was concerned, my mother said that standing up to her on this occasion was one of the best things she ever did, and was a turning point in their relationship: bullies need to be outfaced. How my parents resolved whatever underlying problems there were between themselves I don't know. Certainly they were very different intellectually and temperamentally, but that is by no means necessarily a bad thing. They had a long and devoted marriage.

I remember an idyllic summer: being rowed across the loch to Inveraray to do the shopping; collecting shells; scrambling up the burn behind the house and building dams; watching, spell-bound, the aquatic ballet of seals and thrilling at the sudden eruptions as schools of porpoises raced across the loch, their black backs humping out of the water like the series of loops we had to copy in our PNEU writing books. I was scared if they came too close to our small rowing boat, convinced we would overturn and be devoured like Jonah and the Whale. One day we were the enthralled witnesses to an extraordinary 'miraculous draft'.

This was 1937 and the herring had been missing from Loch Fyne for a number of years, but the summer we were there they suddenly and mysteriously returned in great numbers. We watched as the fishing boats drew up their nets groaning with silver fish: there were far more than they could cope with so that hundreds were thrown back and all the local people, ourselves included, only had to lean out of our rowing boats to scoop them up by the bucketful or even in our hands. An explosion of gannets appeared from nowhere, turning the sky black as they dived all round us in a continuous aerial bombardment. It was extraordinary. No one knew why they had appeared in such numbers or how long the glut would last, but something of the general excitement got through to us and I shall never forget it. We had herring coated in oatmeal and fried in butter for breakfast for days on end—bliss except for the bones.

When my father returned from Canada, we left Loch Fyne to join him at Hinderton Lodge with my grandparents for the end of the summer holidays and as far as we were concerned life went on as normal. Though we may not consciously have known of trouble between my parents at the time, when my mother hinted to me years later that some major crisis had been averted, I was somehow not entirely surprised. Children, even if they do not fully understand a situation, are quick to pick up on atmosphere and usually take in far more than grown-ups think they do.

The following term Hickie left to get married and David, in grey flannel hat, blazer and shorts was sent to the new PNEU school under Scottish Miss Johnston—really the original class from the Lytteltons' house, reconvened, but now taking place in the Vicarage half way along the High Street, courtesy of Olive Parsons, wife of the suitably surnamed vicar of the parish of Eton. Most other Eton children went there too but my mother, ever over-protective, decided for her own reasons that I couldn't cope with school. Years later she was furious with me when I sent my eldest daughter—a strong character and well able to stand up to anyone in her own way—to a small, cosy school aged four and a half. Mum left me in no doubt that she considered I was failing in my maternal duty of care. At any rate when Paquita Morshead, wife of the King's Librarian suggested that I should share a governess with Phoebe, the youngest of the three Morshead children, Mum accepted and that autumn I started to go to lessons every day at the house in the precincts of Windsor Castle where the Morsheads lived.

Watching Seals

What a spoof!
How miraculous, this
sleight of hand design!

First the disguise—
as part of rocky outcrops in
the grey Atlantic surge, next

pretence—
the lumpish drag of handicap,
as weighty flesh is heaved
on hopeless limbs, then

SPLASH!
The shock of elegance,
of streamlined power and pace;
aquatic ballet, ocean-splitting grace

—and I could watch
this conjuring trick all day!

Dynamite

My grandmother taught me
to play Russian Roulette
while she lay in bed
smelling of luxury and violets.

Her weapon was an ivory box
lined with russet wood,
carved and fragrant
—dangerous as a pistol.

Under its inlaid lid
texts stood to attention,
small cartridge scrolls of hope and fear,
close ranked and packed with dynamite.

'Choose only one,' she'd say
reclining in quilted silk
breakfast tray on knees
not giving second chances.

'If I can pick the verse
with angels' wings
I may fly safely through the day:
but here are also words that kill.
Will they explode inside my head
and blow me up?'

It was well understood
her time was precious:
'Hurry up darling make a choice.'
The voice was ripe with yawns.
Small fingers trembled on the trigger.
My pulse still starts to race
when I smell sandalwood.

4

GRANDPARENTS

BOTH my parents' families played a very important part in our lives. They came to see us at Eton; we frequently went to stay with them and, because we never remained at Eton during the school holidays, there was ample opportunity for long visits, so we got to know not only our grandparents but our aunt and uncles really well. The two sets of grandparents were very different.

My mother's delightful father, William Henry Dobie—known as Harry—the eldest of eleven children, came from a long line of doctors, and the medical gene continues to flourish through one of my cousins and her children. Mum idolised her father. Pa venerated his mother. Though the two families knew each other I don't remember ever seeing them together.

The Dobies were originally Border Scots but my great-grandfather started a medical practice in Chester and of his six sons, three became physicians and went into partnership with him. In those days of amateur discoveries, this great-grandfather, William Murray Dobie, as well as being a doctor, was an astronomer of distinction who had his own observatory and spotted through his telescope a previously unnoticed blip on the face of the moon which was subsequently named 'Dobie's Crater' in his honour—a piece of information which impressed us as children.

My grandfather, Harry, after gaining a First in medicine at Edinburgh, then further qualified at St Thomas's Hospital in London, and subsequently worked as assistant to his father's erstwhile colleague and great friend, Lord Lister—famous pioneer in the use of antiseptics. Later he joined his father in General Practice and also became chief surgeon at Chester Infirmary. The fees from private patients enabled him to treat his poorer patients for free. He was especially beloved by the Chester 'barge' families who worked on the canal. My mother said offerings such as duck-eggs or whole chickens—possibly stolen in the first place—were often left anonymously on the doorstep by grateful patients. He held a surgery for them after breakfast and we had to be hurried out of the dining room because it doubled as a waiting-room. The Barge people were distinctly whiffy, and I remember the fusty smell which lingered after their departure. After the last patient had gone there would be much flinging open of windows, and flapping of dusters by Ada, my grandparents' grumpy cook-housekeeper who looked like a bull-frog and fought a running battle with Granny. I suppose in their own unaccountable ways they must have had some affection for each other because Ada stayed with Granny Dobie for years, but it certainly wasn't obvious to the observer. Ada was an ardent Roman Catholic and my grandmother a bigoted Protestant. Ada would deliberately leave her rosary lying about wherever she'd been working and Granny, in a voice as tart as green gooseberries, would ask her—*please*—to remove her 'beads'. They both considered themselves to be extremely Christian.

There is a tragic story attached to one of my grandfather's private patients, the fabulously wealthy Bendor, Duke of Westminster, from nearby Eaton Hall. His precious only son and heir, who had been delivered by my grandfather at his birth in 1899 some eight years before, suddenly became extremely ill and Grandpa was called out. He diagnosed peritonitis from an infected appendix and said he must operate immediately. The Duke however, terrified at the prospect of any operation, wanted a second opinion and sent for a London surgeon, who, on arrival by train, confirmed the diagnosis. He had however omitted to bring his own set of surgical instruments with him and refused to operate without them. By the time they had been sent for and arrived on yet another train the child was dead. My grandfather, who was convinced he could have saved the little boy if he'd been allowed to operate at once, was devastated. What it must have been like for the Duke and Duchess doesn't bear thinking of.

Grandpa and two of his brothers had houses next door to each other. These dwellings, built of glossy red brick, were large, comfortable and hideous. I imagine they must have been built at the turn of the century but they have all disappeared now.

My grandparents lived at Number Two Hunter Street. On the opposite side of the hall to the dining room was Grandpa's study-cum-surgery. To us the great fascination of this room lay in the specimen cabinets containing his valuable collection of birds' eggs, and—more appealing still to children who had never seen wildlife films on television—his preserved examples of birds from all over the world. The latter, clearly labelled, heads and legs intact but bodies unzipped down the front and stuffed with cotton wool, lay in drawers, each more intriguing and colourful than the last. Like his astronomer father, Grandpa Dobie had a second field of expertise and was an internationally respected ornithologist who had written some of the text on hawks and owls in the many-volumed 'Handbook of British Birds'.

One day, thinking they would look marvellous out of doors, David and I transported the more brilliant and colourful examples into the garden and arranged them—with some difficulty owing to their useless feet and floppy bodies—among the shrubs and bushes round the lawn. The quite large but rather boring town garden became transformed into an exotic paradise, with humming-birds, hoopoes and rare pheasants, hawks and water-birds perched in the most unlikely surroundings. Then it started to rain.

I have no idea how much damage we did, and suspect that David bore the brunt of the ensuing row. I only remember that Granny, not surprisingly, was extremely cross but Grandpa, typically, was forgiving. He fostered David's lifelong interest in ornithology and taught us that only one egg must ever be taken from any nest—no matter how desired the specimen or arduous the climb to get it. As a small girl I got rather bored with my family's passion for snooping at all things feathered and invented a 'Bird's Privacy Society' of which I and the birds were the only members—but I am not above hanging a pair of binoculars round my own neck nowadays.

Grandpa wore three piece suits in Lovat blue or green tweed, smelt faintly of surgical spirit and kept peppermints and a stethoscope in his pockets. When he went outside he wore a brownish-grey Homburg hat with a wide band round its high crown. I also remember him dressed up to go fishing in thigh waders and a short mackintosh, a downgraded old hat—of the same model but squashier than his tidy one—on his thick white hair. Casual clothes as we know them now did not really exist for his generation: I cannot imagine either of my grandfathers without a tie or looking scruffy. Their shoes were always brilliantly polished—by someone else.

The kitchens, and what we would now call utility rooms, at Two Hunter Street were in the basement; meals were sent up to the dining room in a hand operated service lift which Ada wound up from below with a sort of cranking handle, before stumping upstairs herself to unload the food and hand it round. I was never sure if the groaning noise was made by Ada or the lift.

At the top of the stairs, overlooking the garden was a big drawing room with solid Victorian furniture, floral cretonne chair covers and charming watercolours in gilt frames painted by various members of the family. Further down the passage were the main bedrooms. Bathrooms in my childhood were not in plentiful supply. People were always trekking down long, cold passages with sponge bags and towels over their arm, and most bedrooms had a cupboard by the bed in which a chamber pot was discreetly hidden, to be emptied in the morning by some luckless maid. This unattractive chore was known as 'doing the slops'. A chamber pot was always referred to by Nanny as The Article, which puzzled me when I was first introduced to the rudiments of syntax. Surely, I thought, shocked, the grammarians could have hit on a more suitable word for naming parts of speech? Brass cans of hot water were brought upstairs to fill the china bowls and jugs on marble-topped mahogany washstands—those bowls and jugs which have now gone up in the world and are much sought after for serving fruit salad at parties, or planting bulbs for Christmas.

A less imposing flight of stairs led up to Ada's bedroom and the nursery bedrooms on the top floor, which had peeling rosebud patterned wallpaper and white painted furniture. These rooms were pretty, shabby and cosy but seemed a long way from the comforting presence of grown-ups after we were tucked up in bed.

When we were little, my mother's older brother John lived with my grandparents. As well as being in the family partnership he was

Consultant Anaesthetist at the Infirmary. After Grandpa retired, Uncle John took over as head of the Practice and my grandparents moved round the corner to a small Georgian house of charm and inconvenience in St Martin's Fields. It had a tiny garden at the back which you could only reach by climbing down a ladder through the bathroom window halfway up the stairs—tricky for Grandpa in his eighties. The garden had a small lawn, just big enough to contain a stone bird bath and a bird table but I don't remember any flowers. From the upstairs drawing room you could see over the top of the Infirmary to the distant Welsh hills. This house too has gone.

My mother's younger sister, Ruth, gave up her career as a nurse at St Thomas's to return to Chester and keep house for Uncle John in Hunter Street until they both made rather late marriages. Aunt Ruth owned a chow called Chung who had a sinister purple tongue and an aloof manner which belied his uncertain temperament. He once leapt at me without warning when I was playing with him and bit me through the lip. I had the scar for ages. Chung later covered himself with glory when he held a burglar down on the stairs for several hours. By the time my aunt and uncle came home after a dinner party, the burglar was absolutely thrilled to see them. He had my sympathy.

To the end of her days, my mother bossed and terrorised her sister—a much loved aunt to us and the member of my mother's family whom I liked best next to Grandpa—and there was never any doubt about their original nursery pecking order. Too much of my mother's company would send Aunt Ruth running for the Valium.

Chester memories include wonderful nursery walks round the medieval city walls, peering down at the canal which, even in the nineteen thirties, occasionally had horse-drawn barges on it like the illustrations from *The Wind in the Willows*. We could view the surrounding countryside and become archers defending the City and we played in the lookout tower from which doomed Charles the First surveyed the battle of Rowton Moor. Sometimes we attended services in the red sandstone cathedral where my parents had been married and where David was christened; we were taken shopping in the famous Rows where the shops, many of them in ancient half-timbered buildings, were raised to first floor level above the street as though on stilts. There had been an important Roman fort by the River Dee. History was all around one in Chester.

To accompany my grandmother to Dutton's, the grocer she patronised, was a particular treat, partly because of the delicious aroma of freshly roasting coffee beans and the smell of cheese, but mostly because after any purchases were made, the payment, plus the invoice, was screwed into special cylinders which were then fired off by a sort of gun and whizzed across the shop on wires to be received by a cashier, who shot them back again with the correct change inside. We never tired of watching this performance.

After tea my grandfather sometimes sat at the upright piano in the drawing room and played and sang for us—a mixture of such old American favourites as *The Campdown Races, Polly-wolly-doodle* and Negro Spirituals—*Poor Old Joe* and *Swing Low Sweet Chariot* always reduced me to pleasurable tears—and songs from Gilbert and Sullivan. We played Spillikins with my grandmother at the baize-covered card table, trying to remove the beautifully carved ivory tongs, hooks, and shovels without moving anything else in the precarious pile. You had to extract a spillikin without disturbing any of the others or you lost your turn and Granny had eyes like a hawk. I was hopeless at the game, trying fruitlessly to control my shaking fingers, and was invariably the first to be out, which was shaming but also something of a relief. I dreaded Spillikins.

Of my mother's many uncles and aunts, I remember plump, pink-faced Uncle Leonard, a bachelor who smelt of lavender water and had soft, manicured hands. He had founded Moorland House, a prep school for little boys on the Wirral Peninsula. Mum's brother John received his early education there as did my father and his elder brother Jack: that was how the Dobies and Nicksons had met.

By the time I remember him, Uncle Leonard had retired and lived with his invalid sister Constance. My mother maintained that Uncle Leonard had such charm that the mothers of his pupils regularly fell in love with him, but though I'm sure he was a model of rectitude to either sex, it strikes me now that he may well not have had the inclination to reciprocate these ladies' emotions. He must have been a good schoolmaster however and when he died one of his former pupils J. F. Roxburgh, the famous founding headmaster of Stowe, gave the eulogy at his funeral and commented on his wonderful kindness and notable ability to inspire enjoyment in others—two great qualities for any schoolmaster. My father had them both in abundance. In my memory, Aunt Connie is permanently perched on top of an enormous bed, a tiny bird-like figure in white with what seemed to us an extraordinary black excrescence sticking out of one ear. This was her ear-trumpet into which we were invited to 'say something to Aunt Connie, children'. 'HELLO AUNT CONNIE' we bellowed in turn with spectacular lack of originality. She must have been thankful when we were removed. No one could understand why I always refused to speak in the presence of Uncle Cyril (Ears, Nose and Throat) who was said to be the cleverest doctor of all the brothers, but shortly before I was born Uncle Cyril had apparently taken out David's tonsils on the kitchen table at Hunter Street—a gory procedure according to Nanny—and I was terrified that if I opened my mouth in his presence he might take a sudden lunge at my tonsils.

Much more fun were Great-Aunts Ruth and Grace—always known as The Aunts—who lived together in a village outside Chester and were cared for by a devoted cook of amazing antiquity who produced marvellous teas for us to eat. The Aunts bred Shetland ponies, and drove their gentle brood mare, Sweetsong, in a trap. I thought it a terrific treat to be allowed to take the reins and was crazy about Sweetsong but was justifiably nervous of her evil-tempered son Dandy, whom The Aunts had failed to break to harness. Instead he had broken Aunt Grace's arm by kicking her over when she was trying to catch him. My joy at giving sugar lumps to Sweetsong was tempered by the dread of a nip in the arm from Dandy's wicked yellow teeth. They also had a white Persian cat, a Welsh terrier and many ducks and hens. A visit to Willow Cottage was a high treat.

Most of my grandfather's brothers and sisters were accomplished artists and The Aunts were no exception. I still have some delightful porcelain plates painted by them, decorated with exquisitely detailed pictures of birds.

The Dobies were a practical, talented, down-to-earth family with no pretensions. They had plenty of artistic talent themselves but not much interest in The Arts as such—and a profound distrust of ostentation which was certainly inherited by my mother.

My father's family were grander, more formidable, and much more complicated. If the Dobie household represented comfort, frugality and common sense, the Nickson one introduced me to luxury, elegance, extravagance and hypochondria.

My sharp-tongued Chester grandmother wore felt hats with small diamond pins aslant the brim, sensible tweeds, ribbed stockings and lace-up shoes. She and David got on badly and rubbed each other up the wrong way. Perhaps Granny was jealous of my mother's open adoration of her son. I don't remember feeling strongly about her one way or the other though I greatly preferred my paternal grandmother Neinie, as she had decreed we should call her, who breakfasted in bed, always smelt delicious, wore luxurious furs and was a monstrous mother-in-law.

Neinie was a very good-looking, statuesque woman. As a child I thought she was completely beautiful—she was certainly glamorous— but looking at a portrait of her in middle age I think handsome might be a better description than beautiful. She ruled over a household staff which included a lady's maid called Norris, a chauffeur called Wright, a cook called Mrs Moran and a housemaid called Ethel. Food at Hinderton Lodge, their house in Cheshire, was always delectable. I'm sure my grandmother had never boiled an egg herself but she had the ability, and insistent perfectionism, to inspire other people to produce sensational food. Though anglicised herself, Neinie had a Welsh grandmother and a special affection for the Conwy Valley where her grandparents had lived and where her family had enjoyed many holidays; she was enamoured with all things to do with Wales, its language and legends and its people, a love with which she infected her family. She was a woman of discriminating taste and wide interests and, so my mother considered, of a regrettably domineering disposition. Her pedigree was full of scholars—a forebear had been Regius Professor of Greek at Cambridge—and Neinie was undoubtedly an intellectual. Her mother had died young leaving her father with three children, of whom my grandmother was the eldest. He had subsequently remarried but his second wife was an alcoholic and from a very young age Neinie had virtually run her father's household and brought up her younger brothers and half brothers. No doubt this responsibility so early in her life encouraged—and perhaps to some extent excused—her controlling behaviour. Her sons, very different in talents and temperament, were always under both her spell and her thumb.

My father, the middle son, a lovely, upright, special man with an offbeat sense of humour and a needle brain, was the only one to get married. Due to bad experiences with her drunken stepmother, Neinie was a teetotaller but all three of her sons liked their drink and were knowledgeable about wine, and two of them in later life suffered from the effects of alcohol. I can see now that my Nickson grandmother must have been a nightmare mother-in-law: by all accounts she certainly gave Mum a hard time in her early married years and never put my parents in the same bedroom when they came to stay, though my mother was not without her own steel core of possessiveness. It says much for both Neinie and my mother that as a child I was largely unaware of the antagonism that existed between them.

I adored Neinie. She talked to me as if I were grown-up, listened to my childish opinions and opened my eyes and ears not only to music but to many visually beautiful things. Although she died when I was only nine, I would still count her as one of the big influences on my life and tastes. Grandpa Nickson was a more shadowy figure and we never got to appreciate his quiet humour till after Neinie's death. He was said to suffer from an 'intermittent' heart. When I enquired what this intriguing word meant I was told that it meant a mechanism that sometimes worked and sometimes didn't—tricky. It sounded like the engine of my parent's old snub-nosed Morris car which often hiccoughed, frequently stalled, and could only be made to start again by arm-wrenching jerks of the starting handle in its bonnet. Neinie always treated Grandpa as an invalid, though my mother said that until old age there was really nothing much the matter with him—but this was typical of my mother's attitude to other people's ailments with which she had scant patience unless she had personally diagnosed their trouble. Mum loved ministering to a chosen few but it had to be on her own terms. Despite being the daughter of a doctor her views on health were highly eccentric. In this case her dismissiveness was probably more a reaction against my grandmother's attitude rather than a reflection of my grandfather's symptoms. She was very fond of her father-in-law.

According to Uncle Dick, a mine of information on family matters, Neinie had originally been in love with Grandpa's eldest brother George and continued to be so all her life, but George Nickson, a formidable clergyman who became first Bishop of Jarrow and then Bishop of Bristol, had inconsiderately married someone else. When Grandpa proposed to Neinie she apparently told him she would only be able to give him 'second best'. He clearly thought it was worth it.

I have a letter from Uncle George to his sister describing a visit to Windsor Castle where he'd been invited to preach in St George's Chapel and stay with King George V and Queen Mary. He gives a marvellously detailed account of the clothes, the food, the company and the etiquette. At dinner he sat next to the Queen who launched into a diatribe against the suffragettes and he apparently told the Queen a racy story about Lloyd George at which she 'shook with laughter' (rather hard to imagine) and insisted he repeated it to the King later. Maddeningly the letter doesn't tell us what the story was!

Whenever Uncle George came to stay there was a tremendous kerfuffle: his every wish was Neinie's law. Perhaps her cosseting of Grandpa, health-wise, was a sop to her conscience because he was never first in her affections; certainly he came after her three adored sons, but one should not make assumptions or judgements about other people's intimate relationships and the only people who really know the truth about a marriage are the couple themselves. Outwardly that of my grandparents seemed to function perfectly well, and clearly she was the star in his firmament.

Grandpa Nickson's hobbies included keeping bees—he won many prizes for his honey—collecting antique clocks and, in old age, knitting grey dishcloths on vast wooden needles. I suppose we should now call it occupational therapy but it seemed an almost farcically unexciting pastime to me as a child. There were many beautiful clocks in the house and I liked to accompany Grandpa when he went round winding them all up with their special keys, some of which were charming objects in themselves. Grandpa always wore a Hunter watch on a chain looped across his waistcoat, and used to make it chime for me when I blew on it. He had a bushy moustache and the aura of an invalid which made me dislike kissing him goodnight—though I felt guilty about this and never admitted it to anyone. Years later, in contrast to my fastidious, shrinking behaviour, I watched one of our own granddaughters come flying across the lawn to hug my husband, also the sporter of a moustache and by then a very sick man, as he drove up in his electric buggy. She put her arm round his neck and laid her cheek against his. I captured this moment on camera only weeks before Charlie died, and always have the photograph by my bed. I wish I had done the same for my grandfather.

A few years after Neinie died, by this time a genuine invalid looked after by a nurse, Grandpa started telling David and me about his schooldays during dinner one night and was so funny he made us roll about with laughter. I have never forgotten that evening. Clearly there was more to Grandpa Nickson than had hitherto met our undiscerning eyes. Sad that we only discovered it so very late in his life.

My grandparents' respective bedrooms were up three steps at the far end of the blue carpeted first-floor corridor. We used to visit Neinie while she was having her breakfast and play on her huge bed. She would be wearing an ivory silk bedjacket, her long hair over her shoulders and we would transform her bed into a stagecoach, lining up the black lacquer and mother-of-pearl chairs in formation to act as a matched team of carriage horses, and driving them along with wild cries and much use of the little plaited leather riding whip that had belonged to Neinie's mother. Sometimes she told us stories or read to us. If I was on my own—for musical activity was not David's scene at all—she taught me songs which we sang together: romantic favourites such as 'My father was a Spanish Captain' and 'Madam will you walk?' Phrases like 'I will give you the keys of heaven' greatly stirred my imagination.

I was fascinated by Neinie's many treasures. There was an ivory box, brought back from a trip to the Holy Land, which contained little scrolls of Biblical texts: I would be invited to pick one out and became nervously superstitious about this, as an omen for the day ahead; I particularly admired a head of Queen Nefertiti which sat on a chest of drawers. Neinie, who was an ardent Egyptologist, occasionally took me with her on trips to the Egyptian museum in Liverpool: her ability to make all the artefacts of riveting interest to a five year old gives some measure of her power to entertain. When my father was a small boy he had asked her to take his teddy bear, Snubby, on one of her trips to Cairo: threadbare, much-hugged Snubby, who in our childhood lived with the other old toys in the big white cupboard in the schoolroom-bathroom at Hinderton, had actually set his paw on a pyramid which gave him a special aura in my eyes. I loved the transparent thinness of the Nantgarw tea service displayed in a cabinet in Neinie's bedroom and her romantic collection of antique fans. The house was full of surprises because she was one of those enviable people who can put together an assortment of disparate objects and turn them into an enchanting whole.

I spent hours sorting out her button box, turning the sets of buttons into families and making up stories about them, and I loved to curl up beside her while she showed me the contents of her jewel case. Sometimes I dressed up and tottered about in her pointy silk evening shoes, a silver fox fur slung nonchalantly round my neck, a garden party hat tipped over my nose and long kid gloves dangling witchily off my skinny arms.

Granny Dobie hadn't got a hope of competing for my favour—but luckily I don't think this was something she coveted at all. I must have been a tiresome, odd little girl and I certainly wasn't Granny Dobie's kind of child.

Neinie's drawing room at the end of the long hall downstairs smelt of roses and potpourri; it was a delightful room with a big bay window looking out over the rose garden. It had pale yellow walls, yellow silk curtains and pretty eighteenth century furniture. I have a satinwood Pembroke table that belonged to Neinie in my own drawing room today, which still has on it the big mother-of-pearl conch shell which I so loved as a child. My grandchildren too have held it to their ears and listened to the mysterious sound of the sea whispering inside it. Best of all the treasures, to me, was Harriet, the doll which had belonged to Neinie's own mother as a child. Harriet was a grown-up doll—so much more interesting than a baby doll—a sort of eighteen-forties equivalent of Barbie I suppose. She lived in a beautiful painted box under the satinwood spinet and could only be played with in the drawing room. She had all her original clothes: wonderfully elegant tea gowns, sprigged cotton morning dresses, a straw hat, a cloak, and best of all a riding habit. Her underclothes went on layer after layer, and included many petticoats, long pantalettes and silk lace-up stays, the finely stitched eye-holes of which were works of art. I thought her delicate porcelain head with the coiled black hair too beautiful for words, despite the metal rivets at the back where her neck had once been broken—a riding accident I decided. Poor Harriet's body, made of cloth and kid, was a let-down; she had disproportionately large feet but luckily her skirts covered them when she was fully dressed. I think the early Victorian head had been added at a later date to the body of a very much older doll. I liked to shut myself in the drawing room, alone, and would play with her for hours, totally absorbed in a world of my own creating. Harriet now belongs to one of my own granddaughters, the fifth generation for whom she has come alive, and she still lives in the same painted box.

The morning room, next door to the drawing room, was very different in character: dark patterned carpet; dark family portraits; heavy curtains; books and an altogether more masculine smell. My grandfather often sat in there, a rug over his knees, doing The Times crossword puzzle. In here also was my youngest uncle's Steinway grand piano. A music stand stood beside it, used by Uncle Dick's glamorous Spanish friend, Alfred Martini, a violinist, who often came to stay at Hinderton. Alfred was soulfully good-looking with a dashing black moustache, which unlike Grandpa's, turned upwards instead of drooping down. Sometimes I lay under the piano with my book while Uncle Dick and Alfred played together. They obligingly pretended they were performing a concert especially for me and explained the music. Sometimes at night, after the grown-ups had dressed for dinner and gone downstairs, I would hear the sound of my talented, black sheep uncle playing Beethoven and Chopin, Scarlatti and Schubert. Then I would creep illicitly out of bed in my nightdress, braving the shadows on the landing, to sit on the stairs as the sound of the piano floated upwards. Chopin's Fantasie Impromptu entered my soul and to this day I can't hear Debussy's *La Cathédrale Engloutie* without recalling Uncle Dick's voice in my head telling me to listen to the sound of the submerged bells mournfully tolling under the sea at low tide. It made my hair stand on end.

Ethel, the housemaid, her dark hair in neat rolls under her frilly white cap, would discover me when she came upstairs to turn down the beds. She would take me back to my bed and tuck me in again— but she never gave me away or told my mother about my secret expeditions.

Uncle Dick had many gifts and wasted most of them. It was a toss-up between a career as an architect or a concert pianist—he became an architect. He was a brilliant tennis player—a Cambridge blue who also competed at Wimbledon. Poor, fascinating, flawed Uncle Dick: my grandparents had longed for a daughter, and when this afterthought baby turned up, they dressed him, and treated him, as a girl till he was seven. He was considered delicate and until he went to university was educated privately by tutors either at home or in Switzerland where my grandmother would take a house in order to give him the benefit of Alpine air.

I dreaded the stiletto-sharp note in my mother's voice whenever she had dealings with Dick, though I realised later that he frequently tried her tolerance—indeed that of all his family and friends—to the limit and beyond, and ruthlessly traded on his considerable charm to get his own way. One of my father's cousins told me he had been the most odiously spoilt small boy imaginable. He was never on time for any appointment and romped through all his own—and a great deal of other people's—money, kept interesting but often disreputable company and ultimately was a disappointment to himself. When Hinderton Lodge had to be sold after my grandfather's death, despite the fact that he worshipped Neinie's memory to an unhealthy degree and insisted that her possessions were not only sacred but all expressly intended for him, he ended up by selling most of them. A homosexual at a period when it was impossible to acknowledge this publicly, he had some disastrous relationships, was blackmailed, was constantly bailed out by his eldest brother and ended up a sad, drunken old wreck—but I always loved him. In my childhood I found him magical and was entranced by his company. In his way he was a wonderful godfather, not in terms of gifts or remembering birthdays, but because he took trouble over me: he made me look at buildings and fostered my early efforts to write poetry. Dick was the original architect of Onitsha Cathedral in Lagos –a prestigious commission, but one which like so many of his ventures was dogged with disaster. The building was not completed in his lifetime because the money kept running out and the only part that was built was destroyed in the Biafran war. Dick had friends from all walks of life, all persuasions, all nationalities and all colours, long before ideas of racial, social and political correctness had been thought up—let alone become fashionable—and he never felt the need to explain or apologise about any of them, something I admire. In his own way he had great courage.

Uncle Jack, the dashing eldest son, was very different—the family hero, idolised by Neinie and revered by my father. He had won the Military Cross and Bar for gallantry at Gouzeaucourt Wood in the First World War, at the age of eighteen. In the last year of the war he was invalided out of the army after being seriously wounded. He was expected to die but my grandmother, at his bedside, persuaded the military hospital to give him one extra dose of morphine and he survived. He would have liked to be a professional soldier but though he remained an enthusiastic officer in the Territorial Army, family expectations forced him to join my grandfather in the family canning business in Liverpool. As soon as war broke out in 1939 he joined up again with alacrity and commanded a battalion in The Royal Welch Fusiliers, though to his regret he was considered too old for active service abroad.

In my childhood he led a busy sporting and social life, hunting, shooting, fishing and playing polo. Hunting was always top of his list, he told me, because of the element of personal risk.

He and my quiet, shrewd, businessman grandfather (his motto apparently was 'Be content with your small profit') must have been poles apart.

We were brought up on the story that handsome, dashing Uncle Jack nursed a broken heart having been crossed in love. He became unofficially engaged to a red-haired Canadian girl called Mary Hendry with whom he was very much in love, but when he sailed out to Canada for their engagement to be made official he was greeted on arrival by a ship's telegraph message to say she was going to marry someone else—a young man called Ronnie Cumming, who later became Sir Ronald Cumming, chairman of Distillers. Uncle Jack never married and the story of this broken romance gave him great added glamour in my eyes. Years later, by a twist of fate, my eldest daughter married the grandson of Uncle Jack's erstwhile love and I learned from her that Neinie's proprietorial attitude to her first-born had been a factor in her decision to break the engagement. When Uncle Jack died unexpectedly of a heart attack aged 69 my father found all his love letters from Mary Hendry in a locked drawer in his desk, together with the engraved silver snuff box which she had given him to celebrate their engagement. Much more strangely, also on his desk at the time of his death, opened but not yet answered, was a letter from her (now Lady Cumming) received the day before, saying she had been thinking of him and asking how he had fared in the forty or so years since they had met.

When Belinda married her grandson, Charles Cox, Mary Cumming gave her the inscribed silver box which Jack had presented to her all those years before, and my father gave her the one Jack had received from her in return. Both boxes are now in Charles and Belinda's drawing room. In my fifth novel, *The Venetian House*, I used this tale of love tokens exchanged in youth and an unexpected meeting of minds in old age. Although the story and characters in the book are not in any other way based on Jack and Mary's story, I was amused when a reader wrote to tell me that though they had very much enjoyed the novel, they thought the bit about the boxes and the telepathic communication at the end of life was too far-fetched—the only part of the story based on truth!

However much my grandmother may have deplored her eldest son's great love, she immediately set about gathering other girls to try to divert his attention from heartbreak. She invited my mother, as the sister of one of Uncle Jack's oldest friends, to join a party for the local Hunt Ball—but it was my father who fell in love with pretty, downright Janet Dobie who had wavy auburn hair, a beautiful skin and definite views. Neinie was far from pleased.

My father was the academic one of the brothers, a brilliant classical scholar and a good athlete who played an elegant game of tennis, was a competent footballer, and a crafty spin bowler. At Cambridge he excelled as a sprinter and hurdler—as a small girl I fancied myself at these too, and used to hare over the boys' hurdles at Eton which were almost as tall as I was.

Uncle George, who had no son of his own—there had been a tragic infant death—mapped out my father's career to his and Neinie's mutual satisfaction and decided he should go into the church, assuring her with unabashed nepotism, that Pa, backed by Episcopal influence, could become a Bishop at a very young age and would have a meteoric career in the church—heaven presumably being the limit. He also wanted Pa to follow in his footsteps and become a Freemason. Pa resisted both these pressures, though his lack of worldly ambition was a disappointment to his spiritual uncle.

The Bishop was much more successful in teaching my father to cast a wily dry fly on a chalk stream than in preaching sermons or taking part in esoteric rituals, and together they shared many happy fishing expeditions. If Uncle George missed a rise, my father would hear him muttering 'Oh Perdition! Perdition!' under his breath—presumably an acceptable ecclesiastical oath. Uncle George was a skilled cabinet-maker and silversmith who had his own assay mark of a bishop's mitre. I have a beautiful inlaid work box he made for his mother and later in life he took up stitching and covered ten chairs with fine needlepoint which my son now has in his dining room—a different league of handiwork to Grandpa Nickson's knitted dishcloths.

By the time I remember him Uncle George was a widower and his house was run by his two spinster daughters. Cousin Dorothy, the elder, had become a Roman Catholic and ensured maximum publicity at the time of her conversion by announcing this to the Press— BISHOP'S DAUGHTER TURNS TO ROME ran the headlines— before telling her father. Not very Christian of her, and a tricky situation for an Anglican Bishop. She often stayed at Hinderton Lodge and I believe my grandmother was extremely good to her, perhaps trying to ease Uncle George's path by giving him the occasional break from his daughter's company. She and my father had endless discussions about their respective faiths, but whenever Pa thought he'd slipped a crafty googly past her guard and was about to bowl her out she would say loftily 'But then you see, Geoffrey, my Church is protected from error'—an unanswerable riposte that drove him mad. My grandparents always offered to send Cousin Dorothy to church in their car, driven by Wright, the chauffeur, when she was staying with them, but she preferred to bicycle uphill to Mass several times a week, suitably mortifying her vile flesh no doubt, but arriving back in such a state of exhaustion that she had to retire to bed afterwards, dowsed in lavender water, and have her meals carried up to her room on a tray. She had bluish hair, always wore black and had some interesting facial ticks—especially a fluttery blinking of her eyes—which I used to mimic behind her back to make my father laugh. Dorothy was said to suffer from what she called *crises des nerfs* about which I once heard my mother say tartly that nerves were no more acceptable in French than in English.

Her younger sister, Cousin Marjorie—said to have a will of iron— was a professional invalid who painted her face a strikingly cadaverous white: the effect was extraordinary. I thought it was natural when I was a child and it wasn't until I was grown-up that I was enlightened about her strange cosmetic quirk. Though she was my godmother, I hardly knew her in my childhood because she never left home. She always remembered my birthday and sent presents wrapped in innumerable sheets of immaculate white tissue paper, each successive layer being tied with narrow blue satin ribbon. Those parcels were a marvel to behold—but the contents were disappointing.

My grandmother's passion for interior decorating had ample outlet between her two houses, and she gave them each a completely different flavour. Cefn, their second house was full of rush matting on old slate floors; Welsh oak dressers and chests, gleamed with the patina of years of beeswax polish; there were William Morris linen curtains and Staffordshire china figures. Hinderton Lodge was much more sophisticated. Neinie and Uncle Dick were always moving things around, re-hanging pictures, discussing new schemes and trying out experiments.

Grandpa and Neinie had bought Cefn as a weekend and holiday retreat when my father and Uncle Jack were small and Uncle Dick not yet born. They also bought some land, including two small tenanted farms. Cefn itself had originally been an old farmhouse— long low and white-washed—and had an incomparable position on the top of a hill with spectacular views in all directions. Look south and you could see miles down the Conwy Valley, a green patchwork of fields spread out between folds of hills, with the river winding its way into the distance; go behind the house and look west and there were the foothills of Snowdonia, mountains with names that had a lilting ring in Welsh, the first language of the local people: Tal-y-fan, Drûm and Pen-y-Castle; the nearest two, Pen-y-Gaer and Pen-y-Gadwr were a pair of mountains, side by side, one hump-shaped as a mole hill, the other pointed like the volcano it must once have been. To sit in the crater on top of Pen-y-Gadwr was to imagine there might be a dragon slumbering beneath. On the skyline at the foot of the rounded slope of Pen-y-Gaer, above the normal tree line, grew a vast ash tree of great antiquity known locally as 'The Ship of the Mountain'—a landmark from miles around. We once found it marked on an ancient map and the name greatly fired my imagination. It stands to this day.

Across the River Conwy, looking east, but hidden by woods lay the famous gardens of Bodnant where Lord and Lady Aberconway lived. The far-sighted second Lord Aberconway, a notable horticulturalist, later presented the gardens to the National Trust with an endowment in 1949. My grandmother had ambivalent feelings towards the romantically named Christabel Aberconway, famous as a society hostess of great skill and charm—two powerful ladies, not much inclined to like each other. Uncle Dick said that when she came to Cefn, Lady Aberconway's first question would always be: 'Now do show me—where is it that you can see Bodnant from your garden?' to which Neinie, would reply sweetly: 'I'm afraid we can't see it at all.' If tea followed this barbed exchange, Mrs Jones would have excelled herself with wafer thin slices of home made 'barabreidd'—the statutory Welsh fruit-bread—sponge cake, orange biscuits and wonderfully soggy ginger cake, but Lady Aberconway would abstain from these goodies and ask instead for 'just the *tiniest* coffee-spoonful of your delicious cherry jam', especially if it wasn't already on the table.

My grandparents had greatly enlarged the original farmhouse, making one large room out of the old farm kitchen, building a new kitchen and staff quarters at the back and adding a second staircase and several bedrooms. There were three bathrooms—quite a lot for those days. It was a lovely house. My father, possibly the most courteous man I'll ever know, taught himself to speak Welsh because he thought it impolite to admire and live in someone else's country without taking the trouble to converse in their language. He was much loved for trying, but I don't think he was very good at it and I suspect his efforts were considered hilarious.

Occasionally Neinie brought extra help with her to Cefn, but beloved Katie Jones, the cook, was always there. She lived in a cottage at Tyn-y-groes, the nearest village, when Cefn was empty, but slept in when anyone from our family was there. There was also Hugh Hughes—dear, gentle Hugh, for whom English was a foreign tongue he never quite grasped—who was officially the gardener, but did just about everything else as well and entered into all our childish ploys with enthusiasm, as he had with those of my father and uncles. His domain was the old stables beyond the kitchen garden where he kept his tools and an amazing collection of old pots and pans, coils of chicken wire and every kind of screw and nail you could possibly want and a good many you couldn't. In my first completed 'novel' written when I was about nine, which I rediscovered amongst my mother's possessions when she died (no Daisy Ashford I—it is remarkable only for its spelling), I describe a male character as: 'smelling delishusly of rusty kettles.' It must have been Hugh I was thinking of. My taste in masculine scent has changed since then but not my affectionate memories of Hugh Hughes.

Hugh was helped in the garden by Obadiah Jones who looked like a cross between Lloyd George and Old Father Time. I was puzzled by Obadiah because I got his name muddled with Oberon, King of the Fairies—surely not a white-whisker type? I loved to trudge along behind him when he was hay cutting because to watch him swing his scythe like a metronome as he walked, was to witness perfect rhythm in action—a sort of magic. There was also the fascinating possibility that he might cut his left leg off. He never did.

Unexpected Passenger
To R.S.N.

Classic FM spills memories in my car
as I drive northwards on the motorway;
landmarks fly past with disconcerting speed
—but I travel backwards: hear again

the muffled boom of bells beneath the sea
a swish of censers swinging through the waves
the chant of salt-corroded psalms
and plainsong drowned by the swell of the tide.

You play Debussy on the Steinway
before dinner and notes float up the stairs
to summon me from the end
of the dark passage where silence is my enemy.

I flit in my white night-dress
to sit illicitly on the top step,
caught in a spell of sound, while you conjure
caverns and shells and a lost congregation.

Now, as the prelude fades,
your presence lingers and I recall
the tolling of another bell on a Welsh hillside
—feel again the airtight disapproval

of the grown-ups at your way of life
and all those talents scattered
with such prodigality, but... I thank you
for the music that you gave a child.

A Mouthful of Pins
In memory of Ethel Langford

She used to stand me on a table
– turning me round and round
like a chicken on a spit –
and spoke with tucked-in lips
sieving her words to a purée
through a mouthful of pins.

She was hard to understand
as she muttered to my mother
about letting-out or taking-in,
buttons versus zips
on something mysterious
called *The Waistband*.

She kept a tin of mints and buttons,
chalk and hooks-and-eyes.
I dreamed of shop-bought dresses
but swivelled round—obedient—
as she tacked me into hand-me-downs
to alter them for size.

Now as I try on writing styles
but search for my own voice
I still seem stuck with 'secondhand'
and I wish she'd come again
with her mouthful of pins
to make a tailor-made one
just for me . . . that really fits.

5

ETON CHILDHOOD

O w e n and Paquita Morshead lived in a charming Queen Anne 'grace and favour' house within the precincts of the Castle, set in its own large garden which Paquita's green fingers made into a delight. It had originally been known as Tennis Court House because it was on the site where Henry the Eighth had his real tennis court, but sometime in the seventeenth century the tennis court had disappeared and the house was later renamed Garden House. When I first started to do lessons there it could be approached by car through the main gates of the Castle and then by turning right towards the cobbled road that ran down to The Royal Mews where the famous Windsor Greys were kept. Ethel Langford, another of Nanny's many friends, who often did sewing jobs for my mother, was the daughter of the stud groom at the Mews and when not stitching away in our nursery at Baldwin's End or with other Eton families, mumbling non-stop gossip with a mouthful of pins sticking out dangerously from her tightly closed lips, she had occasionally taken us to visit these gentle giants in their immaculate stables. I was thrilled when they took bits of carrot from the flattened palms of our hands—an experience which left my brother David unmoved.

Owen Morshead—later Sir Owen—was King George the Sixth's Librarian at the Castle, a man of extreme cultivation, scholarship and charm. His beautiful wife Paquita was an American who had been born and brought up in Tuscany. Paquita's parents had settled in Florence for health reasons and were among the earliest founders of the large American colony which had joined the original British one there. Mrs George Keppel, renowned as the mistress of King Edward VII, was a friend and neighbour of theirs. During the First World War they were one of the international families in Florence who offered to take in wounded British officers for convalescence and had befriended Owen Morshead after he had been wounded. Paquita was a talented young musician, then aged fourteen, who later studied at the prestigious Vienna Academy of Music and was destined by her ambitious mother for a career as a concert pianist. To hear her play Schubert in the drawing room at Garden House was to have your soul pierced. Owen fell in love with her, waited for her to grow up and complete her studies, then married her and brought her to England aged twenty-one after she had completed her first concert tour. Their devotion to each other never wavered. They had three children, Mary, Lawrence and Phoebe.

Paquita Morshead had strong ideas about a good many things, including the undesirability of sending daughters to school, which happened to fit in admirably with my mother's views for me at the time. She and Paquita could hardly have been more different and, though perfectly amicable in a slightly guarded way, I don't think they ever became close.

The curious thing was that my mother had adored school herself: she had been sent to a girls' preparatory school aged seven, where she was the first, and for two terms—until joined by her cousin Meg—the only boarder. I once asked Mum why she had been sent to weekly boarding school at such a tender age—highly unusual for someone of her background at the time—and she said rather cagily that she thought it might have been because she was considered to be 'not always very nice' to her baby sister. I can't feel this was very clever of my grandparents and was surely guaranteed to exacerbate Mum's tendency to jealousy, though she insisted she loved the school and was perfectly happy. She had then gone on to Queen Ethelburga's School in Harrogate, Yorkshire, though she always claimed that she had really been intended for the rival establishment of Harrogate Ladies' College—of which I later became Chairman of the Governors. Apparently the taxi at Harrogate station on her first term had taken her to the wrong school! It seems curious that she was not redelivered to the right one when the mistake was discovered but, as so often with any story told by my mother, if pressed for explanations, she stuck to her story but became vague about details. Whatever negotiations may have gone on behind the scenes, Mum remained at 'Q.E.', a Woodard School, and enjoyed it so much that she later stayed on to be head girl for a second year until she was nineteen. No doubt her lifelong inclination to make up her own rules was catered for in this position and she certainly loved and admired Miss Young, the famous headmistress, but it seems odd that she was so anti school for me; perhaps an example of her inherent dislike of relinquishing control. At any rate she jumped at the suggestion that I should share a governess with Phoebe, the youngest of the Morshead children.

The first governess in question was a German lady of uncertain temper, who smacked our legs and smelled of mothballs. These can't have been very efficacious because moths clearly feasted on the dead pine marten which she wore round the collar of her coat. It had one glass eye missing, I remember, which gave it a malevolent look, and clasped itself round her neck by biting its tail with a long tortoiseshell clip hidden under its jaw. Fräulein, as we called her—I don't think I ever knew her name—had an effect on me like an Alfred Hitchcock film—periods of boredom interspersed with terror—which may make for good cinema, but is not a good mix in the classroom. After Hickie's lucid teaching, Fräulein's lessons were stiflingly dull, and started me on the fatal habit of switching off and withdrawing into my own world of imagination. Perhaps this ability to be present physically while jaunting off on a private mental journey may sometimes be useful for a writer of fiction but it has its drawbacks. I don't remember much about Fräulein's teaching except that I hated all her lessons but arithmetic worst of all. When I eventually went to school, I was to have a report which said 'Figures appear to have no meaning for Mary', a verdict which I have never lived down in my family and which I fear is still true today. I remember a French book about two dreary rodents called Monsieur and Madame Souris. M. Souris appeared in the illustrations kitted out like Sherlock Holmes in a deerstalker hat, but without that great detective's power to hold the attention. When Paquita Morshead taught us herself however—English and History—the lessons were hugely enjoyable and she encouraged the love of words and rhyme that my father had already kindled in me.

I was relieved when Fräulein eventually left because her successor, Trudi, was younger and nicer—though not I think with any qualifications or even talent for teaching. I suspect the pendulum of power now swung too far the other way, as pendulums are apt to do, and, freed from anxieties about Fräulein, we probably led poor Trudi an awful dance.

Gone was Hickie's instruction on flora and fauna. When Trudi took Phoebe and me for walks we ran wild in the Home Park with all its fascinating follies, grottoes and curious buildings—a paradise for children—and always there was the spell-binding Castle itself to fire our imagination. It would have been impossible in these privileged surroundings not to have been imbued with a sense of history. Every stone seemed to tell a story so that it was like living between the pages of a fascinating book, and Owen Morshead, the acknowledged authority on Windsor Castle, had the ability to bring its history to life for us—as indeed he did for many in the book he wrote on the Castle in 1951. We loved to hear him tell the story of King George III, who during the sad years of his insanity used to inhabit a room in the library overlooking the North Terrace. If he heard the tread of soldiers' boots on the terrace below on their way to change the guard, he would stand at the window to watch them pass. Whenever he was there, the command 'Eyes Right' would always be given by the officer in charge and the King would raise his hand in acknowledgement. One day in 1820, while the King lay in his coffin, the Ensign on duty, out of habit, looked up and to his astonishment saw the King in the window. He automatically gave the 'Eyes Right' command whereupon the soldiers saw the King acknowledge their salute as usual. King George V told Owen Morshead that the young Ensign, later Sir William Knollys, Comptroller to the King's father King Edward VII, had as an old man told King George this story himself. It gave us a delicious frisson to look up at this window whenever we passed along the terrace under the Library but we never saw the mad King George.

Phoebe and I loved the memorial statues of Queen Victoria's favourite dogs which were dotted about the park with their names and the dates of their demise. Amongst others I remember Prince Albert's elegant greyhound Eos standing in aloof dignity on Queen Victoria's Walk beside the East Lawn—we thought her incredibly beautiful. Later, I was surprised to discover from Landseer's portraits of royal dogs that the beautiful Eos had been jet black. The stone dogs became part of our games so that I felt I knew each one as a distinct character. I rather fancied a funeral statue of Peggy in the future - 'Faithful companion and loving friend of Mary'. The idea filled my eyes with pleasurably sentimental tears.

Phoebe and I once ran away from Trudi, and finding the door to the Royal Mausoleum at Frogmore surprisingly unlocked, we went inside and hid in there in fits of naughty giggles while we heard the poor woman shouting for us in a crescendo of anxiety. Queen Victoria and Prince Albert must have spun in their graves.

When war broke out poor Trudi was interned as an Enemy Alien. I'm ashamed to say I don't remember that we were much bothered about her miserable plight. We imagined her to have been caught out in all sorts of hitherto unsuspected crimes, though all the poor young woman had done was to find herself in the wrong place at the wrong time.

We spent a lot of time playing on the flat roof of Garden House and kept cages of pet mice up there. Mine was white, banally named Snowy, and I found his red eyes, pink tail and shivery whiskers entrancing. This is not a taste that has lasted with me. Inevitably our mice got loose, bred, overran the house and fell prey not only to the family cat but to traps set by Evie, the Morshead's cook-housekeeper, which resulted in some graves in the garden, not quite up to the standard of Queen Victoria's dogs. Mouse-keeping was then banned.

At home, level-headed Hickie had been replaced by lachrymose Mademoiselle, a young French woman who, as well as helping with domestic chores, was supposed to converse with me in her mother tongue but actually learnt English from us. I think she was terrified of David and me and I fear we must have teased her dreadfully because to our astonishment we once reduced her to tears. She was the first adult I ever saw cry—I had not known till then that grown-ups ever actually did so. It was a salutary lesson on how unpleasant the effects of what the perpetrators consider to be amusing teasing can feel like to the recipient. Luckily these revelations so appalled us that we were filled with compunction and became much nicer to her from then on. She was a spectacular seamstress and helped me to make a hideous tea cosy for my mother while she made an exquisite miniature family dressed in eighteenth century clothes for my dolls' house. These works of art were greatly treasured by me until Peggy, bored at being shut up in the nursery one day, ate them. Their tiny mangled bodies, made out of pipe cleaners, were a harrowing sight and this time Mademoiselle and I both cried together, snivelling away in a perfect harmony of mourning.

I missed David dreadfully when he was sent off to prep school to become a boarder at Sunningdale School. We would both have been amazed to know that by the age of twenty-one I would be the Headmaster's wife there—though not of course married to the headmaster of David's time, the alarming, deadpan Mr Fox.

I remember three things about David's first term: my father, holding out a formal hand as David rushed to him on his first Sunday out, and Pa saying that from now on they would only be able to shake hands, not hug any more. I felt deeply upset at the time and thought it was sad for them both—and quite unnecessary. I still think so today. Though David and my father—very different characters—always adored and admired each other and achieved one of the best father/ son relationships I've ever witnessed, it seems a shame that a deeply instilled inhibition in the English male upbringing of the time stopped my father from embracing his little boy of eight. Years later when he did exactly the same to my own small son he was extremely surprised when I said: 'Oh Pa you've done this *twice* in my life now! Do stop it.'

The second memory is that at the end of his first term David announced he would now be too grown-up to play with me any more. I rushed upstairs, shattered, to hide myself away in my distress—but of course ten minutes later he'd forgotten all about this lordly attitude and we continued to be boon companions. The third memory is of David's own misery whenever he had to return to school; I used to be taken along to try to take his mind off his impending doom and comfort my mother on the return trip, and remember my despair because I could help neither of them. He claims not to have been unhappy when he was actually at school, it was the prospect of leaving home that was so awful, as I was to find when I went to boarding school myself, much later.

There were not nearly as many Eton beaks' children in our time as there are today when a far greater proportion of masters are married and have families. David had more contemporaries than I did and after I went to do lessons at Garden House, I inevitably saw less of my own friends anyway. The two little girls who were nearest my age were Margaret Horton—later Horton-Fawkes—whose father George taught French, and Penelope, daughter of housemaster Charles Gladstone, the grandson of the 'Grand Old Man' of English politics. Penelope had two older brothers, William and Peter—there would be more Gladstone children later, but they were much younger and never entered into our orbit. William was to have a distinguished career as a headmaster of Lancing College, as Chief Scout and later still as a Knight of the Garter; Peter was also to become a successful schoolmaster and a notable zoologist. As a boy at Eton he was the first to discover the presence of a well-established colony of Coypu rats on Slough Sewage Farm which generated great interest nationwide. These huge, beaver-like creatures, once valued for their fur, could be up to twenty pounds in weight. At about the same period another surprising sight might also have been spied at the Sewage Farm when my brother got permission to shoot snipe there one particularly snowy winter; feeling his armed expedition might be more successful if he was camouflaged, he threw a chorister's surplice over his tweed jacket and sported on his head one of the floppy white cotton sunhats normally worn in high summer by the rowing fraternity. The camouflage must have been successful because as far as I know this strange apparition went unnoticed. Perhaps it puzzled the Coypu rats. Back in our nursery days, however, Peter Gladstone was the *enfant terrible* of the nannies' gossip, rumoured to be UNMANAGEABLE which gave him terrific cachet with other Eton children. I remember going to a party at Penn House when Peter sneaked away from the festivities to put all the nannies' hats up the chimney. We were most impressed by this subversive and no doubt enjoyable act of sabotage. Penelope had tremendous screaming matches with her mother, the talented and artistic Isla, which left them nicely invigorated but left me, as an open-mouthed spectator, shattered. My own rebellions against my mother were not to come till much later and were not of this noisy and extrovert variety. There were blood-curdling shrieks between mother and children from the household next door to us at Baldwin's Shore too when Sylvia Horton usually out-screamed her children. Shrieking was not my own mother's style at all. In later life mercurial Sylvia—rather disloyally—used to tell the story of attending an Eton and Harrow match at Lord's when they had just added Fawkes to their surname in order to inherit Farnley Hall. An old acquaintance, spotting her in the social throng, swooped down on Sylvia gushing: 'Sylvia Horton!! My dear, how lovely. I haven't seen you for ages!'

'Oh, but I'm not called Horton anymore…' Sylvia started to explain, but before she got any further, back came the disastrous reply: 'Oh my dear I'm so pleased I always thought George was the most crashing bore!' No getting out of that one.

Round the corner from Baldwin's End lived a housemaster and his wife who had one treasured small boy of exactly the same age as David. He was the idol of his elderly parents' life but the bane of David's. He was a flabby child—a sort of undercooked drop scone of a boy—and though he always wanted to play with my energetic, extrovert brother, he didn't actually enjoy doing any of the same things. Years later, when David and I were both parents of young families ourselves, we were playing that dangerous game concerning mutual acquaintances, 'What Would They Be If They Were One?' It was David's turn to think of a person, and mine to ask questions and guess the identity:

'I've thought of someone,' said David. 'Male—but you'll never guess him.'

'What sort of paper would he be?' I asked.

'Blotting,' said David, unhesitatingly.

'What sort of bird would he be?'

'Boiled chicken with white sauce.'

Into my head, after about thirty years of absence, popped the right answer.

Other contemporaries included Anthony Butterwick who could sprint faster than David over a short distance but had less staying power—so the winning post was always in question, at any rate in David's view. 'We haven't finished yet,' David would gasp, grinding back to the other end of the lawn after Anthony had stormed past him on the first length.

Anthony was the youngest of the Butterwick children and his parents Cyril and Desiré, who were senior to our parents, were glamorous, sophisticated figures in our eyes. Desiré had a memorably husky voice to match her sexy name, and Cyril Butterwick, who was a renowned expert on silver, joined Sotheby's when he retired from Eton.

Memory flips up random snapshots of many Eton characters: eccentric Lionel Fortescue, gardening in a hair net. He was to be much more successful as a horticulturalist than as a schoolmaster and the garden he created in Devon at Buckland Monachorum after he left Eton is still justly famous; I can see Czechoslovakian-born Mitza Weatherall, with her Slavic cheekbones and individual pronunciation of the English language, inhaling rapturously when the coal lorry, no longer pulled by Bonnie but still loaded with tarry-smelling black sacks, pulled up beside her and hear her saying 'Oh zat vonderful smell! How I hev always loved the smell of sex!' Kind Mary Jacques could look holy even when riding a bicycle. My father, religious too, but not overly impressed by piety, once greeted her with: 'Hello Mary. I needn't ask how you are—you have the fulfilled look of one who has come fresh from hemming altar cloths.' She was very puzzled.

George Lyttelton (father of 'Humph' of jazz and broadcasting fame) was one of the famous Eton masters—someone who illuminated the English language for many boys. He was also notable as a great games player but a terrible loser. Partnered by my husband on a week's golfing holiday at Troon, (well pre me, in Charlie's bachelor days) George was so incensed when Charlie missed the final putt and lost them the match that he immediately stormed off in a rage and caught the next train to London, only to return next day as if nothing had happened. He was notorious among other beaks for his *bons-mots*. 'Have you just lost a castor?' he once greeted the stout and temporarily lame Mr Mayes, and famously described that same gentleman as having: 'A body by Chesterfield; legs by Burrows and Watt and fingers by Palethorpe.' Cruel, but unforgettable.

So steeped were we all in Eton sights and customs that another contemporary of ours, William Wilkinson, aged three, once felled a starched and be-muslinned Julia Birley (whose father, Robert, was to become a future headmaster of Eton) to the floor at a children's party crying 'Wall game, Wall game' as he sank his teeth in her white-socked ankle in imitation of the mysterious Eton game of that name, at which no one ever scores a goal, but where everyone has a highly enjoyable time fighting each other in the mud.

Of our parents' friends, easily the most important to us when we lived at Baldwin's End Cottage, were the Hartleys who lived next door but one to us at Baldwin's Bec.

How to describe Grizel Hartley—that binder of spells? Their house was a magnet to all ages and all comers and we had the freedom of it. We were constantly in and out of her flower-filled, delicious-smelling drawing room with its be-cushioned bay window jutting out over the lane below; a room where piles of books competed with children's toys and precious antiques—and where dogs were most definitely allowed on sofas. Grizel, who had longed desperately for her own children, had that generosity of spirit that enabled her to enjoy other people's offspring despite her own aching void. She kept one of David's woollen gloves, left behind after some visit, in the drawer of her desk for years. I remember her showing it to me when I took my own first child to visit her. 'Oh darling—I did love you both so,' she said. Grizel was tall, athletic and beautiful in a Valkyrie sort of way with a wild mop of red hair and a golden presence. She had a mind like an idiosyncratically compiled encyclopaedia, a sense of humour that forever changed one's way of looking at life, a passionate interest in people and an infectious sense of adventure. A spectacular correspondent, she had the most original handwriting of anyone I've ever known; all her life she wrote hilarious, touching—and frequently libellous—letters to her innumerable friends. She was to become a huge influence on me.

Hubert Hartley was a giant personality too—they were both larger than life characters whose long marriage was not without its dark undercurrents despite genuine devotion. Hubert, a Coldstreamer in the first World War who had survived that terrible carnage, rejoined the regiment in 1940 and disappeared for the next six years. For over three years Grizel never heard from him at all, an omission that was not entirely explained afterwards by his reputedly undercover exploits.

I dearly loved them both and they were endlessly good to me. When Hubert died I was astonished and deeply moved to learn that a copy of one of my poems was folded in a book at his bedside. They had first met at Cambridge where Hubert had gone up in 1919 and where he stroked the Cambridge Eight to victory in the Boat Race for three successive years. Grizel read Natural Sciences at Girton and something of her charm and glamour was later to be depicted by Rosamund Lehmann, a friend and fellow undergraduate, in her first novel, *Dusty Answer*.

Grizel had originally wanted to be a vet, and animals were very important to her. The dogs I remember in my childhood were a portly black and white Springer Spaniel and a series of Golden Retrievers starting with a mother and daughter duo, Copper and Clover, and ending with Feather, her last dog. The sight of Feather in her final years filled me with sadness: she and Grizel had become so alike—two once Titian-haired charmers, now both heavily arthritic, nearly blind, grey-haired and stout, but still beautiful to those with eyes to see, who had known them in their golden glory years.

When we lived at Baldwin's End Grizel grazed her horses on Fellows' Eyot during the summer, though she also had stables for them in Windsor for the winter. One of her most beloved was Kandy, a foal she had bred herself and of which she was immensely proud. This unpleasant animal had the habits of a brigand and used to hold people up as they crossed Fellows' Eyot to Luxmoore's garden— and woe betide them if they hadn't any sugar with which to buy him off. Grizel adored him: 'Darling he's a *lamb* really,' she would insist unconvincingly, but there were lots of complaints and eventually her horses were banned from Fellows' Eyot. She also owned Mist—an enormous, half-gelded grey of eighteen hands with a charming nature but a mouth like iron. Grizel, typically, had bought him because the Master of the Garth Hunt couldn't hold him, a challenge she couldn't resist: neither could Grizel hold him—or anyone else, come to that, including me. After I'd left school and was working in London but weekending at home I used to ride Mist—by then nearly thirty but still with the pulling power of the Flying Scotsman—most Saturdays, while Grizel or Eva Mackinnon exercised the horrible Kandy. Grizel had a permit to ride in the Great Park and in those days we were able go anywhere—no restrictions about sticking to approved routes. Thundering up the three miles of The Long Walk, the double Avenue of trees leading from the Castle to the famous equestrian statue of George III at Snow Hill was huge fun. So enormous is the so-called Copper Horse that when it was being assembled on site in October 1831, sixteen men are said to have got inside its body to have their picnic lunch of bread and cheese. As Mist never deigned to stop at the road that runs below it at the top of The Long Walk, I always prayed there wouldn't be any estate workers' cars coming as we roared across it. Once he reached the rocks at the foot of the statue, Mist would stop of his own accord. Luckily I never came off on any of our cavalry-type charges up hill, because without either a mounting block or a leg up I wouldn't have had a hope of remounting. Unlike Grizel I was not a particularly intrepid horsewoman and nothing would have induced me to get on Kandy, of whom I was frankly terrified, but no great prowess other than good balance was required to ride Mist because he never did anything unexpected—apart of course from the fact that it was like driving a bus without brakes. Grizel was also one of the few keyholders to the St Leonard's Gate at High-Standing Hill, another section of The Great Park between Ascot and Windsor, where there was also an unforgettable view of the Castle. To come across this view while riding on a crisp autumn morning and see Windsor Castle apparently floating on the clouds, framed by a cartouche of golden beech leaves was an unforgettable experience. In late May, at dusk, nightingales sang in that part of the park and I remember before the war being kept up late as a special treat and taken up there by Grizel to hear this magical bird music on a moonlit night. No wonder Keats wrote that ode.

Grizel and Hubert were adored by their staff, all of whom stayed with them for years—their butler Heath was like a stage butler from a pre war 'drawing room' comedy and Edwards, the groom, had been Hubert's devoted soldier-servant in the army. Unlike anyone else, he had unbounded faith in Hubert's driving ability: 'Mr Hartley has such wonderful judgement' he would say proudly after Hubert had managed to skim the paint off a passing bus without actually having a serious accident—like the Regency bucks who 'drove to an inch' in Georgette Heyer's romantic novels perhaps.

In my teens when I was staying with them at St Catherine's, Hubert once nearly put me through the windscreen of his car by jamming on the brakes with extreme violence when he suddenly noticed the dozing Highland cow which lay in the middle of the gated road down which we were hurtling. 'Can't afford to kill a cow at the moment,' said Hubert as we stopped inches short of the surprised animal, leaving me in no doubt that had it not been for his latest financial crisis we would have soared straight over the top of it. Hubert's terrific laugh rings down recollection's corridors like a gong and his occasional outbursts of rage were memorable too, certainly to anyone unfortunate enough to have triggered one—though I was luckily never on the receiving end myself I witnessed one or two of these volcanic explosions. Hubert managed to make the shy and uncertain blossom. 'How lovely so see you. You're looking *very* pretty tonight my dear' he would say with apparent conviction and a total lack of truth when I was at my most gauche and gawky. It did wonders for social confidence.

Another housemaster's wife of whom I was especially fond was Ruth Colquhoun—later to remarry and become Ruth Birchall. She was a good deal younger than my mother and before she had children of her own—she had been told she shouldn't have any but was to have five—she used to 'borrow' me to have tea with her and read aloud to me. I have the happiest memories of Ruth introducing me to all sorts of books, both then and later. We were still corresponding about books well into her old age.

After the departure to Shrewsbury of Jack Peterson, my father's closest friend among Eton beaks was undoubtedly Dennis Wilkinson, a man of endearing enthusiasms and a fellow classicist who shared my father's passion for wildfowling but unlike Pa was fond of standing on his head. Another companion was Jack Upcott, an eccentric character whose hobbies of religion and dry fly fishing also provided common ground with my father. They had deep theological discussions while munching soggy sandwiches on the banks of the Kennet or the Test, eyes glued to the river in case of a rise.

Being surrounded by so many powerful and eccentric personalities wonderfully widens the perception of what is normal. Among other notable Eton figures was the wealthy Claude Beasley Robinson, a high church housemaster who was passionate about God, hunting the fox, and cars. I remember him careering about on a grey hunter or roaring round in a vintage Vauxhall known as The Yellow Peril. He had a room in his house consecrated as a private chapel, veered wildly between piety and worldliness, and was famous for the gourmet 'Hellfire' dinners he gave for other beaks on Shrove Tuesday, before inflicting a stringent Lenten diet on himself. All through the war the boys in his house were far better fed than in many others because, unlike my law-abiding father, he had no qualms about dealings with the black market. When he retired from Eton he exchanged his flamboyant hunting pink for a humble brown cassock and joined the Cowley Fathers as a monk. He hunted for the whole of the week before he disappeared to his Monastery—six days in England in the Shires, and then over to Ireland for the final Sunday. After that he used occasionally to turn up at Eton on a much more mundane mount, having pedalled all the way from Oxford or London on an ancient bicycle, his long monastic garments greatly impeding progress. 'The headwind made it difficult today' he told my father once, arriving at our house in a state of exhaustion. My mother had another pathetic story about Beasley: on joining the order he was asked what he would like to do by way of manual work, and had answered that he'd happily do anything except perhaps gardening which he detested. Back came the horribly hair shirty reply: 'Then that, Brother Claude, is what you are called upon to do.'

Rare Birds
A Rondeau

Too rare a sight to see him fly,
blue shriek, green gasp and fiery cry
and watch him plunge his skewer wit
to spear fun on the end of it
while shoals of laughter minnow by;
then, shaking carefree arrows dry,
arrest the current with his eye.
Too rare a sight!

Children with nets of hope may try
to scoop out starfish from the sky
when fires of fantasy are lit—
but as years pile on, bit by bit,
daydreams and kingfishers grow shy:
too rare a sight.

Spies

Five grey men
meet by the riverside.
Cold winds of espionage
blow round about them;
they hunch their shoulders
against knives.

Expressionless
they exchange secrets
through thin beaks and are
impersonal as station waiting rooms.
They reek subversively of menace
and the dark.

Cautiously, the secret police
approach with binoculars,
but the men were always
watching out for them
and disperse quickly—
but with no apparent haste.

Loosely attached
as cigarette ash and
rising casual as smoke
they take to the air,
their drab anonymous raincoats
flapping out like monstrous wings.

They nearly fooled me, those spies:
I could have sworn they were herons.

6

WAR

I have a vivid memory of being told about the outbreak of war in September 1939. It seems surprising to me now that I knew nothing about what was happening in Europe—probably David did—but I have no recollection of any previous knowledge of hostilities with Germany, no memory of the Munich crisis. I learnt later that my peace loving father thought Neville Chamberlain had been right to attempt to negotiate with Hitler at that time—though like many he came to change this view later. With the advent of television and in this media-dominated age I think it would be almost impossible for modern children to be quite as unaware of what was going on in the outside world as we were, but on that September day in 1939 the news of war burst on me with all the suddenness of the bombs that were about to fall on England. Whether this blinkered protection was a good thing or not I don't know. As usual, I expect there are pros and cons to either scenario. When my first novel was published my grown-up children were highly amused to read in the blurb on the cover that 'this book is about the art of compromise'—which was news to me. 'Good old Mum—can't help seeing all points of view,' they said, falling about with laughter.

We had spent August in a borrowed house at Burnham Beeches after moving out of Baldwin's End Cottage because my father was about to become a housemaster in the Michaelmas Half and we were in the process of moving into Common Lane House, an old house with a wonderfully central position. We had then gone to spend the last part of the school holidays at Cefn, in North Wales, my paternal grandparents' second home.

All the grown-ups seemed very preoccupied and David and I were playing in the garden when my parents called us in because they had something important to tell us. We went into the house where my grandparents and the uncles were assembled and my father told us that England was at war with Germany.

I have no memory of the explanation which he surely must have given us, only of the terrible atmosphere of anxiety, the gravity on all their faces, and the sick feeling this gave me in my stomach.

Afterwards we were sent back into the garden and immediately dived into the dense hedge of viburnum tinus that that ran below the croquet lawn, dividing the manicured part of the garden from the rough grass of the shrubbery. In early spring this area was always a golden shimmer of daffodils and a little later clouded white with the Pheasant Eye narcissi so specially prized by my grandmother, but by September the grass was scrubby and brownish after being scythed for hay by my friend Obadiah. David and I often had a secret den in this hedge—a good place to hide from authority and a happy hunting ground for the lost croquet balls which over-enthusiastic grown-ups had whacked out of bounds during needle matches.

Crouched in our leafy hideout, we discussed what war would mean— killing people, certainly: even I knew that. Would our father have to join the army and fight for England? Possibly—petrifying thought—be killed himself? David, far more knowledgeable than me about anything to do with fighting, announced solemnly that he thought it likely. Writing this so many years later with both my parents long since gone, I suddenly realise that I have no idea whether joining up was a probability for my father or not. He may have been over the age for compulsory call-up and schoolmastering was for some a protected profession; certain of his colleagues went to war while others like my father manned the home front. Was it a question of choice and, if so, possibly a very difficult choice for him? Unlike his elder brother, Jack, Pa would have had no natural inclination for military life, but it would have been very out of character for him to evade anything if he felt it his duty to do it. I wish I knew. One of the inescapable regrets when someone dies is that so much information, even of a trivial nature, dies with them—part of my excuse to myself for writing these memories down.

My ideas of battle were confined to illustrations from H. E. Marshall's wonderfully romantic children's history book *Our Island*

Story: Boadicea (who seems to have changed her name recently to the less attractive-sounding Boudica) looking ready for anything in a coronet, espadrilles, arm bands and a white nightie, careering about in a chariot with knives on the hubcaps of its wheels; Harold being hit in the eye by an arrow; Henry, glorious at Agincourt; Cavaliers and Roundheads and the future King Charles II, heart-stoppingly handsome, hiding in his oak tree—and also David's regiments of lead soldiers laid out on the nursery floor in front of the toy fort which played a key part in his imaginary games. We had been told we must be extra helpful, but had no idea what form this helpfulness should take. David, ever practical, said he thought we should dig a trench so we went to find Hugh Hughes, who was as much beloved by us as he had been by my father and his brothers when they were children. Hugh provided us with spades so that we could start immediately to put this plan into action, and suggested the kitchen garden—well away from the house—as a suitable site for our war work. I expect it was indeed helpful if it kept us occupied for the next few days, though I had only the haziest idea of what the purpose of a trench actually was. One of my grandmother's half-brothers, Uncle Joss Scholefield, a lawyer who had emigrated to the States and settled in California, generously offered to have David and me for the duration of the war, an offer my parents considered but refused. It must have been tempting with the serious threat of a German invasion looming, and many parents who were offered similar opportunities sent their children to America or Canada, but I can't really imagine my mother agreeing to be parted from her children under any circumstances.

Our life style, like that of everyone else in England, was about to change.

The first immediate change I remember after war was declared was the blackout—that bane of our lives which was to become a nightly ritual and a constant worry for every British household. Drawing-pins were the essential accessory and by the end of the war the wood round most people's windows was pockmarked with tiny holes where curtains or blinds had been pinned to the surrounding frame in an effort to eliminate the smallest chink of light. David and I watched in amazement as grown-ups clambered up ladders in an effort to rig up extraordinary contraptions over windows and skylights, but it must have taken a nightmare of resourcefulness to meet the challenge of making the whole school with all its quirky old buildings blackout-proof. All sorts of unlikely materials were pressed into use such as carpets and sacking—almost anything that was dark and heavy would do—and official cotton 'blackout material'—was sold by the mile.

With the black out, volunteer A.R.P. Wardens became feared bogeymen as they went on inspection tours each night—those with a liking for power over their fellow civilians could indulge their taste. Among beaks any existing antipathies were in no way modified under these circumstances. My father, the most unmilitary of men, joined the Home Guard, and—even more unlikely—became an officer in the Corps. He looked as ill at ease and unconvincing in his khaki uniform as someone who has been bullied into taking part in amateur dramatics. In after years, my brother, who was for five years a regular soldier, always described Pa at funerals as standing to 'Home Guard attention.' It was all very 'Dad's Army'—but serious stuff this time: no more practical jokes with stuffed crocodiles.

My mother, along with other Eton wives and Dames, (the Eton name for house matrons, derived from the original landladies, or dames, who had run local boarding houses in order to enable fee-paying boys to share the tuition given to the seventy King's Scholars in College) became a V.A.D., and took her turn at day or night duty in the Gymnasium, part of which was turned into a First Aid Post. Gillian Elliott (pronounced with a hard G), the Headmaster's powerful wife—a natural chief amongst some rather bolshy Indians—was their Commandant though I don't think she knew any more about first-aid than the rest of them. I suppose the Dames must have had some rudimentary knowledge of nursing and presumably the rest of her band must have done some sort of crash course in basic skills. I have a vague memory of my mother unwillingly attending lectures. Perhaps she passed on a few of her own surprising medical tips? Later in the war when the house of Dr and Mrs Ley (the Precentor and his wife) received a direct hit, Gillian Elliott was said to have rewarded a boy for his helpfulness over their rescue by allowing him into the First Aid Post to see her amateur nurses at work, including watching the doctor stitching up the bottom of a girl injured by shrapnel. The story of this unusual good conduct prize spread through the Eton bush telegraph like wildfire and didn't need the School Messenger to pedal it round Eton.

All car headlights had to be partially blacked out: a small cross of light in the centre was all that was allowed—this went for traffic lights too—and of course street lights were totally extinguished. The night world was in darkness and I remember being taken along in the car by my mother—for dubious moral support—while she made a wavery trial trip through pitch black streets to Windsor and back. It was like someone trying to find their way to the bathroom at night in a strange house by the glimmer of a fading torch. It must have been incredibly difficult and I was conscious of her unvoiced anxiety.

It's hard to remember now how much information of what was really going on filtered through to us children; my recollection is that we varied between bemused fear and fascinated excitement at all the new goings-on. All signposts were painted out or removed, as were place-names on railway stations. The idea was to confuse any Germans who might parachute in, but of course it confused everyone else too. Map-reading your way about small country lanes without the help of signs or place names became an essential skill. The only hope of knowing where you were when any train stopped on interminable wartime journeys was if you were lucky enough to catch the announcement of the station's name as it was croaked by some ancient porter, dredged from retirement while younger men were conscripted to serve in the armed forces as he—or increasingly often she—tottered down the platform. Knowledge of a train timetable was no help because trains might stop anywhere, scheduled or not, for any length of time.

There were constant warnings to be on the alert for German spies—nuns were particularly suspect, and we were always hopefully on the lookout for black-habited mother superiors fluttering about in the sky like rooks. Eva Mackinnon, wife of the Assistant Bursar, told the story of how she had actually given mugs of ersatz coffee to two frail, hungry-looking nuns who came to the door with a collecting box for some charity. After they had departed she saw to her horror a large red lipstick mark on the rim of one mug, and instantly feared she had been entertaining The Enemy in disguise—until she remembered that 'Bee' Mackinnon, her husband, had done the washing-up the night before and the lipstick mark was her own.

Advertisements on hoardings gave way to dire warnings: 'Careless talk costs Lives', 'Make do and mend', 'Dig for Victory', and the mysterious 'Be like Dad—keep Mum' which I found puzzling. There was also an evil cartoon character called The Squander Bug who apparently caused citizens to do reprehensibly wasteful things if not resisted. I've always felt a guilty affection for The Squander Bug, and succumbed to his wiles years ago.

At Eton, boys made chain gangs to fill and then pile up banks of sandbags outside buildings to protect lower windows against bomb blast, gloomily obliterating all light from outside. Sticky tape, criss-crossed over the window panes of town houses was a common sight during the war and rubber solution was sprayed on all our windows at Common Lane House in order to protect the boys from flying glass should the windows be blown out in an air raid. It made the house incredibly dark and dreary giving every room the feeling of a lavatory with frosted glass. Needless to say we children picked out little spy holes through which we could peer at the outside world. You had to scratch hard with a thumb until you got a good wodge of rubbery goo under your nail and then you could peel bits off in the most satisfying way. The trick was to know when to stop because it was so tempting to go on pulling, making the hole ever larger—but no hole could remain undiscovered for long and there would be repercussions afterwards. A discreet peephole might be overlooked but the demolishing of the protective layer from whole window panes could not be excused, as I learnt to my cost.

As the war progressed all sorts of restrictions and shortages came into play which would seem extraordinary to my children and grandchildren, though with our new awareness of global warming, recycling is beginning to enjoy a renaissance. I grew up at a time when no envelope was ever wasted if it could be used again—probably several times—with an 'Economy-Label' stuck on top; bits of string and brown paper were hoarded; tail ends of soap were melted down and gunged together again; old jerseys were unravelled so that the horrid crinkly wool could be washed and knitted up again into something else; newspapers were torn up and screwed into 'spills' for lighting fires: matches were very precious. A red line was painted at the end of baths, three inches above the bottom, to stop one running too much hot water—thereby conserving precious fuel; there were frequent power cuts and constant power restrictions on electricity and gas so that the gas fire or single-barred electric heater often gave out little heat. Coal and coke were rationed and the cold in winter was intense—none of our houses had central heating. Chilblains, those appallingly sore and itchy swellings on toes and fingers, became commonplace and most of our fingers looked like chipolata sausages. Petrol was rationed and later the car had to be laid-up till the end of the war; food was rationed; clothes were rationed. Soon practically everything was rationed.

Nearly everyone who could lay claim to the smallest backyard space—let alone a real garden—kept hens to eke out the revolting powdered egg ration. We brought our hens down from Wales on one of our many memorable wartime journeys as we now spent all school holidays at Cefn in order to have a respite from the air raids.

Hens do not make ideal travelling companions—especially when the string round the box in which they travel keeps breaking. My mother, having failed on the last lap of the journey to get them into the Guard's van along with our bicycles—another vital bit of wartime equipment—was anxious that our fellow passengers should not realize what was in the increasingly smelly parcel she had defiantly put onto the overhead rack in our compartment. Strange noises started to come from our luggage, and one or two people made insinuating remarks which my mother loftily ignored. Luckily the train was so crowded that anyone fortunate enough to have got a seat was not going to risk losing it by moving, so nobody investigated. My mother made fiercely quelling faces at us in case we said anything which might let the cat— or in this case the birds—out of the bag.

It was typical of her that we had to obtain our eggs in quite such a difficult way: there must surely have been plenty of hens for sale in

Berkshire? But once she had been struck with an idea she was not one to abandon it, and anyway she considered anything from Cefn had a special magic—our eggs would be far more nourishing if they came, however indirectly, from Wales. We had to change trains at Chester and Crewe, cross London by taxi (always agonizingly long waits in the cold and dark in taxi queues) to get from Euston to Paddington and thence to Slough—but we got the hens to Eton. Brown Henrietta—my favourite—white Amelia, black Susan and Fiery-Lizzie—the most beautiful of the four, who had a flame-coloured rear and an elegant smoke grey neck—did sterling war work for us. They were joined later by my beloved bantams, Rachel and Rebecca who used to ride about on my shoulder when not earning their keep in the nesting-box. Chickens, however, especially when fed on scraps, also brought rats to the garden: not so nice. Rats were caught in a barred cage-trap and it was David's job, when at home from school, to drown the rats in the water butt in the garden. At some stage he taunted me that I was too feeble and girly to drown a rat myself and when I foolishly protested, dared me to prove that I could really do it. I expect I must have been being particularly annoying—or was badgering him to take me on some expedition when he didn't want to have me trailing along—to have caused this teasing, because he was usually my kind protector, but I remember my efforts to prove my valour and equality all too well. Next time there was a rat in the trap, the rat and I looked at each other for what seemed like an age before I could bring myself to lower the contraption into the water butt. I had to stand on a large box in order to be tall enough to achieve this and peered down with horror at the stream of bubbles that rose to the surface as I held the rat under water before I hauled the trap up again. The saturated rat lay limply in the bottom, its sinister aura pitiably diminished in death, while I rushed to the rubbish heap and was violently sick. When I returned, green and shivery, to collect the evidence of my would-be boyish bravery, the rat, like Lazarus, had undergone a miraculous revival. It was sitting up, much refreshed, and cleaning its whiskers. I let it out.

Of course people living in the country who grew their own vegetables and had access to cows and pigs never faced the same food shortages as town dwellers. When we went to Cefn for the holidays we ate like gourmets compared to the term time. Katie Jones made delectable rabbit stews—the rabbits shot by David with the ancient .410 hammer gun that had belonged to Uncle Jack and my father when they were boys. Farmers occasionally offered extra ham or bacon rashers and even—a rare treat—small amounts of butter. I'm amazed my mother never hit on the notion of transporting a pig—Welsh, naturally—by passenger train from Cefn to the garden of Common Lane House.

Feeding ravenous teenage boys must have been a nightmare and as the war dragged on and rations grew smaller my mother had the unenviable task of catering for a household of about fifty people, dealing with all the ration books and trying to engage and then keep a domestic staff in competition with all the other Eton houses. Mum came into her own with these challenges and was at her enterprising, busy best. Despite all the difficulties of the job however, on a personal level the hardest thing for her was probably having to share her house with another woman—the dame. This was not something she ever found easy but it must have been especially difficult to start with because my parents' first dame, an extremely efficient but emotionally needy character, played on my father's ready sympathy and openly adored him. I was very aware of the tensions between her and Mum, without really understanding the cause, though years later as a young headmaster's wife I understood all too well and felt much retrospective sympathy for my mother. The first dame only lasted for about a year and Mum certainly preferred her breezy but inefficient replacement who drove my father crackers and nearly caused a medical catastrophe by failing to summon medical help quickly enough to a boy with a head injury. She didn't last long either.

For a while Mum kept bees—you could claim an extra sugar allowance for doing this—and got much advice from Grandpa Nickson. For some reason she and our doctor Wilfred Attlee, a good friend of my parents, kept their beehives down the Eton Wick road at the school Sanatorium of which—as one of his extra wartime jobs— my father was in charge. Every Sunday afternoon I used to walk there with him on his routine visit to see Matron. I looked forward madly to this potentially dull expedition because it meant that on the way to and fro, I had my father's sparklingly good company all to myself—a rare treat. I presume that unlike hens, bee-keeping was not encouraged in the gardens of boys' houses, in case any boy with an allergic reaction got stung, but I suppose at the Sanatorium medical attention for this emergency would have been on tap. Mum always claimed that she was never stung by her own bees but only by Dr Attlee's bees which, according to her, had more aggressive temperaments, though it must have been hard to tell which was which. When my mother did get stung, whether by alien bees or not, she used to swell up alarmingly and her eyes disappeared into her face giving her an unnerving resemblance to the picture of an Eskimo lady in my Geography book, but she insisted valiantly that bee venom was good for her rheumatism. She used to pedal off down Judy's Passage en route for the Eton Wick Road ready-dressed in full anti-bee regalia—the navy blue woollen trousers she wore during air raids with bicycle clips round the ankles, leather gauntlets and a straw boater with the dense black bee veil attached to the brim, hardly able to see out through the veil and looking extremely strange as she wavered blindly along on her rusty old upright bicycle with the high handlebars and uncertain brakes.

Mum's pretty auburn hair turned grey in one month at the start of the war and, never one to fuss about her appearance, she grew it and took to wearing it pulled back from a centre parting in a severe bun, bustling defiantly into middle age. After the war, still only in her early forties, she cut her hair short again and looked years younger although by this time it had turned a becoming shade of silver. She was always mistrustful of elegance in other people—not that those who possessed it were too thick on the ground at Eton, Mrs Wykes and Mrs Tatham being two exceptions. I secretly admired them both but didn't dare say so to my mother. Mrs Wykes wore bright yellow stockings which greatly impressed me in those days of subfusc hosiery and soigné Mrs Tatham was often accompanied by two sinuously elegant Afghan hounds which flowed along after her like mobile fashion accessories.

I couldn't imagine my mother bursting into such flashy plumage or sporting that kind of designer dog.

Our household, with boys, domestic staff and family, must have consisted of about fifty people and each week Mum measured out everyone's butter, sugar and revolting-tasting margarine allowance into screw-top jars and saucers with initials painted on for consumption in the dining room. Some percentage of course was withheld for cooking. We all had our own character-revealing ways of dealing with this, and on the whole people were divided into hoarders or gobblers. Did you have an invisible scraping of butter on toast or bread for most of the week, for instance, or one great gorgeous mouthful once a week? I was of the gobbling school of thought, preferring 'a crowded hour of glorious life', but one couldn't help envying the hoarders their irritating self-discipline by the end of the week. Children of today would be amazed at how little fat we had. High cholesterol and obesity were not our problem.

In the summer holidays of 1939 my parents had been building on much needed extra bathroom and lavatory facilities to the boys' side of Common Lane House—though still inadequate by today's standards. William Hope-Jones, from whom my father took over the house, had made do with only one bathroom for himself, Mrs Hope-Jones, their six brilliant children and all the domestic staff. The workmen employed to undertake this improvement were Italian and the moment war was declared they downed tools and rushed off to join Mussolini. There was great difficulty in getting the building work finished before the beginning of the half. In those days each house and all its running costs were the personal responsibility of the housemaster to whom the boarding fees were paid. My parents had to take out a significant bank loan to cover the costs of the improvements in the expectation that they would eventually not only recover their money but actually make a profit. Their finances never did recover and as well as the terrible wartime anxieties I think my father was constantly plagued by worries about money. The days when housemasters made money from their houses were gone, but their salaries did not rise to reflect this till well after the war.

William Hope-Jones, known as 'Ho-Jo', was one of Eton's great eccentrics, a brilliant mathematician, a kind man, and much loved— if mocked at—by the boys in his house. He espoused a Spartan way of life and was known for his addiction to jolly fresh air, views on the sacredness of the human body and a dislike of wearing socks. Apparently when Claude Elliott, the headmaster, remonstrated with him about the latter, objecting to the sight of bare ankles beneath the turn-ups of beaks' uniform trousers as undignified, Ho-Jo took to painting his ankles black, which looked even stranger when he was seen bathing in the (otherwise) buff in Cuckoo Weir—that unsavoury backwater of the Thames which served as a swimming-pool throughout my childhood for all Etonians. Ho-Jo was arrested for indecency when he dived, starkers, off the top of Windsor Bridge into the powerfully flowing River Thames below. Woad would no doubt have been his favoured outdoor cladding if he'd had the choice: he produced some witty verses in praise of it which the Scouts used to sing to the tune of 'Men of Harlech':

> What's the good of wearing braces,
> Vests and pants and boots with laces,
> Spats or hats you buy in places
> Down the Brompton Road?
> What's the use of shirts of cotton,
> Studs that always get forgotten?
> These affairs are simply rotten:
> Better far is Woad.

> Woad's the stuff to show men:
> Woad to scare your foemen:
> Boil it to a brilliant blue
> And rub it on your back and your abdomen.
> Ancient Briton never hit on
> Anything as good as Woad to fit on
> Neck or knees or where you sit on,
> Tailors you be blowed.

Mrs Hope-Jones, on the other hand, was more modest and could often be seen at Cuckoo Weir wearing a bathing-dress made from checked cotton dusters, two for the bottom arranged in a cunning sort of triangular fold and joined at crucial places—and two for the top. Even during the war, when rationing caused people to be inventive with their clothes, this garment was remarkable. She was extremely thin and I can visualise her poised on the bank, scrawny arms pointing upwards like a church steeple, hair stapled on top of her head, before she upended and disappeared into the murky depths of the river, dusters clinging round her skinny frame.

As the young and able-bodied of both sexes joined the services, getting staff, either teaching or domestic, became a struggle. If you were lucky enough to find someone to fill a post, then you were certainly prepared to put up with a few eccentricities. Over the next few years we had some pretty strange types working at Common Lane House including Miss Jackson, the cook, a sparse-haired, one-toothed lady with a terrible temper who cooked in a red felt hat. I can't remember anything about her culinary skills but I do remember that she once burst into my father's study wielding a nicely sharpened carving knife and uttering blood-curdling threats against various other members of staff—and especially against my mother. My father never doubted for a moment that her intentions were serious, but his courtesy did not desert him: 'How nice to see you Miss Jackson,' he said, pulling out an armchair for her. 'Now do come in and sit down and tell me what the trouble is. I wonder if you might let me relieve you of that rather inconvenient-looking knife? Oh, thank you *so* much.'

She calmed down, my father somehow managing, as he so often did with all sorts of people, to draw out the best in her. I don't suppose anyone had ever listened to her with such concentrated or courteous attention before. Perhaps in more peaceful times she would have been asked to leave immediately, or even rushed off to the nearest psychiatric hospital, but you didn't lightly part with a school cook in wartime. She told my mother later that she was lucky to be married to such a perfect gentleman, and no one was murdered.

I think this ability to bring out the best in people was probably my father's outstanding gift both as a teacher and as a housemaster. As my brother later put it in *Two at a Time*, his own book of memoirs, 'He created virtue by imputing it and gave boys confidence in themselves.' After his death in 1983 my mother had countless letters from Old Etonians on the theme of my father having enabled them to perform beyond their natural ability by giving them belief in themselves. He had an off-beat sense of humour and an engaging ability to poke fun, primarily at himself, but sometimes, in the kindest way, at other people if he thought they were taking themselves too seriously. I never heard my father be rude to anyone, but if angered he could, very occasionally, be formidable.

Thanks to Pa Miss Jackson remained, but one helper who did have to leave was beautiful Welsh Joan of the lovely soprano voice and beguiling smile, who ran the boys' dining room with impeccable efficiency. At twenty she had been turned down as medically unfit to join the forces or do strenuous war work in a factory, and my mother had been thrilled to find her—until she announced her engagement to a seventeen year-old boy in John Herbert's house (The Hop Garden) opposite. They had conducted their courtship across Common Lane from the pantry window in our house to his bedroom opposite, Joan serenading him with love songs as she did the washing-up. One of them had to leave and the headmaster decreed that it should be my mother's parlourmaid. Mum was very put out. Another member of the domestic staff whose time with us was also cut short was tottery old Mrs Harris who looked so like a witch that I constantly expected her to fly off astride the yellow 'Ewebank' carpet sweeper she pushed slowly round the passages. Unlike Joan, whom she loved, my mother intensely disliked Mrs Harris, partly because she reeked overpoweringly of TCP, a smell Mum detested, and partly because she was given to uttering dire warnings about my state of health. 'Mark my words, you'll bury that child one day—you see if you don't,' she predicted with gloomy relish whenever I was laid low with some childish ailment. The tables were to be turned. One morning Mrs Harris herself was discovered dead as the proverbial doornail outside her bedroom on the top landing, Ewebank lying uselessly beside her.

'Well now *I'm* going to bury *her*,' my mother triumphantly told my father, to his huge amusement, as she bicycled off, dressed in black, to attend Mrs Harris's funeral at Eton Wick cemetery.

A sombre reminder of the tragedies of war were the daily lists in the papers of those killed in action, missing, believed killed, or wounded, and the sadness and anxiety on my parents' faces as they looked at these columns made a great impression on me. The first of my father's boys to be killed was William Palmer, a boy we had got to know well because his home was in South Africa, so from the moment war broke out he had been cut off from his family and had spent part of the holidays with us. This was the first time death had claimed anyone I knew and that it should be someone who had so recently been chatting to me, teasing me in a big brotherly sort of way and playing cards with me was shattering. He was eighteen.

Everyone makes a great fuss about any suggestion of identity cards nowadays, but in the war we all had to have one in order to be eligible to claim a ration book and we all had an individual number which we had to wear so that our remains could be identified if we were killed. My identity disk was on a silver bracelet and my number, engraved on it by the School Stores jewellery department, was easy for me to remember because it rhymed: DVJ E stroke thirteen stroke three. My mother told me I had to wear it in case I ever got lost, which seemed rather a cosy idea, and it was from other children that I discovered that its real value would be in identifying my dead body if I was hit by a bomb. We also had to have gas masks with us at all times; they were packed in a cardboard box and slung over the shoulder in a special case—no euphemisms about this: we were all told about 'mustard gas' and its potential horrors. Carrying our gas masks became an unquestioned routine when leaving the house, no matter for how short a time, like putting on outdoor shoes. How I dreaded gas mask practices and inspections and the terrible, claustrophobic panic of being strapped into this suffocating contraption! I can still smell the horrible rubber smell and feel the dreaded choking sensation of it closing in round my cheeks as the webbing straps were tightened at the back of my head. Grown-ups' encouraging jokes: 'Pretend you're an elephant with a funny trunk' fell very flat as far as I was concerned.

Soon after the war started, during the first few months of what came to be called the 'Phoney War' there were the first 'false' air raid warnings when the sound of wailing 'Alert' sirens bansheed into the darkness as we all trooped down to the smelly 'Anderson' shelter which had been urgently built at the bottom of the gardens of all boys' houses. Soon the single-noted 'All-clear' went and we were able to troop back into the garden again. I was thrilled to be pushed on my swing in the moonlit garden by various members of the 'Library'—the Eton equivalent of house prefects. I had always spent a lot of time on the swing in the daytime, playing my own imaginary games, sailing up towards the clouds and taking daring leaps into the garden below— but soaring up and down into the night sky in my dressing gown was glorious. Aged eight, I fell deeply in love with Eddy McGrigor, one of the swing-pushers who was about to become captain of my father's house. Eddy was to remain a family friend for life.

All too soon real air raids began in earnest and were anything but fun. The shelters were long reinforced concrete bunkers lined on each side with double tiers of slatted wooden bunks. When the siren sounded, everyone pulled on a jersey and a pair of trousers, seized a torch, a rug, a pillow and the ready-packed emergency bag which we all kept at the foot of our beds, and scrimmaged out to the shelter and settled for the night. A few lucky people managed to sleep, but the horrible dank dampness of the shelter brought on my mother's asthma within minutes of being down there, and eventually the doctors decided that it was far more dangerous for her to go into the shelter than to risk the bombs, so she and I would lie under the grand piano in the drawing room while she read aloud to me above the crackle of gunfire till that most reassuring of noises, the 'All Clear', sounded. We would no doubt have been pressed out flat like gingerbread men if the house had collapsed from a direct hit, but it gave us a false sense of security that was comforting. Daylight was comforting too, when it came—no air raids till darkness fell.

I have a memory of my mother stretched out under the piano reading me *White Fang* by Jack London, wearing evening dress—short, blue, Chinese silk jacket with tiny buttons down the front, long straight black skirt, pointy-toed shoes, discreet string of pearls, no make-up—so raids must sometimes have started early in the darkness of winter and for a short while dinner parties must have continued to be formal despite the war. I remember peering down through the banisters of Common Lane House as Lord Quickswood, the Provost, (formerly Lord Hugh Cecil) arrived to dine with my parents clad in the black knee breeches and silk stockings he still favoured rather than the more contemporary dinner jacket. Stories about 'Linky', as he was called, were legion: he always read the lessons in College chapel wearing a green celluloid eye shade more suitable to a female tennis champion at Wimbledon. Whether this was supposed to help poor eyesight I don't know, but he certainly sometimes got the words wrong and once famously convulsed the boys at Evensong by announcing in his squeaky voice: 'We will now sing the Narcissus'. He fought a running battle with the headmaster, Claude Elliott, and their dislike of each other was legendary.

The cracking and booming of continuous anti-aircraft gunfire at night, which seemed to shake the house to its foundations, became a constant dread of my childhood. Always 'gun-shy', with a hatred of loud noises, I was more terrified by the explosive sounds of our defences than the thought of bombs themselves, though I remember the sickening whoosh and crump made by falling bombs. Even though the sound of the 'All Clear' was always a blessed relief, indicating that enemy aircraft were no longer overhead, the sound of gunfire could carry over a twenty mile radius. Eton is only twenty miles from London and very close to Slough which was a major target for the German bombers because of its vital munitions factories.

Despite the proximity of the heavily guarded Castle, the home in which the Royal Family stayed at weekends and where the princesses were evacuated during the whole of the war, I don't think Windsor received any direct hits in the blitz. London and Slough were the real targets.

Kippers and Cow Parsley
Remembering my mother, with love

Talking of kippers and cow parsley
I thought immediately of you.

Both would be luxuries if they were rare:
the one so highly flavoured,
pungent, strong—
caviar for unpretentious homes—
the other hedgerow lace
of beautiful simplicity
and quite without artifice.

We never had to guess
your stream of thought:
no muddy waters, stagnant pools or tributaries,
your little burn flowed clear and bright
straight down a narrow channel;
its force and energy
could well have turned a mill wheel
and ground corn—good wholemeal flour
for family consumption—
but not to be gobbled up
by stray lame ducks.

Children you loved, and birds,
looked not unlike
a small pied flycatcher yourself
—so darting and alert—
watchful to snatch at any chance
for nurturing your chicks.

I borrowed your car once
and moved the driving mirrors
'Don't worry, darling, that's alright,'
you said, 'I never use them anyway.'

Not for you the backward glance,
careful avoidance of collision
or keeping to the inside lane.

You were never much inclined
to dwell on shelf-life:
no silly nonsense about sell-by dates
or 'best before...'
at ninety you applied for a new Railcard
answering the question 'Hobbies and Interests?'
with a single word:
LIVING you wrote, heavily underlined.

You kept no airs and graces
in your wardrobe, and could be sharp
with flashy dressers rash enough
to wear them in your presence
  —yet now my post brings tributes to surprise you:
'She was a great lady' and
'We shall not see the like of her again'
Life will be very dull without you, Mum,
but thank you for your generous years
of *biased* love.

7

WINDSOR CASTLE

BEFORE the outbreak of war, my mother had driven me to Windsor every morning in the boxy little black Morris Eight—successor to the ancient, open, two seater snub-nosed Morris of my very early years. I remember the excitement of this car arriving because we had been two years without a car, my parents having parted with the old one in an attempt to economise, but my mother had unexpectedly been left a small legacy and decided to blue it all on a car—a brand new car! We thought it incredibly dashing. It was to last us for years—David and I both learnt to drive in that car—and we were to do many family journeys in it after the war. I marvel now that we all four squeezed in as David and I grew larger: we sat in the back, clutching our knees, so tightly wedged in with clobber that it was a major operation to get out again especially as there were only two doors. There was no boot, only a small rack that let down at the back on which suitcases, in theory, could be roped. I don't think my father was very good at doing this because they tended to fall off—which caused my mother to have one of her innovative ideas. She designed a large wooden box— rumoured by the boys to be a coffin—and had it fixed to the back of the car. It had been bad enough when our suitcases dropped off en route, but it was much worse when the coffin itself fell off as it once did on one of our many journeys to Wales. It weighed a ton and even unloaded it was hard to move from the middle of the road. We could have done with the horsepower of a lorry because our progress up hills was always extremely slow and unreliable. If we didn't get what Mum euphemistically called a 'good clear run', there was always anxiety as to whether we would make it to the top of any steep incline. Sometimes we didn't. Then the passengers would have to clamber out and walk. Sometimes David and I had to push, first searching for sizeable stones to put behind the back wheels to stop the car from slipping while my mother, if in the driving seat, roared optimistically but fruitlessly on the accelerator, or my father 'rode the clutch' with great skill and delicacy, keeping the car stationary but making no progress up hill. Somehow we always got there in the end—however that was still in the future and after the war the luxury of having a car again more than compensated for such trivial trials.

The wide wrought iron gates through which tourists now enter Windsor Castle were closed during the war and entry was only through the heavily guarded, arched entrance known as King Henry VIII's Gateway. Only those with a special pass could enter and the Guardsmen in the sentry boxes on either side no longer wore ceremonial plumed bearskins and scarlet tunics but purposeful tin hats and khaki 'battle dress', and their rifles, with fixed bayonets, were loaded. There were always two policemen on duty too, with whom we children became great friends. My special favourite, unbelievably well-named for an official in a royal residence, was called Mr Courtier. He was as bald as Humpty-Dumpty and much the same shape and could make his helmet jiggle either up and down or side to side in the most satisfactory way by moving his scalp. While on the subject of names, there were three workers in the gardens and parks at Windsor Castle when I was a child, called respectively, Christmas, Easter and Pentecost, all of whom served in the Home Guard during the war. Easter was also the Morsheads' gardener. Berkshire abounds in surprising surnames, supposedly due to the famous Foundling Hospital at Reading which flourished in the eighteenth and nineteenth centuries, where foundling babies were allotted names for a variety of reasons, including the days or times of year when they were brought in, or the unlikely places where they had been found. The Reading telephone directory used to be a great source of unlikely surnames. All the many gates inside the Castle grounds were locked and guarded but certain residents, such as the Morsheads, were issued with sets of huge keys which were themselves carefully kept under lock and key. I now caught a number 441 bus which stopped outside Upper School and went up Eton High Street, over the bridge and to the top of Windsor Hill; I then walked to lessons on my own, a freedom I relished. After a chat with the policemen (the only way a soldier on sentry duty was supposed to acknowledge anyone's presence was if he had to leap into action and shoot you dead as an enemy alien, though sometimes I could get the flicker of a wink, which always felt deliciously subversive), I would trudge up Lower Ward, opposite the breathtakingly beautiful St George's Chapel, round the right-hand side of the Round Tower (in the filled-in moat of which, at a later stage, we used to go roller skating until we made too much noise and were banned by Lord Wigram, the Governor), through St George's Gate—a pause to look up at the carving of the dragon-slayer above—and down the hill to the Morsheads' house. It was a wonderfully romantic walk with which to start my day and I meandered along in a happy daydream.

After the outbreak of war when Mary was thirteen and Phoebe and I were eight, we were joined by three other little girls. First to come was Louise Cockcraft—later to marry David in St George's Chapel and become my sister-in-law. Louise was an only child and her father, Colonel Louis Cockcraft DSO—always known as Beetle—had just been made a Military Knight. He and his wife Jane came to live at Number 8 Lower Ward, one of the houses in the row of ancient 'grace and favour' dwellings which I walked past every morning and where distinguished retired soldiers of slender means traditionally lived and carried out ceremonial duties. When on parade they wore wonderfully becoming uniforms of scarlet tailcoats (invariably adorned with rows of medals), dress swords and glamorous cocked hats with white plumes. During the war their duties and dress were far from ceremonial and these gallant elderly gentlemen became the backbone of the Home Guard and the A.R.P. and responsible for the safety of the Castle. It fell to Beetle's lot to tell the King that he and the Queen and the two Princesses really must not to go out on the top of the Round Tower during air raids to watch the firework display in the sky. This was not at all popular with the Monarch who had a notoriously short fuse and Beetle probably deserved another medal for bravery.

Beetle and Jane Cockcraft had been given an introduction to my parents by my Great Uncle George, the retired bishop. Next to join us were Anne and Carola Verney, whose parents had taken a house locally so that they and their small brother Harry could be near their handsome and alarming mother Esmé, who was commandant of the FANY (First Aid Nursing Yeomanry) training centre stationed at Combermere barracks in Windsor while their father, Ulick Verney, known to friends and family as Peter, was a career soldier and spent much of the war in India. Arklow Cottage, at the gates of the Great Park, provided Nanny and the children with a wartime base. Nanny Verney was a force to be reckoned with—a tall and immensely distinguished-looking figure, who was said to be the illegitimate daughter of the 5th Earl of Harewood—though we children didn't know this bit of gossip at the time, nor would it have meant much to us if we had. Years later when I came to know the redoubtable and delightful Madge, the Dowager Lady Boyne, born Lady Margaret Lascelles, the resemblance between these two unacknowledged half-sisters was unmistakable.

As far as Phoebe and I were concerned, the arrival of other children to share our lessons greatly enhanced our lives. Paquita Morshead now did most of the teaching herself, and Mary, who up till then had done her lessons in a separate room, joined us too. How Paquita managed to cope with a class of such varied ages and stages, ranging from eight to fourteen, as well as all the many other things she did, I don't know. Perhaps the answer is that wonderful though she was, a good deal of the time she couldn't cope with it and there were yawning chasms in our education which were to prove difficult later. We all ended up with such widely varied levels of knowledge and attainment that those of us who were eventually sent to school never fitted into any class and were either miles ahead of, or far behind our contemporaries in most subjects. We were more or less allowed to concentrate on the lessons we enjoyed most, and certainly never learned a disciplined approach, but at least we now started to partake in activities which involved other people.

On Monday afternoons we trekked down to Eton to join one of Miss Grace Dempster's gym classes for the children of Eton masters. Our class was usually held in a secondary, upstairs gym because the main one was bristling with beaks' wives knitting, chatting and rolling bandages in starched caps and aprons with huge red crosses appliquéd on the bosom, waiting to administer first aid to war casualties who mercifully seemed in short supply. Miss Dempster and her sister were physiotherapists attached to Eton College who gave boys treatments for sports injuries and held remedial exercise classes for those that required it, while their brother, masked and white-suited, taught fencing. I can't remember what Mr Dempster's face looked like because we seldom, if ever, saw it except behind his protective wire mesh face guard. When we were read stories in History lessons about The Man in the Iron Mask I always imagined him as the faceless Mr Dempster lunging about on a rubber mat with squeaky shoes and a rapier. Unlike her white-clad brother, Grace Dempster was a symphony in brown; she wore a very short box-pleated brown gym tunic over a fawn shirt with long sleeves, chocolate woollen bloomers down to the knee, brown lisle stockings and sand coloured plimsolls. Her brown hair was knotted into a big bun and she had brown mottled splodges on her face and hands to match her outfit. I don't think I ever saw her in any other clothing until she attended my wedding in a flowered hat and patterned dress and I hardly recognized her. I adored gym, at which, surprisingly for such a weedy child, I shone. Vaulting over the 'horse', balancing on the bar, shinning up ropes and hanging upside down by my feet transformed me—temporarily—from a timorous wimp into a daringly agile monkey. Though small for my age, I held the record for high jump among all Miss Dempster's classes.

One afternoon a week we endured two hours with wizened Mademoiselle Bouige who looked like a walnut and attempted to engage us in French conversation with conspicuous lack of success. On another afternoon bald little Mr Beech in grey suit and stiff collar and tie came to instruct us in drawing. Perspective was his forte. I don't remember ever drawing anything but square boxes and the blue and white ringed mugs and saucers out of which we drank our milk at our mid-morning break. Alas, I have no talent for drawing or painting but I could still dash off a reasonably recognisable mug if the need arose, though it's not a skill I have been called on to put to much use.

Mr Beech had a large mole on top of his shiny pate, out of which a bristle grew upright to about two inches like an unexpected thistle in the middle of an otherwise well kept lawn. When he came round to correct our work, he used to sit in our places while we stood behind him watching as he transformed our lopsided mugs and curiously angled boxes with a few deft strokes of the pencil. We thought it enormously funny when standing behind him to convulse our giggling fellow artists by pretending to tweak the offending hair. One awful day, Carola unfortunately misjudged the distance and tweaked it right out. Mr Beech said nothing, but gathered up his things and quietly left. His silence and unhappy dignity were far worse than a punishment for us all. The following week six chastened little girls waited in trepidation for the drawing lesson. As far as I know nothing was ever said about the matter.

History and Geography we learnt by playing educational card games on the lines of Happy Families. You had to collect the major events of each reign, or, in the case of Geography the major industries of each country. For instance for India, Burma and Ceylon you would need the cards for rice growing, tea growing and teak. Canada mysteriously listed salmon canneries and due to my inability to spell I always had a delightful vision of lots of little song-birds, all dyed pink, flying round the pine forests serenading the grizzly bears.

We started on Shakespeare at a very early age, reading the plays aloud, taking different parts and learning great chunks by heart, as we learnt much other poetry too. Unlike my abysmal efforts to learn tables or anything to do with figures, remembering words came easily to me and I was in my element. Paquita Morshead had a great knowledge and appreciation of English literature and even more importantly, as far as we were concerned, the ability to transmit her enthusiasm to us. She was a remarkable and unusual woman, combining a mixture of rare insight and wisdom with what some might consider considerable crankiness. After Owen Morshead retired and they went to live in Dorset, she practised as a Radionics Healer (using the controversial and mysterious 'black box' said to transmit healing to invisible energy fields) and had a following of devoted patients.

With increasing food shortages Paquita now acquired two goats for milking—one draught of the revolting liquid they produced put me off the taste of goat's milk for life—and she also started breeding rabbits to sell for the pot to help augment the meagre meat rations. Their hutches stretched all the way up one side of the kitchen garden and it was our job to help look after them. As a sop for assisting with this war work, we were each allowed to name one rabbit as our own and supposedly build up a special relationship with it, but of course torrents of tears ensued when the progeny of our particular doe became ready to be transformed into rabbit pie. I also remember our shock and horror in the early days of this venture when Bun, the friendly buck rabbit who was exceedingly tame, was mistakenly left in the cage with one of his wives and a new-born litter and gobbled up all his own babies—not the sort of paternal behaviour we had been brought up to expect. Lessons might be suspended at any time to enable us to go on long foraging expeditions in the Home Park to pick great trugfuls of coltsfoot leaves—apparently a sort of rabbit equivalent to smoked salmon—to augment their diet or to clean out their smelly cages, an occupation I loathed. Lessons were also suspended on summer mornings when Paquita traipsed us down to a backwater of the Thames which oozed along below the North Terrace of the Castle and somehow taught us all to swim with the help of discarded rubber motor tyres. As she (wisely) never entered the water herself, I'm not sure how she achieved this, but learn to swim we did, chins in the air so we shouldn't swallow the unwholesome water. My children and grandchildren consider my particular head-in-the-air style of breaststroke extremely funny to this day and childhood conditioning has left me with a dislike of putting my face underwater that I've never been able to overcome. We ploughed through the reeds along the edge to start with, where we were still well within our depth and could put a toe down into the reassuring black sludge if need be, but finally the ultimate test came when we had to swim through the lily pads across to the other bank—and of course back again—where the water was quite deep in the middle. I have no idea if Paquita could swim herself, should lifesaving skills ever have been required, but

Health and Safety rules did not impinge on my childhood. Anyway my mother, always darkly suspicious of unknown *other people* would have considered it far riskier to contemplate an outing to the public baths, where, in her opinion, one might pick up absolutely *anything*. During two particularly hard wartime winters we learnt to skate on the lake at Frogmore, wheelbarrowing a couple of kitchen chairs along to the lake's edge so that we could push them round the ice until the great moment came when we got the hang of the rhythm and could take off unaided. Oh the freedom of that moment—like learning to fly! Less adventurously we learned to knit—mostly long khaki scarves for the troops, which were dull but straightforward, though some of us graduated to the production of socks, involving four needles and the complicated operation known as 'turning the heel'. We were not allowed to have idle hands and had to knit for the war effort whenever anyone read aloud to us. It may surprise my children to learn that I became a reasonably proficient knitter and quite enjoyed it as long as my mind was occupied with whatever book was being read to us at the time, but because I could never master the art of reading to myself while knitting at the same time it never appealed to me as an occupation in its own right. I think I once managed a pair of khaki socks, of a distinctly strange shape, before settling back as a producer of military mufflers. When I first went to boarding school this experience stood me in good stead because until the end of the war, everyone was expected to take knitting in to meals and we all busily clicked away, while we waited to be served with food, with our chilblainy, chipolata fingers more limping than flying. Three wartime dishes I remember were 'sausage slush' made from rehydrated potato, gristly pork pie said to be composed of blood and sawdust from the floor of the nearby Harris Bacon factory in Calne, and pink semolina pudding, so solid it had to be cut into squares with a knife. Perhaps the knitting helped to take our minds off the disgusting food but it seems strange to think of today. Paquita Morshead herself was an expert knitter and could read aloud—and very well too—while rattling off socks for soldiers, jerseys for her children and making her own extraordinary skirts, strange tubular garments in purple wool, knitted at enormous speed on one great circular needle with pointed ends. In between our patriotic khaki contributions we were allowed to make something for ourselves and all six of us managed to achieve identical sleeveless pullovers in Fair Isle patterns of red, grey and white, which we wore to Miss Dempster's class with our unbecoming navy blue gym knickers.

At some stage we fell under the spell of guinea pigs. Our mothers, fearing a guinea pig explosion, decreed that we must discover what sexes our respective pets were since both males and females keep their reproductive organs discreetly tucked away internally and it's hard for the uninitiated to distinguish males from females. We were duly dispatched to consult a vet. Quite why we decided to go to a vet in Maidenhead when there must have been perfectly sex savvy vets in Windsor I can't remember, but five of us set off together on a country bus accompanied by a picnic lunch in one basket with two other baskets containing our assorted guinea pigs. I suspect the attraction of the jaunt was an eight mile bus ride unaccompanied by any adults. We duly had our pets 'sexed' in Maidenhead (it strikes me now as rather a suitably named venue for such an enterprise) and they were divided into separate containers. All would have been well had we not taken the little darlings out to play with on the bus on the return journey... got them mixed up and been unable to remember which was which. Of course we did not dare admit this to our mothers and agreed that subterfuge was the only option. I never did know what sex my beloved Chilawee and Chickanee were, (named after the two beavers in *Sajo and Her Beaver People*, that enchanting children's book by the so-called 'Grey Owl') but they must have been two of a kind and it was a great disappointment to me that they never produced any babies. Perhaps nowadays gay guinea pig couples of the same sex manage to acquire ready made families but there were no such opportunities in the nineteen-forties. I was deeply envious when Louise's Salty, originally presumed to be a boy, suddenly popped out an enchanting litter of mini guineas in front of our fascinated gaze. I recommend guinea pigs as a first—if misleading—introduction to obstetrics-as-spectator-sport since they arrive fully clothed and ambulant and with no apparent discomfort to the mother, well able to sit up and wash themselves from their very first breath. Would that the human birth process was always so simple and tidy!

Soon after the outbreak of war, our extra-curricular activities started to include two Royal engagements every week. I always assumed that this honour came my way because of my connection with the Morshead family, but my mother told me later that it also came about at the suggestion of Miss Marten, the formidable spinster sister (known to Eton wives as The Acid Drop). She kept house for Sir Henry Marten, the Vice-Provost, who became History Tutor to Princess Elizabeth and taught her about the British Constitution. Perhaps Miss Marten specially approved of my parents or perhaps it was to make up for the dice with death I had endured at the hand of Sir Henry's chauffeur, but apparently this mark of favour caused considerable resentment among the mothers of other little Eton daughters. I was quite unaware of this at the time but apparently my mother suffered. I don't think there was normally much communication between the two rather self-absorbed and esoteric communities of Castle and College so having a foot in both camps, as I did, was unusual. However it came about, for two hours on Tuesday afternoons we now joined Princess Elizabeth (our present Queen) and Princess Margaret for Girl Guides, and on Saturday mornings we did dancing class with them.

I can't now remember which came first—the dancing or the Guides. I think it was Guides. The King and Queen were great admirers of the Scouting and Guiding movement and as Duke and Duchess of York had both been much involved with it before the war. A 1st Buckingham Palace troupe of Guides and Brownies had been formed in 1937 for the two Princesses and after they were evacuated, this was transformed into the 1st Windsor Castle Company, of which Mary and Phoebe Morshead, Anne and Carola Verney, Louise Cockcraft and I were founder members. We were soon joined by a selection of children from the Royal School in the Great Park for the families of the Crown Estate workers, plus some pupils from a London school which had been evacuated to Windsor to avoid the worst of the blitz. I suppose about fifteen children in all, from these two schools, were brought up to the Castle to join us each Tuesday, arriving in an open horse brake, there being of course no spare petrol. The London children were needle-witted, sharp-tongued and amusing—they greatly increased our vocabularies and must have added a welcome dash of spice to the rather bland dish provided by the rest of us. Sometimes the six of us from Garden House used to go to the Cockcrafts' house in Lower Ward where Louise's mother Jane gave us an early lunch before we changed into our Guide uniforms. Because there would often be an inspection parade during the afternoon meeting, much tweaking and smoothing of our second-hand regulation blue cotton dresses, much buffing of leather belts, *Duraglitting* of badges and re-folding and tying of our ties ensued. The latter consisted of large squares of coloured cotton which when folded in the traditional way became the trademark stumpy Girl Guide ties, but could, in theory, be whipped off in an emergency, opened out and folded diagonally to make a triangle and used as a sling should one happen to encounter anyone wandering around with a broken arm. After applying the Duraglit, I remember how violently we then polished our brass 'trefoil' badges on Louise's bedroom carpet—good for the approved gleam of the badges but not much cop for the carpet, I imagine. Despite our efforts at sprucing ourselves up, I think we always looked pretty shabby compared with the glossy appearance of Princess Elizabeth and Princess Margaret, whose well-ironed dresses positively gleamed and crackled with starch and whose shoes shone with military brightness. We would always be expected to arrive before them, crossing the big Quadrangle, or Upper Ward, the very heart of the enclave of the Castle buildings, passing the great equestrian statue of King Charles II and then entering the State Apartments through a door in the projecting State Entrance designed by the architect Sir Jeffry Wyattville for King George IV. From there—a gaggle of slightly overawed but giggling little girls— we made our way up the Grand Staircase with its gun carriages, display of ancient weaponry, impressive suits of armour (including that of King Henry VIII), and the two huge armoured models of horses at the top, to the enormously long St George's Hall, revamped, like so much of the Castle by Wyattville. Here, in these historic surroundings, we would be joined by the two Princesses, accompanied by their governess Miss Crawford—known to all as Crawfie—who later notoriously became *persona non grata* with the royal family for writing about their childhood, albeit in the most flattering way. In the light of the kind of revelations and disclosures that are now all too commonplace her indiscretion seems pretty innocuous but at the time it obviously caused great offence. Sad for both sides that those seventeen years of devoted service should have ended on a sour note. We liked Crawfie, who would be wearing the uniform of a 'Guider' or Guide's officer. She was pleasant to everyone and was disposed to set us at our ease—though not so much at our ease that we were not conscious of an invisible line that must not be overstepped. We always curtseyed when the Princesses first arrived and addressed them as Princess Elizabeth and Princess Margaret. There was never any question of lapsing into the use of their Christian names only. We took this completely for granted at the time, but looking back I can see what a barrier it was. I think the Princesses themselves were probably unaware that this was so, but we most certainly were not. We were always on our best behaviour and treated them with a certain deference, and this does not make for normal relationships between children. Waiting for us would be Miss Violet Synge our Guide 'Captain' who had previously run the Buckingham Palace Company, a jolly, statuesque lady of whom we were somewhat in awe, and her more larky and approachable second-in-command or 'Lieutenant', Miss Ramsay, with a drawly voice, elongated vowels and infectiously cackling laugh.

There was much about this privileged Guide Company that was enormous fun, but as far as I was concerned there was also something to dread. My constant bugbear was 'signalling', the sending and receiving of messages by means of waving flags in either semaphore or Morse code. I don't know which system was worse, or whether transmitting or receiving was more terrifying to me, for though no one else seemed to find either particularly difficult, no matter how hard I tried, I was completely incapable of remembering the various arm and flag positions of the former, or the 'dots and dashes' representing letters of the alphabet of the latter. As it was usually a competitive exercise between one patrol and another, I was constantly letting down the fellow members of my patrol and became extremely unpopular on these occasions. Perhaps it was lucky that I was still only a child when the war ended and never had to join the services and practise signalling to serious effect. I would have been a disaster.

In the winter or on rainy days our meetings took place in the immensely grand surroundings of St George's Hall with the moulded and painted shields of all the former Knights of the Garter on the wooden ceiling overhead. Each patrol—I think there were three— would have its own special 'HQ' in the bay of one of the huge windows and we could run races the whole length of the chamber. We learnt to tie all sorts of nautical knots, first aid and the theory of childcare; we lumbered about doing country dancing and we sang jolly campfire songs. In good weather, out in the Home Park, we occasionally had real campfires for which we collected firewood—to augment and add a bogus authenticity to the pile of logs already chopped for us by the Grenadier Guards! A type of bleached dead wood called *punk* was particularly desirable for its burning qualities, I remember. No such aids as paper or firelighters were ever allowed—or indeed available, and to use more than one match to light a fire was much frowned on. I can still lay a mean fire to this day. We learnt how to make a ring of flat stones as a fireplace on which we could balance a saucepan; how to place two forked sticks either side holding a cross bar capable of supporting a billycan; we made revolting concoctions of much kneaded grey dough from flour and water called *dampers*, which were rolled into grubby worms, twisted round sticks and poked in the embers. When cooked, we thought these indigestible corkscrew-like confections, flavoured exclusively by wood smoke, tasted positively ambrosial.

The Grenadiers featured largely in our outdoor life. They built wonderful assault courses for us to swarm up and through and over and a sergeant came and drilled us—apparently the King, for some reason, was particularly keen for us to learn proper drill—so we could Quick March, Dress by the Right, Form Fours, Left and Right Wheel and Halt in a highly professional way and felt well equipped to take on the German Army single-handed. I hope the Guardsmen enjoyed these unusual duties and that it amused them while they trained at Windsor to face deadly enemy fire which the invasion of France, which lay ahead of them, would bring. They also obligingly acted as 'bodies' when we had mock incidents to test our first aid knowledge. A crumpled yellow elastic band in the ear of a 'casualty' signified a head injury, when the patient should on no account be moved. Some wag told us that this represented the yellow discharge that would be caused by brains running out of a cracked skull and for ages I believed that an ear inspection was necessary to diagnose such a perilous condition. When the papers reported some years ago that our present Queen had been hit on the head by a falling grouse while out shooting at Balmoral, I couldn't help wondering if Her Majesty, also presumably privy to this esoteric bit of medical knowledge, had demanded an ear inspection for herself on the spot! Luckily her brains clearly didn't leak out.

A camp was organized for us at Frogmore which was a great excitement. We arrived to find large, round, military tents already erected for us by the ever helpful Grenadiers, though they had thoughtfully left one tent for us to put up ourselves—under their supervision—just so that we would know how to do it; food was sent down from the Castle kitchens by the Queen in case we did not have time to cook. Camping de luxe indeed—but we fondly imagined we were roughing it.

The King and Queen drove down to see how we were getting on, inspected the camp, shared our much brewed billycan campfire tea out of enamel mugs and joined in our singing. The Queen always looked as if she was attending a wedding or garden party in high-heeled shoes, ropes of pearls and a smart summer hat tipped dashingly over one eye which I would now think most unsuitable for such an informal, outdoor occasion but, as always, she captivated everyone with her warmth and charm. The King, shy himself and lacking her natural ease with people, was a much scarier figure to us, but was clearly adored by—and adored—his daughters. One Tuesday two horse brakes were sent from the royal stables to collect us all for a special outing and take us for a picnic at Royal Lodge with the King and Queen. We clip-clopped blissfully up the Long Walk behind the Windsor Greys—at a much more sedate pace than I was to achieve a few years later on Grizel Hartley's Misty. I remember being entranced on this visit by the adorable thatched miniature cottage *Y Bwthyn Bach* (The Little House) belonging to the Princesses which was in the rose garden at Royal Lodge. It was every small girl's dream and we were deeply envious, though it was probably no more fun to play in than the dens all children make for themselves with the help of a few old props and a lot of imagination. It had been presented to Princess Elizabeth by the Welsh nation in 1932. Sometimes we went on hikes and went tracking down exciting trails laid for us by the Guiders in the Home Park, following arrows made from sticks and interpreting other mysterious Scout-law signs—all very ecological.

Looking back I think how extraordinarily lucky we were to take part in all these activities in such magical surroundings. I suppose we were partly conscious of this at the time, but as a child you tend to take whatever is part of your everyday existence for granted—be it bombs and blackouts, food shortages, or royal privileges. We all liked and admired Princess Elizabeth enormously. She was outstandingly kind and considerate; always nice to everyone. Talented, mercurial Princess Margaret was more unpredictable and could blow hot or cold. No one could be more fun or better company to those in her favour, but this state, enjoyable while it lasted, could vary without much warning, leaving the suddenly discarded one feeling the draught when the chill wind blew.

Dancing class on Saturday mornings did not include the Guiding children from the two schools. Because it involved fewer of us, it was more intimate in one way and yet more formal in another. I don't think there were ever more than twelve of us altogether. Our age range spanned six years. Princess Elizabeth and Mary Morshead, the eldest, were joined on Saturday mornings by three other friends of their age, Anne Crichton, Alethea Fitzalan-Howard and Libby Harding, all of whose families lived in, or had connections with the Castle. Princess Margaret, Anne Verney and Louise were in the middle age-wise, with Phoebe and me next and Carola as the youngest.

We always wore party frocks for dancing—strange creations, some of them, for as we grew larger and clothes rationing became more difficult, our mothers had to be resourceful: second-hand dresses passed down from older children were the best bet, but some of our wardrobes also featured such garments as cut-down evening dresses that had belonged to grandmothers or surprising creations made of furnishing material. I well remember a glossy, rose-sprigged dress which was made for me by Nanny's friend Ethel Langford from a remnant of chintz which my mother had found in a drawer at Cefn. I thought it too pretty for words until another child gazed at it in astonishment and told me it was the same material as their bathroom curtains! Later in the war my un-sartorial but enterprising mother got Ethel to run her up a suit made from a roll of hairy green baize normally used to line the silver drawer in the butler's pantry. After I had gone to boarding school I remember praying that my mother wouldn't be wearing this curious outfit when she came down to visit me, but God wasn't listening.

Dancing took place in the Crimson Drawing Room and we changed out of our outdoor clothes in the Dining Room next door. To get there we had to pass the glass case displaying the bloodstained collar worn by King Charles I for his execution, which held an awful fascination for us and before which we lingered ghoulishly before skipping hastily on to put on our dancing shoes. The class was taken by Madame Vacani, who had taught dancing to generations of embryonic society debutantes. She must have been a considerable age by then but was still a glamorous figure to us. She wafted lissomly about in layers of sweet pea chiffon always impeccably made up and with immaculately coiffed gold hair. 'Dyed of course,' said my mother disparagingly. Madame Vacani was helped by two assistants, both called Betty, one of whom was her niece, so the ratio of teacher to pupil was high. Sometimes we did ballroom dancing, sometimes we learnt the basic rudiments of ballet movements—though none of us were budding Darcey Bussells—sometimes we did tap dancing which was more successful and for which we wore special red shoes with metal discs on the bottom. We tapped away happily if not always accurately while one of the Betties rapped out instructions: *Shuffle, Ball-change, Toe-heel, Toe-heel, Toe-heel.* Sometimes the King and Queen would appear to watch our progress. Luckily the Princesses were genuinely good dancers, especially Princess Margaret who at a later stage could probably have had a career in entertainment.

An off-shoot of dancing class and Guides were the two Wartime Christmas Pantomimes, first 'Cinderella', then 'Aladdin' the following year, which were organized in aid of the Queen's special wool charity (to supply knitting wool for making garments for the armed forces e.g. my misshapen khaki socks) and performed in the famous Waterloo Chamber before invited audiences. The Princesses, both of whom had good natural singing voices, took leading parts as did Mary Morshead and a boy from the Royal School in the park called Cyril Woods, whose elder sister Iris, together with Princess Elizabeth, was one of the original Patrol Leaders in the Windsor Castle Guide Company. Cyril was a natural comic whose performances regularly brought the house down and I'm amazed he didn't later take to the boards as a professional. The inspiration and guiding hand behind the pantomimes was the headmaster of the school, Hubert Tannar, a Gilbert and Sullivan buff, who not only wrote the scripts but produced and took part in the performances. The invaluable Grenadiers once more turned their hands to unusual duties and became stage hands and scene shifters. Because I lived further away than any of the other members of the class, I was not allowed to take part in Cinderella. I do see now that it would have been extremely difficult for my mother, with no car, to get me to and fro for any evening rehearsals especially with the very real threat of air raids, but at the time I minded very much and felt horribly out of it with the others so involved. As an example of how thoughtful Princess Elizabeth could be, I remember during a Saturday morning dancing class which had turned into a pantomime rehearsal for the chorus line and was taking place on the newly constructed stage, I was the only one not taking part so was sitting alone at the back of the Waterloo Chamber when the King and Queen with Princess Elizabeth came in to watch the rehearsal and went to sit at the front. Princess Elizabeth must have noticed me as she entered as she immediately came over and said, 'Oh Mary you can't sit all by yourself—do come over and sit with Mummy and Papa and me.' So I did. I thought then, and think now that it was a very kind gesture on the part of an older girl—let alone a royal one—to a much younger and very shy one. By the next year I was considered sufficiently grown-up at eleven to stay on at Garden House after lessons and come home alone on the bus, even in the dark, so I was able to join the chorus line to dance in 'Aladdin' and share in all the fun and excitement of the performances.

At about this time our tight-knit little group at Garden House was joined by one more member, Brigid Westenra, whose mother Lady Rossmore was temporarily living in a rented flat on Windsor Hill while endeavouring, like so many wartime wives, to achieve the difficult balance of following the Flag while trying to keep the family together. I think Paquita, typically, had taken pity on them because there had been some drama over Brigid's schooling. This would hardly have been surprising for Brig, as she was always called, was a one-off—a free spirit—who would not have fitted in easily at any traditional school, but slotted seamlessly into our unusual set-up. Brig was very small, slight and undeveloped for her age, with fair curly hair, bright blue eyes, a deceptive air of childlike innocence reminiscent of those naughty little angels in Renaissance Art—and even less academic grounding than the rest of us. She was in fact nearest to Mary in age, but looked and behaved as though she were several years younger. At Garden House this didn't matter at all and we thought her a great addition to our coterie. She was very good company and having spent her earliest years running wild in Ireland had little regard for rules— but however unconventional our education might be, no one ever took liberties with Paquita Morshead, so though in some respects we were allowed a great deal of freedom, we were by no means undisciplined. Brig automatically joined us at both Guides and Dancing.

As the tide of the war was beginning to turn in the Allies' favour we had a new threat to contend with on the Home Front in the form of flying bombs or *doodlebugs*, those randomly destructive terror machines. Having no pilots they were as likely to arrive by day as by night. Night after night again had to be spent in the air raid shelters—though not by Mum and me—but if the sirens went off during the day we were supposed to dive for the nearest cover and crouch down with our arms over our heads, like the recommended brace position in an air crash. Everyone knew that when the engine of a bomb cut out there were only moments before it exploded. The four of us had a lucky escape on our way back from Wales. We were on our way back to Eton at the end of the holidays, had crossed London and were waiting, together with several hundred other passengers, on a platform at Paddington for our connection to Slough when the sirens sounded. We heard the by now all too familiar drone of an approaching bomb. Then it cut out overhead. A great shout 'GET DOWN' went up and my mother tried to shelter David and me as we all flung ourselves on the ground and almost immediately there was a most terrific crash. It was only as we shakily got to our feet again that the realisation hit us that while we had been incredibly fortunate, other people very close by most certainly had not.

A year before the end of the war in Europe our class at Garden House split up. I had been the first to arrive and was to be the first go. I had started lessons with Phoebe when I was six and I was now twelve so perhaps it was time for me to move on. Within the next year Anne and Carola and Louise had all moved to different schools too. I imagine our parents had suddenly decided that perhaps School Certificate (the GCSE of our day) might prove useful to us in the future and woke up to the fact that our present education, so unique, so special in many ways, took no account of such things as exams. Mary and Phoebe continued to be educated at home but though the day to day association between us all was over, the bonds between us were certainly not. We have remained close friends and are still in touch. We were all influenced by Paquita Morshead in many different ways. We celebrated her 80th and 90th birthdays in Dorset with her and her family and remember her with great love.

Katie

The grown-ups called her Katie
—we called her Mrs Jones.
Rembrandt would have seen beauty
in her hunched and knotted bones,
mapped the fine pathways of experience
on her face; captured the shine
of gentle eyes and reproduced it
as a pool of light.

I thought it a wonder
that she had button shoes like mine.
In the mornings
she wore flowered overalls
(black for the afternoon
under a bibbed white apron, brisk with starch).

Sometimes she staggered under heavy trays.

She called us 'cariad',
let us lick bowls and spoons
while we regaled her
with the stop-press trivia of our days;
she told us where to find
snake's head fritillaries whispering in the grass,
knew where white violets grew
and taught us how
crushed dock leaves can bring ease
to nettle stings on scrubby knees.
She laughed at jokes,
listened to crotchet moans,
kissed bruises better when we made a fuss.
I wish that she could kiss me better now.

If she bubbled music in her mother tongue
words were incomprehensible, and yet
—always—we understood
the language of her love.
I hope that some of it rubbed off on us
for we shall not forget
dear Katie bach—whom we called Mrs Jones.

CEFN

IN 1940 my grandmother unexpectedly died of a heart attack while she and my grandfather were at Cefn. It was an awful shock to everyone and her sons were devastated. I remember being terribly upset at the time and wracked with misery later as the realisation sunk in that I would never see her again. She had seemed indestructible to me—one of the certainties of life.

We had often stayed at Cefn, but usually when my grandparents were there too. After Neinie's death however my grandfather remained at Hinderton Lodge with Sister Chapman, the white-shod and white-capped nurse-housekeeper who came to look after him—a scarlet lipsticked, chain-smoking lady with a curiously bouncy walk whom David and I unfairly loathed on the erroneous suspicion that she was trying to entrap Uncle Jack into marriage. She and Grandpa did The Times crossword together and she read Georgette Heyer aloud to him by the morning room fire, a lighted cigarette hanging perilously from one corner of her mouth while she did so. I had a go at this myself and found it as impossible as I had found Ethel Langford's trick of talking though a mouthful of pins. I think Grandpa probably enjoyed more real companionship with her than he'd had for years. He now lent Cefn to us for all the school holidays. He was glad I think not only to have the house used and enjoyed, but to hand over to my mother the responsibility of running it.

Increasingly, although it never belonged to us, we came to look on Cefn as home.

After her gesture of defiance three years earlier when she had removed us to Scotland for the summer, my mother's relationship with my grandmother had improved and I think she was genuinely sad when Neinie died. All the same, in the way that certain married couples whose unions have been acrimonious in life can mysteriously

Geoffrey Nickson   Janet Nickson

Granny Dobie, David, Mary, Janet Nickson, Sweetsong

David, Geoffrey, Mary

Mary and David

'Aladdin', Windsor Castle, 1943

David

An Eton wedding

Susannah, Nanny Featherstone, Belinda, William

Aunt Evelyn and Uncle Charles Sheepshanks

Charlie

Arthington

The house from the River Wharfe

The flying staircase

Mary and Charlie with the Arthington Tapestry (incomplete)

The Arthington Tapestry

Mary, publicity photograph in *The Times*, 1995, by Joan Russell

Mary's 80th birthday in Corfu
Susannah & Robert Tamworth, Mary, William & Alice Sheepshanks,
Charlie & Belinda Cox

enjoy retrospectively idyllic marriages after widowhood, it was noticeable that my mother's affection for Neinie became a great deal stronger once there was no longer any danger of them treading on each other's toes.

Cefn now represented a blessed retreat from the blitz—oh the relief of knowing there would be no air raids. Imagine the contrast between the nightly noise of gunfire, the wailing of sirens and the fear of bombs and suddenly the utter, dependable quiet of this deeply rural backwater. In fact Liverpool was only sixty miles from Cefn, but it might have been on another planet as far as we children were concerned, so little were we aware of the terrible bombing it was receiving at the time. As the main link with American destinations, the Mersey ports were of crucial strategic importance and played a vital part in the Battle of the Atlantic, not only providing anchorage for naval ships but handling over 90% of all the war material brought into Britain from abroad. More Liverpudlians lost their lives during the blitz than those in any other industrial area, including Birmingham and Coventry, terrible though the bombing of those cities was. The government was desperate to hide from the Germans just how much damage they had already inflicted on Merseyside, so reports on the bombing were kept to a minimum. I certainly don't remember being aware of the full awfulness that was going on so close to our sheltered Welsh existence, but this may also have been because my mother tried to shield us from anxiety. Later in the war, as we asked more questions, could read the newspapers for ourselves, and reports of the unspeakable atrocities being committed by the Nazis in Europe filtered through, it was no longer possible to remain in ignorance of what was going on in the world. No one of my generation who saw the first pictures of the piles of barely breathing skeletons to come out of death camps such as Belsen can ever forget the horror of them.

For my mother Cefn provided a sanctuary from the constant problems of trying to run a school boarding house under wartime conditions; a chance to revert, for a few weeks, to the private life she so much preferred and concentrate her energies on her family. For us children there was better food, freedom from fear and a more relaxed atmosphere. The meagre standard food ration was no bigger than anywhere else of course but fresh vegetables and fresh eggs were plentiful and I can't describe the luxury this was—such conveniences as deep freezes, which we take for granted now, had not yet come into our lives. Diminutive Katie Jones, who could make a rabbit stew taste delicious out of the simplest ingredients, would be waiting at Cefn to give us a welcome. She was one of those people who made the world seem a better place. We were lucky indeed. Many people had no such breaks during the war.

The journeys to and fro were grim enough and often seemed interminable, but it was well worth it once we got there. London had to be crossed, always an anxiety especially on the return journey which might end after dark and therefore coincide with air raids; trains were packed, unheated and invariably delayed; sometimes they stopped for hours in the middle of nowhere for no apparent reason and with no explanation. Information on journeys was hard to come by and billboards at stations were plastered with propaganda cartoons of the 'Careless Talk Costs Lives' variety depicting an eavesdropping Adolf Hitler hiding in the most unlikely places—crouched under the table of tea-drinking ladies, or peering out from cupboard doors in hotel bedrooms, so that as a child one half expected Hitler the bogeyman to crawl out from under the seat in crowded railway carriages or be found secreted on the luggage rack along with our smelly hens. There were no open coaches then, such as there are today, but compartments, and the corridors were crammed with soldiers leaning against the windows, chain-smoking, their heavy kitbags cluttering up any spare space; there would often be civilian passengers sitting on suitcases as well and if Mum had been unable to book seats we frequently had to do this too, at any rate for part of the way. Sometimes we might manage to get one seat to share between us and would take it in turns to sit down. Fighting past all the bodies and their impedimenta for a dreaded trip to the lavatory made one very unpopular with standing passengers—which of course not only increased the desperate feeling of urgency to get there, but produced an immediate desire to pay another visit the moment one had clambered apologetically back over everyone on the return trip! We would each be in charge of one small suitcase—like hand luggage on an airline now—and my mother would have organized a picnic as there was unlikely to be anything to eat or drink on the train. A large trunk was packed a week before our journey, taken by carrier to Slough station and sent off as 'Luggage in Advance' though it often arrived after we did. Most vital equipment of all, there were our bicycles to be organized. Sometimes these would be dispatched in advance too, sometimes we would have them with us and heave them in and out of the Guard's Van whenever we changed trains. To add to the complications of the journey we usually had Peggy with us, who didn't enjoy travelling any more than I did, but hated being left behind in boarding kennels even more. The minute the suitcases appeared from the cupboard under the stairs, Peggy would drag her blanket over, pack herself in my case and refuse to get out unless bodily removed. Even enticement with a tiny piece of sausage—a rare treat for which she would normally sell her soul—failed to budge her.

Those journeys must have been a major undertaking for my mother.

My father usually came along later. There were not only school reports to be written and much end of half business to be done but he often had to remain at Eton for home guard or firefighting duties. Sometimes he had to go on army-run courses in his unlikely role as an officer in the Corps but he usually managed to join us for part of the holidays.

We would eventually be met at Llandudno Junction station by concave-chested Austin Williams, the local taxi driver in his huge hearse-like car, a sepulchral figure himself, with his grey Homburg hat, dark overcoat, five o'clock shadowed chin and slicked back black hair. Austin was like a character from *Under Milk Wood* and was a self-appointed purveyor of all bad news. He and his elder brother Bob owned the local garage and the Smithy. Austin did the driving, manned the petrol pump and collected the coupons from those who were entitled to a petrol ration, while Bob shod the horses, mended farm machinery and was an expert blacksmith. I loved to spend a morning sitting on the wide back of whichever farm horse Bob Williams happened to be shoeing while he whistled through his teeth or chatted away in Welsh regardless of the fact that I didn't understand a word he said to me. No two brothers could have been temperamentally more different. Bob was always smiling while Austin's hatchet-faced gloom was legendary and the speed at which he drove—more suited to a trip to the crematorium than a homecoming—reflected this. But however slow his progress, nothing could dampen our spirits as we greeted every familiar landmark during the six mile journey from station to house.

First we drove over the famous suspension bridge across the estuary of the River Conwy. Churning waters swirled under the bridge at high tide, but if the tide was low a vast expanse of mudflats would stretch as far as the eye could see, populated by wading seabirds scurrying purposefully about like city crowds at rush hour. Once over the bridge we skirted the town and harbour to pass under the dark bulk of Conwy Castle, perched strategically on its rock so as to command the estuary—one of the great medieval fortress castles built by Edward I between 1283 and 1289 during his drive to subdue the Welsh; thence on through a narrow archway in the walls that encircled the town and we were headed along the road for Tyn-y-groes, our nearest village; on past the Red Lion pub and the Post Office, down the long hill out of the village, turn right; through the twin farms of Llichan Isaf and Llichan Ucha which belonged to Grandpa and finally up the steep, potholed half mile of drive and we were in the courtyard of the long, low, whitewashed house we loved so much. However awful the journey might have been, what sticks out most in my memory is the magic of those arrivals at Cefn: the smell of the air the minute you got out of the car; the scent of wood ash from log fires; the peaty-smelling water from mountain streams which gushed pale brown from the taps and was so soft you could make suds by swirling a cake of soap in it—very different from the hard water of the Thames Valley; the beeswax polish Mrs Jones used on the furniture and the faint, spicy whiff from bowls of Neinie's special potpourri in various rooms. If I was dropped, blindfolded, back in time, I would know the smell of that house anywhere.

Next day David and I would walk the couple of miles up to the village to go with Austin to collect the trunk and our bicycles, which would all have been put at Llandudno Junction on the little local train to single line Tal-y-cafn station overlooking the River Conwy—still tidal for several more miles—at the point where the Romans once had a ferry. Austin, would have fixed a roof rack on his car to which he now secured Mum's ancient, sit-up-and-beg bicycle and then roped the trunk to the rack at the back, and David and I would ride our own bicycles the three miles—mostly uphill—home. No matter how furiously we pedalled or how funereally he drove, Austin always got there first. My mother had an ambivalent attitude to Austin Williams. On the one hand his negativity irritated her to distraction and found her at her most brisk, bracing and least conciliatory; on the other hand his services were quite indispensable to us and we depended on his goodwill for all transport—a balancing act which was not Mum's forte. I suspect a good deal of behind the scenes diplomacy from my father was required to prevent them falling out.

We went everywhere on those bikes, desperately seeing how far we could ride up the hills before we were forced to admit defeat and push them up the last bit—inevitably David always got much further than I could—then we leapt on again to freewheel blissfully downhill, hurtling along with our feet off the pedals and the wind in our hair until we had to brake violently in order to negotiate some hairpin bend. We were always needing new brake pads to be fitted by Bob or Austin Williams. There was hardly ever any traffic except for the occasional country bus: to meet a car was a rare event. Even in rural areas, few children today can enjoy that sort of freedom.

Social life at Cefn in the war was non-existent—something we didn't miss—and we made our own amusements. During the day there were expeditions on foot or on bicycle. Looking back after well over half a century I marvel at how much independence we had as children. Nowadays we teach our children not to speak to strangers; then we were brought up to greet anyone we met—known or unknown. Because we were thrown so much on our own resources we reaped a huge and lasting benefit: we were never bored.

David and I used to disappear for hours, armed with his split-cane trout rod, to fish the mountain streams. He became a highly skilled catcher of the little pink-fleshed scarlet spotted brown trout, on either a worm—if the stream was in spate—or a wet fly tied by my father, often striking so enthusiastically at the first tweak on the line that the trout would come whizzing out over our heads to land kicking on the bank. Katie Jones would fry them for our breakfast and if we had managed to gather mushrooms as well, this made a feast. There was one particular pool, known as the Mill Pool, which involved clambering down steep, stone steps of extreme slipperiness beside a disused old watermill. The pool itself was deep and the mill race a powerful force; to cast a fly we stood, wobbling precariously in our black wellies, on moss-covered boulders at the edge. I don't think at this stage we could either of us swim.

To get to any of our favourite haunts we had to run the gauntlet of farm dogs, usually tied to their kennels, but always leaping threateningly about on the end of their chains, barking ferociously. Occasionally however one would be loose and would creep up behind us and snap at our heels. I was petrified of them. David was much braver than me and it must often have been a pain to have me along but he was endlessly tolerant and protective. I had my uses though; however skilful his casting, there would occasionally be the inevitable 'birds nest' when the catgut cast and dangling flies became hopelessly entangled and then my small fingers were useful to unravel knots. Fields of cows or bullocks were another hazard because there was the very real chance that there might be a bull amongst them. I was always privately planning my escape routes, skulking along wall or hedge so that I could scramble to safety in an emergency. A few years later I did indeed witness David being chased by a bull and it was truly terrifying. It had broken through a gap in the hedge of the field below the house in order to join some ladies—gaps in Welsh hedges frequently being closed with nothing more substantial than a broken old iron bedhead tied up with frayed string—no barrier to a randy bull in search of romance. David had been ferreting and I was on the point of walking down to meet him when I heard a terrible bellowing and reached the garden gate just in time to see my brother hurl himself over it as the bull, head down, was about to treat him like a Shrove Tuesday pancake. It continued to roar and rage round the gate for ages, leaving us in no doubt as to the seriousness of its intentions.

A favourite picnic place, where we had often been with Neinie before the war, was the ancient Roman Bridge across the Afon-roe, the stream at the foot of Tal-y-fan which scurried its way downhill to join the Conwy. With Neinie, the expedition had involved my father or an uncle driving a car to the track that ran below the mountain, the car laden with fitted picnic baskets and rugs; thermoses of tea and homemade lemonade; tomato sandwiches and ginger cake. I well remember the first time David and I managed to get there alone, on foot and entirely under our own steam. We had not intended to go so far—nor even thought that we could—but there had been a blizzard on the high ground in the night, the hills were white and we kept climbing higher and higher to try to reach the snowline till we suddenly realised where we were. Then of course we had to go on to the little stone bridge itself where Roman soldiers' feet must once have marched. The feeling of triumph and achievement was intoxicating. We were Centurions; we were Stanley and Livingstone, Scott and Oates. It was dark by the time we staggered home and we must have been gone for hours but I don't remember that there had been undue anxiety about our whereabouts.

After that we felt we could get ourselves anywhere, though the snag at the end of any expedition from Cefn was always the final flog up the last steep hill to the house itself.

Sometimes we went on fishing trips to one of the mountain lakes—Crafnant above Llanrwst, or Lake Elsie above Bettws-y-coed, but for the latter expedition we usually had a grown-up with us because it involved first taking our bicycles on the train from Tal-y-cafn to Bettws. For either venue there was a difficult decision to be taken: after leaving the road, did we push the bicycles up a steep mountain track on the outward trek in order to be able to come wildly bumping and spinning down—gloriously if dangerously—on the homeward trip, or leave them at the bottom and walk both ways?

David and I spent hours playing croquet on the sunken lawn below the house. To make the matches sufficiently exciting I had to be given a two hoop-lead because he was much better than I was, though I could occasionally have flashes of unexpected brilliance which upset the game plan. It would be hard to know which of us was the more surprised when this happened. The ancient croquet mallets, the wood of which had become brittle over the years, had a rough life because we were given to slamming the heads down angrily on the ground when we missed a vital shot and the shafts would sometimes snap. Then we had to bicycle up with them to the Smithy where Bob Williams would cut off the splintered ends and put a sort of metal collar on to fix them together. This happened so often that the handles gradually got shorter and shorter till by the end of the war we were playing with mallets that looked like stumpy little boots. Sometimes David managed to coerce me into playing cricket. I would go in to bat as Australia and make eleven ducks in quick succession before David, as England, put up terrific scores while I spent the rest of the session flogging up and down bowling and fielding. I greatly preferred croquet.

In the evenings Mum read aloud to us indefatigably—a mixed diet from Dickens to Arthur Ransome, Louisa Alcott to Wilkie Collins; we played cards and mah-jong or pencil and paper games and we read voraciously to ourselves as well. When my father was with us we learnt to play bridge, a game my father adored but I think was never very good at, but which became a lifelong pleasure for David who excelled at it. I look back on those wartime holidays at Cefn as a wonderfully happy time when, for a few weeks at a time, the war could be forgotten by us children—though no doubt not by our anxious parents. At six o'clock every evening they would endeavour to listen to the news though the reception was poor and necessitated someone crouching by the ancient bakelite wireless to squeeze the aerial between finger and thumb in order to get any recognizable sound out of it at all.

On Sunday mornings we walked to the little mediaeval church of St Mary by the River Conwy at Caerhûn, where we could hear wigeon calling from the marsh above the squeaky sounds of the ancient harmonium played by rickety Miss Jones. As one of her legs was much shorter than the other, which necessitated the wearing of a special boot with a six-inch thick sole, it must have been a tricky procedure and perhaps accounted for the extraordinary noises she sometimes managed to produce. Many of our family are buried in that churchyard and though we none of us live there any more it is still a place of pilgrimage to us all. We always attended the English service, but there would already have been one in Welsh first, and this linguistic split meant that both congregations tended to be sparse—especially as the majority of locals were 'chapel' rather than 'church'.

The vicar of our childhood years was known to all as Will-the-Liar, a soapy-faced man with a notoriously scant regard for truth and a passion for the sound of his own voice. He was given to wildly dramatic gestures from the pulpit and David wiled away the tedium of the interminable sermons by playing prayer book cricket. The vicar, unknowingly cast in the role of bowler, whirled his arms like a windmill while David, book held as a bat and with a look of profound concentration, carefully blocked the ball or hit the occasional thrilling boundary with a left hook over his shoulder, while he kept a careful score in his head. We sat in the family pew below a stained glass window commemorating our great-grandparents and a brass plaque which exhorted us to *Grow old along with me, The best is yet to be.* After the service we went round to pay our respects to Neinie's grave, the headstone of which was designed by Uncle Dick in grey Welsh slate. I tried not to think of what might be lying under the oblong of grey gravel on top, but fearful imaginings filled my head, triggered no doubt by the exhumation of the dead canary, and I secretly dreaded this ritual.

Because of the paucity of surnames in Wales people tended to be known by their occupation or the name of the place where they lived. Apart from Will-the–Liar I particularly remember Willy Shop, a father figure in the neighbourhood, who kept the Post Office. Mrs Willy Shop, of the refined accent, floral overalls and corrugated cardboard waves in her hair, had delusions of grandeur, having been before marriage lady's maid to Lady Aberconway which apparently gave her a special standing, particularly in her own eyes. As well as helping her husband in the shop she worked the local telephone exchange (a great way of picking up information because she could listen in to all conversations), handed out free advice and terrified other local wives with the threat of her disapproval. Willy Shop stocked most of the basic necessities of life but what he did not supply could usually be ordered by telephone from E. B. Jones & Sons, the grocers in Conwy—provided of course there were enough coupons in our ration books for whatever was required—and it would be put on the local bus to Tyn-y-groes. We then collected the parcels on foot from the Post Office and staggered back home with them—and very heavy they seemed too. Also in the village were red-haired Tommy Butcher, supplier of the minute portions of meat that made up the weekly allowance, and Davvy Jesus who delivered the Sunday papers.

In the farm below Cefn lived Mr and Mrs Owen Llichan, so called because of the name of their farm. Scary Willy Owen was a relentlessly dour character and my father had got into trouble during the First World War for pretending to his little brother that Mr Owen was really Kaiser Wilhelm in disguise, an unlikely tease which apparently caused poor Uncle Dick to have nightmares. Friday-faced Mrs Owen was in charge of the dairy and David and I would be sent down the hill every few days to collect milk. My mother found Welsh names quite beyond her. She had trouble addressing people correctly anyway and habitually called all acquaintances Mr or Mrs Er, but in a valiant effort to personalise her would-be friendly greeting, she once offended Mrs Owen by saying 'Oh Mrs Owen, how nice to see you again. How are you and Mr Roberts keeping?'

On Sunday afternoons, all sporting activities being taboo on the Sabbath, David and I often went to visit Hugh Hughes in the tiny, stifling cottage at Llandbedre, full of framed texts and lustre jugs, where he lived with his wife Maggie, who may have had a heart of gold but also had the distinction of being the most alarmingly hideous woman we had ever seen. We thought she was a witch. Hugh would be sitting by the fire reading the Bible to himself in his mother tongue and wearing curiously matted mittens on his arthritic old hands. These had been knitted for him by me from fluffy, pale pink, angora baby wool—anything more unsuitable would be hard to imagine—in an excess of loving concern after he had once complained of the cold. He wore them every Sunday afternoon.

As well as enjoying the sporting rights on the two small farms owned by my grandfather, my father rented other rough shooting and he and David walked for miles in search of elusive coveys of partridges in September, and the occasional woodcock and pheasant in the Christmas holidays. Hunting for the pot had an importance during the war that is hard to imagine today and any game or rabbits shot by David and my father greatly enhanced our diet. Astonishingly, David even shot a grouse once—his first, and possibly the only one ever seen on Drûm, the largest and furthest away of the five 'home' mountains on the edge of Snowdonia which provided the backdrop to our view from Cefn. The poor bird was a strange looking creature by the time David got it home, its neck having been stretched like a piece of elastic to at least twice its natural length in the process of being hung by its head from his game belt to be carried down the mountain, and then held triumphantly aloft for photographs to prove its existence. I hated shooting as a child, so my mother and I would join Pa and David for lunch in various barns, lugging the picnic impedimenta for miles—loyal camp followers, if sometimes rather grumpy ones, as the two shooters were invariably late at whatever rendezvous had been planned. This would cause my mother to be sharp with my father, which I dreaded. I was always hotly on his side—unfairly so, I now think, as in matters pertaining to sport my beloved Pa was an inconsiderate husband and tried her patience quite hard. I was used to all the males in my family being fanatical in their pursuit of sport, but the laid-back attitude of one family friend who occasionally came to stay on leave from the army during the war—though he was known to be a keen and very good shot—gave us children a surprise. On a day of especially inclement weather, of driving sleet, snow, and freezing wind, to my brother's utter astonishment he chose to stay indoors sorting his vast collection of cigarette cards by the fire rather than face the elements and go on an armed walk up the mountainside in search of a mythical pheasant and a probably non-existent woodcock.

This was Charles Sheepshanks, a favourite visitor, whom we all adored and who was to become my husband, though nothing could have been further from anyone's mind, least of all his or mine at the time. David, who had been taught by Charlie during his first year at Sunningdale before the war, admired him as a dashing role model and was seriously shaken to discover his hero could make such an extraordinary choice. I remember being equally impressed but deeply admiring of such independence of mind. I must have been nine or ten at the time and I also remember Charlie promising that when I grew up he would take me to the ballet. Ten years later, he did.

The North Wales climate is generally mild—though frequently wet and windy—but I remember two particularly hard winters in the war when we were snowed in for days and could not get back to Eton—no question then of four-wheel drives or even tractors to dig us out. We stayed put. I tamed a robin which would come and sit on my finger and eat out of my hand—not a member of the Birds' Privacy Society, presumably. During warmer weather I showed scant respect for the privacy of the colony of ants which lived under the verandah that ran along the front of the house, a place where adults gathered to inspect the weather and discuss alternative plans if the rain blew sideways down the valley. A vine provided welcome shade in summer but though its bitter little black grapes never seemed to ripen into sweetness, its roots had conveniently lifted and loosened some of the terracotta tiles at the far end so that I could temporarily remove them and enjoy a secret window on another world—a complex yet ordered world of hectic activity, drama and sometimes cruelty involving soldiers and civilians, royalty and slaves. It was rather like having a private box at the opera from which to watch a performance of *Aida*.

In the summer every reasonably active person, regardless of age or sex, helped with the harvest. Though the war inevitably had much less impact in rural areas than in towns or cities, life in the country was not without its own hardships and the lack of able-bodied young men to do the heavy agricultural tasks was one of them. By the middle of the war they had all been called up—many of them would never be fit for heavy work again and some would never return at all. There was a POW camp between Tyn-y-groes and Conwy, with first Italian prisoners, dressed in dark brown, and later German prisoners who wore grey, but I don't remember them being available to work on local farms before the end of the war. The Italians were sent home soon after the end of the war, but some German prisoners were not repatriated till as late as 1948. Uncle Jack certainly had POWs to work in the garden at Cefn. The Italians were much jollier, singing love songs and snatches of opera, making jokes, lying in the sun and laughing, but I suspect the Germans got more gardening done. They thought it very funny to spring to attention and say 'Heil Hitler' every time they saw my uncle, with his ram's horn walking stick, striding towards them. Uncle Jack normally had a very good sense of humour, but he possessed a short fuse and could be irascible, and this was a joke he found hard to appreciate. I'm afraid we thought it hilarious. During the harvest we followed behind the horse-drawn reaping machine, driven by grumpy Willie Owen, and learned to gather up and bind great armfuls of corn which were later 'stooked' by hand. Even I, though small for my age, became adept at these tasks. The only necessities were gloves and a long sleeved shirt because patches of nettles and thistles could make the gathering up a very painful business.

For me, the most magic time of year was undoubtedly the April holidays. The hedgerows would be thick with primroses and tiny sweet-scented violets and there were drifts of wild daffodils in the fields. Azaleas and camellias were in flower in the garden, and wild cherries in blossom in the hedgerows. Every green looked different and the air smelt of honey. I remember as a very small child lying with my face buried in the grass, convinced that I could actually hear it growing. I think this sense of being part of nature, sharing the identity of a flower or a blade of grass is quite common among young children but sadly the vision does not last and this 'third eye' closes so that we can remember, but never completely recover, the sensation— Paradise lost indeed. Years later I turned this memory into a poem which later still was turned into a song and set to music by singer– guitarist Caroline McCausland who performed it at many concerts. Wherever we went David and I looked for birds' nests, though he was always much quicker at spotting them than me. Our most exciting discovery was a treecreeper's nest, so cunningly tucked behind a loose bit of bark half way up a tree that if David hadn't seen the parent birds flying in and out we would never have found it.

There was a second Nickson house on the hillside below Cefn. It had been built for my great-grandfather by the distinguished Edwardian Welsh architect Edward North, and he and my great-grandmother lived there in retirement with the unmarried daughters from their large family of children. After we were grown-up, it too came to be a house of great importance to David and me and our respective families because it was the house where my parents went to live in 1955 after Pa retired from Eton and where they were extremely happy for many years, but during my childhood it was let, and I don't think we ever went into it. Sadly, Hinderton Lodge had to be sold after my grandfather died and it became a housing estate on the edge of the village. I have never been back and I believe about twenty houses were built where Neinie once lovingly tended her rose garden and in the walled kitchen garden where we used to feast illicitly on raspberries and strawberries. Once the war was over and Uncle Jack had reluctantly retired from the army he made Cefn his permanent home and ran the family business in Liverpool from there. He also threw his considerable talents and energies into local affairs and public service, greatly enlarged the already charming garden into something spectacular and, generously, still allowed us to invade him every holidays, so Cefn continued to be a second home for the four of us and remains in my memory as a place of enchantment.

Awareness

I hear the sound of thistledown floating:
listen and hear the spiders spin.
Listen—oh listen—to the green grass growing
with the silver sound of a violin.

Feel through your fingers the snowflakes whisper,
breeze on your cheek from a butterfly's wing;
touch the petals of falling roses
dance to the music that songbirds sing.

Marvel at pearls in rain-drenched flowers,
diamond dews and feathers of frost;
watch on the wind for seabirds sailing—
search in the fire for dreams you have lost.

Skimmed Milk

Llichan Ucha: liquid name of farm
where hand in hand we went
for milk. The dairy smells
of slate-slabbed cleanliness
and chilling rectitude in chapel pews.

Mrs Owen blows the fat aside
scoops pale blue fluid up
and fills our can;
if we are sent
for cream—immoral thought—
she skims it off the pan
with surreptitious dips
into the blue below
then tips it in our fluted jar
for luxury should be diluted so.

Mr Owen cannot smile
in case his waxed moustaches crack.
a parcel tightly tied with string,
cords below knees and elbows,
is he afraid that fantasies may weave
up trouser leg or sleeve
and make him sin?
Did Mrs Owen on their wedding day
rip all the wrappings off
to peep inside?

Did they find love
in their great feather bed
or only copulate for procreation's sake,
a Biblical pursuit and thus allowed?
Before he bound himself with knots
against the wicked dew,
perhaps he blew
the cream off her teetotal head
and filled her veins
with thin skimmed milk instead?

9

GROWING UP

F ROM the time I went to boarding school at nearly thirteen until I left school after the end of the war in 1948, I spent very little time at Eton. David left Sunningdale in 1943 and the following year I went away, so I wasn't at home for the main part of his Eton career. The relationship of father and son could have become difficult for Pa and David but they both said it was never a problem. David was a very successful Etonian, ending up for his last year as a member of Pop; my father was a popular and well respected beak and Eton is a large place. The close friendship they enjoyed, which was to last all their lives, was in no way jeopardized by those five years in the school together as beak and boy.

I was sent to St Mary's School, Calne, in Wiltshire. It was the first time I had ever been to school, let alone one so far away from home, and to begin with I was very homesick and the school found me difficult to place. I was moved several times between three different forms during the first half of the term—up down, up down, up down—before the school despairingly gave up and decided to stick me in the middle one and hope for the best. I was so far behind in some subjects, Maths in particular, that I soon ceased to make any attempt to understand what was going on at all and resigned myself to a fog of incomprehension that never cleared, whereas in English and History I was so far ahead that there was little necessity for me to make the slightest effort for a long time, which in some ways was worse. What a bore I must have been to the school, but I don't remember being offered coaching in any of the subjects in which I was so backward, or of being allowed to work to a higher standard in the few where I excelled, so I can't think the situation was very cleverly dealt with. No doubt, like all schools at the time, they were short of staff and very dependent on elderly teachers who had nobly postponed retirement during the war because so many younger women were in the Services. It can't have been easy for St

Mary's and I was not a good schoolgirl, with an irreverent attitude to sacred cows and not averse to breaking those rules which, in my quite unjustified arrogance, I considered ridiculous. Coming from Eton, I had expected far greater freedom and independence and thought some of the restrictions extraordinarily petty.

During my first term my mother got a letter from the Queen's lady-in-waiting, saying that Princess Margaret would like to hear from me from boarding school. I duly wrote a letter full of schoolgirly gossip and a few days later got an answer sent by registered post and franked by Windsor Castle. It never occurred to me that this would arouse curiosity let alone cause a stir so I never said anything about it and I was disconcerted to be sent for by St Mary's famous and formidable headmistress of thirty years' standing, Miss Marcia Matthews, always referred to as Matt, who asked me who the interesting-looking letter I'd received was from—though she must have known—and when I told her, demanded to see it. I was reluctant to produce it, mostly because it was full of references to childish naughtiness such as talking after lights out and I feared it might get some of us into trouble but also because I felt it was my private letter. I was summarily dispatched to get it however and was left in no doubt that refusal was not an option. I complied with a sense of outrage!

If asked at the time I think I might have said I hated school, but this was not really true. I made some good friends; I had a lot of fun; I adored acting and took part in every possible production and because I was a natural mimic was in demand from my contemporaries to pillory various members of staff—but I never really felt I fitted the mould and made woefully little attempt to do so, remaining a quiet rebel. I longed for the holidays, when I could shin up a rope (a skill learnt from Miss Dempster in the Eton gym), and disappear with my book up one of the two big lime trees in front of the house at Cefn and read, uninterrupted, for hours.

Once I left school however, there was a price to be paid for the isolated rural idyll at Cefn in terms of social ineptitude; a price too for having such a loving but over-protective mother who did not at all wish to see her daughter try her wings and take to the wide sky. When

I first grew up I was so shy that parties of any kind were an endurance test. This state of affairs did not last very long, but while it did it was painful and I would not wish to be seventeen or eighteen—often regarded as golden years—again.

I spent nearly a term in London at an establishment with the grandiose title of The House of Citizenship—it later moved to Ashridge—and was just beginning to enjoy it when I picked up a virulent bug which was hard to shake off and pulled me down. I was not considered sufficiently recovered to return the next term and subsequently spent a year at home doing absolutely nothing—I don't think this was really necessary health-wise and it was certainly not a good idea in other ways. That this period of inactivity in an environment so full of academic possibilities should have been not only allowed but encouraged by my parents seems extraordinary to me today. I mixed very little with the boys in my father's house, never had meals with them and was firmly discouraged from straying over to the boys' side of the house, even to visit the dame—by this time the charming Miss Pearson. Looking back, I think my father was terrified of having a pubescent daughter at large in a boys' school while my mother wanted to envelop me in emotional cotton wool and guard me from the adult world. In Mum's eyes sons were for achievements, adulation and the outside world; daughters were for cosseting and keeping at home. David meanwhile had left Eton and become a regular soldier, heading for Sandhurst and a commission in the Coldstream Guards. I missed my childhood companion. I felt desperately unsure of myself but also very constrained.

Grizel Hartley came to my rescue. I stayed with them in Scotland; at Eton she not only took me riding on the iron-mouthed Mist, but she and Hubert frequently asked me to their twice-weekly dinner parties where I learnt that shyness is no excuse for sitting in tongue-tied silence—if anyone is kind enough to offer you supper, then you must be prepared to sing for it. Grizel was a brilliant hostess but her guests were definitely expected to contribute—a useful lesson. Another unexpected and life-changing invitation came my way. Soon after my eighteenth birthday, Charlie Sheepshanks, now demobbed from the army and back to schoolmastering again, invited me to join the skiing party which he and his bachelor uncle, an ex-Eton housemaster—another Charles Sheepshanks—took to Switzerland each January. Charlie's father had died when he was two and uncle and nephew were devoted to each other.

That fortnight in Lenzerheide was the first time I'd been abroad and the first holiday I'd spent away from my family—it was a notable milestone on my belated road to growing up. I loved everything about that fortnight, from the sensational Alpine scenery and the thrill of skiing, to the fun of dancing to an accordion in the evenings; from the glamour of dressing for dinner and eating delicious Swiss hotel food—in contrast to the continuing gastronomic dreariness of rationing in post-war England—to the banter and laughter of the mixed-ages party.

My father was a friend of both uncle and nephew and before the war my parents had often stayed at Arthington Hall, the Sheepshanks' family home in Yorkshire, to shoot grouse on Pockstones, their grouse moor. Now that the war was over this tradition started again. Charles Sheepshanks senior—Lt Col A. C. Sheepshanks DSO—always known in Etonian circles as The Sheep—had retired from Eton just before the war and his elder sister Evelyn had given up her London life to keep house for him. During the war he took on the directorship of the Yorkshire Red Cross of which his friend and neighbour, Princess Mary, the Princess Royal, at nearby Harewood House, was President and he continued in this position to the end of his life.

I loved a story told about him by his sister. In the late summer of 1939, when everyone was preoccupied about the probability of war with Germany, Queen Mary was due to come to stay at Harewood with her daughter and son-in-law for her annual September visit. Charles and Evelyn Sheepshanks had been approached about the possibility of them bringing their famously demanding guest over to Arthington for lunch, and according to Evelyn, her brother Charles, the most socially unassuming of men, who hated fuss and liked nothing better than a quiet life, was awaiting confirmation of this plan with considerable lack of enthusiasm. Queen Mary was a passionate collector of antiques with a well-known tendency not only to admire her host and hostesses' most treasured possessions but to drop the broadest hints about how much she would like to have a particular object in her own collection. She invariably accepted with alacrity if her loyal subjects lost their nerve and offered it to her as a gift. Apparently the Arthington house party were all listening anxiously to the news when there was a telephone call for The Sheep. He returned looking so despondent that everyone assumed it was indeed war. 'Bad news,' he said. 'She's coming!' Shortly afterwards war was indeed declared—and Queen Mary never came to lunch.

When the house was taken over as a military hospital in the war, Charles and Evelyn moved into the stable cottage with their elderly cook and parlourmaid. After the war was over, they couldn't face moving back into the big house again with all the upheaval it would have entailed, because by this time the privations and anxieties of wartime existence had taken its toll, they had run out of energy and the house had become very dilapidated. As it seemed unlikely at the time that anyone in the family would move back into it, they sold their biggest pieces of furniture and stored everything else in the squash court which had been built in the 1930s. They also sold their biggest picture, Constable's enormous *Chain Pier at Brighton* (which had been sent to the States for safe keeping during the war) for what today seems the unbelievably small sum of £19,000 to the Tate, where it still hangs today.

I didn't remember The Sheep from pre-war days, but it didn't take me long on that Swiss holiday to fall under his spell. An incredibly tough little man physically, who had fought in the trenches in the First World War and been decorated for gallantry, he may have been small in stature—5ft 2 inches—but was huge in personality, with a dry sense of humour and a marvellous sense of the ridiculous. Behind a deadpan face, he was also a terrific tease and until I got his measure almost had me believing 'six impossible things before breakfast' every day like the Red Queen in *Alice*, to his huge amusement. He was endlessly kind to me and Elizabeth Henson—later Rickards—the only other female in the party. Elizabeth, who was six years older than me, had recently started on a career as an actress and was just beginning to get parts in West End productions. We shared a room together and were to become lifelong friends, but she seemed very glamorous and sophisticated to me then. She lent me her make-up and taught me how to apply mascara which horrified my mother when I got home. Neither of us had skied before so for the first week The Sheep took us both in hand. He scorned to use ski lifts—not that there were very many then—and preferred to climb everywhere with sealskins on his skis, so we did the same, floundering and puffing up hill like a pair of enthusiastic puppies while he plodded ahead at a level pace, hopefully exhorting us to: *Aequam memento rebus in arduis servare mentem* as we stopped and started and stopped again: *'Remember when the path is steep to keep an even mind'*—not something I was good at then. When we eventually got to the top of whichever run he'd decided to do, he revived his two wilting pupils with orange segments while we unclipped the skins from our skis, packed them into our rucksacks with the packed lunch we each carried and then crashed our way downhill completely out of control, learning to ski in soft snow before we ever went near a piste. I adored it. Because we skied off the beaten track we often put up wildlife—partridges, ptarmigan and black game, mountain hares, roe deer and very occasionally, if we went high enough, chamois. If we looked through powerful binoculars we could sometimes pick out the hugely horned steinbok, a species of ibex, that roamed high up the mountain on the opposite side of the valley, but I never saw one close to. The squirrels which abounded in the woods had much darker fur than their red-haired, Squirrel Nutkin cousins round Cefn. As our skiing improved we started to join the rest of the party on all day expeditions. Charlie, who was an immensely elegant skier but not one to follow in anyone else's tracks, always chose the route and led the party down. Except for the war years, he had been coming to Lenzerheide since he was nine and knew the mountains like the back of his hand. That holiday was my first experience of his penchant for eye-poppingly bright colours and his flamboyant taste in clothes, which would not be so remarkable now but certainly was then, and he cut a dashing, not to say eccentric, figure on the slopes. A passionate gardener, he always held that in nature colours never clashed—a debatable horticultural theory anyway and certainly not one that worked sartorially. I thought him marvellously entertaining, as I had as a little girl, but he was twenty years older than me and I regarded him as my father's friend, and certainly didn't consider him in a romantic light at that time. What that holiday did start for me was a love affair with mountains.

When I went home I felt like a jack-in-the-box that had suddenly popped through the lid of its enclosed world and knew I would not be able to settle back for long inside that safe, padded little box again. I was quite unqualified for any specific career, but realized that I needed to leave home. In order to earn the money to go skiing I had worked during the Christmas rush in Caley's, the Windsor branch of John Lewis, selling handbags and leather goods and had thoroughly enjoyed it. One day, without telling my mother what I really had in mind, I went up to London to meet a school friend, Susan Chevasse, who had recently started working in London, and came back having found lodgings to share with her in Kensington Church Street and a job for myself. Thinking that the only thing I was any good with was books, and with my six weeks' experience as a shop assistant as the only useful work experience I had to offer, I had walked into Harrods Book Department and asked if they had any vacancies for a sales girl. They hadn't, but they sent me up to the 4th floor to see the Head Librarian of Harrods' then famous lending library, a desiccated little man appropriately named Mr Page, and I talked myself into a job as a trainee librarian.

I felt exultant in one way, but also horribly aware that it seemed a shabby, underhand way of repaying my mother's devotion and constant care. I knew that if I'd consulted her beforehand her objections would have been legion and had decided that a *fait accompli* was my only hope, but I dreaded telling her. The upset that greeted my announcement was awful and Mum was not only convinced that I would never stand up physically to working in London but was deeply hurt that I could have taken such a step without telling her. I had to enlist my father's support but I was determined not to be deflected and as I intended to come home at weekends it was hardly the most earth-shaking of decisions. Mum eventually came to terms with the idea of both my job and my independence and was generous enough not to bear a grudge.

In fact working in Harrods Library, though extremely badly paid, was great fun. It not only catered for customers who lived in London, many of whom came in to change and choose their own books in person and expected to have discussions and suggestions about the latest publications, but there was an enormous out-of-town clientele whose books were either delivered or posted to them. Most of these would ring up with requests or send us lists of what they wanted to read, but some of them expected the librarians to choose for them, and getting to know their tastes and probable opinions was an interesting challenge. In order to give a highly personal service, the members were split alphabetically into sections and administered at twelve 'desks' ranged round the enormous book-lined room, each desk run by a senior librarian and a junior assistant. For the first few weeks every new trainee had to spend the days stacking shelves—sorting and replacing returned books. This entailed pushing huge, heavy trolleys round and constantly climbing up and down ladders—hard physical work—but an invaluable way of getting to know where everything was kept. I found it an endurance test but the knowledge of Mum's expectation that I would soon crack kept me going. It was a relief when I was promoted to work on a desk. My boss was a delightful woman called Mrs Flischer from whom I learned a great deal not only about books but about life in general and she was wonderful to work with. She widened my reading tastes, revolutionised my ability to deal with all sorts of people and boosted my self-confidence. What had started as a rather desperate bid for freedom turned out to be an excellent job for a future novelist and good training for life in general. I was lucky.

Every morning I caught a 52 bus from Kensington Church Street to Knightsbridge. Staff entered Harrods by a door on the far side of Hans Crescent, punched their time of arrival into a machine—lateness was not tolerated—and walked via a tunnel underneath the road into the basement of the main store. We wore grey overalls with the Harrods logo on a pocket on the left bosom. The hours were 8.45 a.m. to 5 p.m. Mondays to Fridays and 8.45 a.m. till 1 p.m. on Saturday mornings. We had two weeks' holiday a year. On Saturday afternoons I caught a Green Line Coach to Eton via Slough, which stopped conveniently opposite School Hall—a minute's walk from Common Lane House— and was usually home by half past two. Riding and dinner parties with Grizel continued.

Mr Page had an office in the Library and was treated with great deference when he occasionally emerged to make a ponderous progress from desk to desk, but his deputy, elongated, crop-haired Miss Robinson, scarved like Isadora Duncan and with bracelets jangling up ropey arms, sat at a kneehole desk at the top of the room, keeping her beady eyes on us at all times from behind vast tortoiseshell-rimmed glasses. She reminded me of a cartoon we had thought funny as children when we poured over the old bound editions of *Punch* in the Neston schoolroom; it depicted heavily made up twenties ladies and was entitled *Shingled Heads, Bangled Arms and Bungled Faces.* I always imagined Miss Robinson slapping her pancake make-up on with the sort of spatula that builders use for applying putty to bricks. She was rumoured to be conducting a passionate affair with wispy, doe-eyed Paula, one of the senior librarians.

After I'd been working at Harrods for about six months I was joined by my childhood friend Carola Verney—scholastically no better qualified after our Windsor Castle education than I was. Carola's arrival livened things up no end and led to us being summonsed to Mr Page's office where he informed us portentously that Harrods Library was not to be used as a meeting place for our young friends and he deplored what he described as '*the unsuitably frivolous cocktail party atmosphere*' we were introducing.

After a very slow start, my social life was beginning to pick up.

Sometime during my Harrods period, Charlie Sheepshanks, who was a frequent weekend visitor to Common Lane House, remembered his old promise to me as a ten year-old child to take me to the ballet and invited me to go to Covent Garden to see Margot Fonteyn and

Michael Somes in *The Sleeping Beauty*. I was completely overwhelmed by the whole evening: the music, the dancing, the glamour of The Royal Opera House—and of course the electrifying presence of Fonteyn herself. From the moment she first erupted on to the stage something extraordinary always happened; I was lucky enough to witness this magic countless times in the future. I applauded till the palms of my hands were almost raw. Charlie had introduced me to another lifelong passion.

After this we often used to go to Covent Garden together, after which he would take me out to dinner at Rules in Maiden Lane or The Savoy, or to eat Lobster Newburg in Prunier's in St James's Street. Sometimes we went to dine and dance at the recently restored Café de Paris, which had received a direct hit in the blitz. We enjoyed each other's company enormously but I must have been extremely slow-witted about his real feelings. Because I had known Charlie all my life it did not occur to me that he was seriously falling in love with me and the first time he proposed to me I was astonished. I thought he was mad—but he didn't give up on the idea.

In the summer of 1952 I was staying with friends in Aberdeen-shire to go for the second year running to dance reels at a highland ball at wonderful Haddo House, at the same time as Charlie was also staying with friends of his, Derick and Midi Gascoigne, at nearby Leith Hall. He offered to drive me home from Scotland to Eton, stopping en route for a night at Arthington with Charles and Evelyn Sheepshanks. The plan had to be altered at the last minute because Charlie's great tank of a car—an American Packard—broke down and there was difficulty in getting the required spare part. Somehow he prevailed on the Gascoignes to invite me to stay with them until the car could be repaired. I wasn't at all keen on this scheme as I'd never met the Gascoignes and couldn't feel they really wanted a strange girl foisted on them, but Charlie was very pressing and Derick and Midi were wonderfully warm and welcoming. Midi had inherited the Leith estate from an aunt and at some stage the house, a vast, spooky, turreted pile, was made over to the National Trust, but at the time Derick and Midi were living there with their three clever and original children: Bamber, a scholar who was about to leave Eton, Veronica still at school, and Brian who was due to start at Sunningdale. In the end I had an enormously entertaining three days with them, the start of a friendship with both generations. Bamber had been a pupil of Charlie's and later he and his delightful and talented wife Christina were to become friends of us both and very favourite visitors whenever they came to stay with us—but that was in the future. While we were staying at Leith Hall, Charlie again proposed to me—but I still said no.

During this time romance was in the air for David too, who became unofficially engaged to another friend of mine from Garden House days—Louise Cockcraft. Unofficially because there was opposition from his regiment and a good deal of anxiety from my parents who couldn't see what on earth they were going to live on if they married so young, since no marriage allowances were granted to officers under the age of twenty-five and David was stationed in North Africa at the time anyway. They went ahead despite the difficulties and got married in St George's Chapel in Windsor Castle in October 1952.

A few weeks later Charlie proposed to me for the third time—and this time I said yes.

The Bird of My Loving
For Charlie

To all the air I vainly cried:
'This octopus possession strangles me.
Can't I be loved, and love,
and still be free?'

But no one heard or listened,
none replied
until upon the green horizon of my view
you came to stand.
The bird of all my loving flew to you.

You held it for a moment
in your hand,
then opening up your fingers
to the sky you said:
'Our love is liberty.
Feel free to fly
—but know that I am true.'

Because you never tried
to pinion it,
the bird of all my loving
stayed with you.

Time to Straighten Your Tie
G.W.N. for D.W.N.

Be careful with prayers:
they can be dangerous, ignite unexpectedly;
perhaps they should carry
a Government Health Warning.

Hearing of your friend's death
as he dropped a dry fly
over a rising trout, I said:
'Oh Pa, wouldn't you like
to go like that? To cease mid-stream,
mid-cast—no long farewell?'
And you were horrified. Not for you
such wild, untidy, impulse of departure.
'That is not how I want to die,'
you said: 'Before I meet my Maker
I would like time to straighten my tie.'

And it was granted you!
Oh, it was granted you
this wish, this dangerous prayer:
two long painful years, while the flesh
was honed to the bones
—but your tie was straight,
so very straight.

You showed me much:
the values of integrity, humility,
unfailing courtesy—the brash
could bark their shins on your politeness—
and you were master of the soft answer
that may turn wrath away, but can annoy.
Old-fashioned virtues, yours,
but not the worse for that.
If you were too fastidious for compassion
—which is essentially an earthy gift—
then you were still exceptionally kind.

You had a flair for laughter:
your wit a kingfisher's beak,
humour a syncopated rhythm.
You showed me words:
always in set metre, patterned rhyme,
but words that had a ring.
You did not teach me how to have a fling.

Was it a comfort to you, your faithful,
disciplined, pew-steady Churchianity?
I really do not know: support, possibly, yes
but comfort, sadly, no. If consciousness
survives the jumble-sale disposal in the earth
I hope you got a wonderful surprise.
I hope some infinitely gentle angel greeted you.
(Surely not God who must be hierarchies on).
I hope it said: 'My dear chap! Lovely to see you!
You must be quite exhausted. Come on in.'
I hope it said: 'Your laces look so straight,
do slacken them—it's quite informal here.
Judgement Day? There's no such thing:
it's D.I.Y. You've judged yourself too hard
these last two years. Besides we're modern here:
continuous assessment—not exams.
Sin? Why, yes, perhaps you ought
to learn to sin a little bit—
you who were always so afraid of it.
There are a few harmless ones that you may care
to re-evaluate sometime. But later—
not just yet: you are too tired
and we're so very pleased to see you.'

Was it like this? I'd like to think it so—
but, oh alas! One thing that's certain is
… I do not know.

10

AN ETON WEDDING

As my father and I walked up the aisle of College Chapel on the eighth of April 1953 it was questionable who was supporting whom: my legs not only felt wobbly from nerves and spike-heeled shoes, but my father leant so heavily on my arm that I was afraid I might not be able to hold him up. He had been ill for three months—hit by a mystery virus which affected his joints and all his movements. At the height of his sickness he had been unable to grip a pen sufficiently to sign his name or even hold a spoon to feed himself; quite unable to get out of bed or walk unaided. Other masters had covered his teaching and an assistant master had temporarily taken over the supervision of the boys in his house, so there was serious doubt about whether he would be able to attend my wedding, let alone give me away, though he was determined to try. Two weeks before our wedding I had taken him down to Brighton for a few days' sea air and we had practised little walks, arm in arm, for very short distances along the pier. Pa was eventually to make a complete recovery, but we did not know this at the time and we were a shaky pair as we tottered uncertainly over the ancient, uneven flagstones and I wondered if we would manage to make it as far as the altar and what I ought to do if he collapsed halfway. Somehow we got there, and as we approached, Charlie, who had been watching our uncertain progress with considerable anxiety, gave me a brilliant smile.

Pa was exhausted but we exchanged a look of triumph, both hugely relieved to have made it up the aisle, albeit so slowly that the last verse of our processional hymn, *Come Down Oh Love Divine*, had finished before we arrived at our destination. As the final accompanying notes of the great organ died away I remember thinking with surprise that there had been something missing in the singing of the congregation. All my life I had been used to hearing the tremendous volume of noise made by several hundred young male voices belting out the hymns in College Chapel. It is a very particular sound. Anyone who has been brought up in a similar type of boys' school will know what I mean.

On that sunlit, breezy April day I was a very immature twenty-one year-old—compared with many of the university-educated, gap-year-experienced young of today it is hard to realize quite how unsophisticated and less self-reliant many of my generation were at that age. My wedding not only marked a prospective move between two very different academic establishments but underlined a change in status from single girl to grown-up married woman.

Charlie was soon to take over as headmaster of Sunningdale School and I found the prospect daunting. Though he had been courting me with great persistence for over a year, the fact that I had finally fallen in love with him did not reconcile me to the thought of the job which, so everyone—except Charlie himself—impressed on me, I would have to take on along with the man I had chosen to marry. I had little taste for what I thought of as the kind of stuffy, middle-aged responsibility which would now be expected of me. It had not been until after the announcement of our engagement that the long-standing previous headmaster unexpectedly decided this was an opportune moment for him and his wife to retire and hand over the running of the school to their chosen successor. As far as I was concerned it was very unwelcome news. I had got more than I bargained for.

To say I regarded my future home with suspicion would be an understatement. I had unhappy associations with Sunningdale, remembering how David had hated returning there as a small boy at the end of each holiday or Sunday outing. I used to be taken along too in order to try to cheer him up on the outward journey and console my bereft mother on the return trip and had always been miserably aware of my inability to comfort either of them. When Charlie proudly took me over to the school to introduce me as his wife to be, my first visit there since childhood did not go well. I felt no more disposed to like the place than I had before and the thought of actually living in the school filled me with doom.

I was invited to tea by Mrs Wilson, the fearsome Head Matron who crackled with starch and wore a sort of upturned paper doily on her tightly permed hair. She informed me over tiny sandwiches that she had been very surprised to learn of our engagement as she thought Charles was sure to marry the divorced mother of one of the boys in the school with whom he played a lot of tennis. Because Matron Wilson seemed to me so old at fifty it did not occur to me at the time that she could be jealous of me and was herself half in love with Charlie—as, I was to discover later, were several other female members of the staff. She insisted that I accompany her upstairs to one of the dormitories to see a photograph of the parent in question, looking horribly glamorous against the flatteringly cloudy background that was the trademark of the Society photographer Lenare. In Mrs Wilson's sweet-sour presence I was temporarily at a loss for words, though I found plenty to say to my betrothed as he drove me home to Eton. He was highly entertained at my account of this ordeal by tea party and thought it uproariously funny—but I had a sense of humour failure.

My reunion with Mr and Mrs Fox, the poker-faced and poker-playing headmaster and his blue-rinsed, world class bridge playing wife was not much more successful. As the small sister of one of the school's pupils, Nancy Fox's alarming appearance and terrifying teeth had made me feel that she might first bite me and then spit me out; now we regarded each other with mutual suspicion.

I'm sure the Foxes genuinely tried to be friendly to me but their efforts to draw me out felt more like a grand inquisition and my attempts to make conversation to them were clearly regarded as frivolous inanities. I can sympathise now with the dismay they must have felt at the arrival of the green girl I then was, not only twenty years younger than Charlie but woefully unsuitable in their eyes to take part in the running of the school which they both loved and which had been their life's work. Worse still, I didn't play bridge or golf or know anything about racing, their three great passions (all of which Charlie shared with them) but when Nancy Fox asked me politely what I enjoyed doing and I said I loved reading she looked baffled and raised her eyebrows.

'I don't suppose you'll find much time for doing that here!' she said.

I couldn't help thinking that golf and bridge took up quite a bit of time too.

We tried to find some shared ground but the only thing we really had in common was a well founded doubt about my capability of stepping into her formidably competent shoes.

Perhaps if the Foxes had met me first they would not have been so quick to announce their retirement. Perhaps if I had realised quite what the lack of privacy of living actually in, rather than over, 'the shop' would entail so soon after marriage, I might have refused Charlie's pressing proposals for a third time and he might not have asked me again—and that would have been a pity for both of us. At any rate the Foxes agreed not to retire till the end of the following summer term, which would give them time to find a house they liked in the neighbourhood where they had always lived, and would give Charlie and me one precious term together before we had to move into the school... but that was certainly not at the forefront of my mind as I heard my father respond to the question 'Who giveth this woman to be married to this man?'

Eight years after the end of the war England was beginning to emerge from its long period of shortages and restrictions but many things, including clothes, were still rationed; by means of swapping, bartering and saving up, it was usually possible to obtain enough clothing coupons for something special and I don't remember it being particularly difficult to get enough of the silk organza for the big skirt and train of my wedding dress. Less successful were the dresses my unfortunate bridesmaids had to wear but that had nothing to do with rationing. I had two grown-up bridesmaids—Mary Nicholson, my great friend from St Mary's Calne—still a very special person to all my family—a cousin Jennifer Clare-Lees, and three little girls, Fiona Peterson, Joanna Glazebrook and my cousin Elizabeth Dobie. They can't have been very pleased at having to use up clothing coupons for their wedding regalia. Though Mum always looked nice herself in the country clothes that suited her preferred lifestyle—good tweed skirts and cosy cardigans—I would never describe her as a snappy dresser and she was given to some curious notions when faced with challenging sartorial occasions. Perhaps it might not seem immediately obvious that the window above the altar should provide her with the inspiration for my bridesmaids' dresses, but so it was.

The glass of the great East Window in College Chapel which had been blown out during the war had recently been replaced by an exciting new stained glass window representing the Crucifixion, at the top, with Christ and his disciples at the Last Supper below—Judas with a green face clearly feeling bilious at what he was about to do.

The design eventually decided on was by the notable Dublin artist Evie Hone, who worked on the window itself between 1949 and 1952. The window, though not to everyone's taste, is now regarded by many as one of the masterpieces of modern stained glass but it was a bold and divisive choice at the time. It aroused powerful passions both in the Eton community and the Art world. Some thought it unsuited to the age and architecture of the fifteenth century chapel, less glamorous sister to King's College, Cambridge; some felt that only a potentially great modern work of art representing our age was a permissible choice for such an important commission. Controversy raged between those who admired the East Window's hugely dominating impact, its Celtic influence, vibrant colours and distorted but strangely moving figures, and those who hated it; I remember that some people disliked it so much they could hardly bear to look at it. Emotions ran high. I don't remember my mother expressing any particular opinion about the artistic merits of the glass—that was not really her sort of thing— but she became obsessed with the peculiar notion that the window must not overshadow the bridal procession.

She seemed to be under the impression that if only Evie Hone had realised my wedding was in the offing, she might have designed a window with more subdued and tactful colouring to set off the occasion. Clearly, in my mother's view, my traditional bridal gown had to be white and wasn't expected to compete in a colour contest with the disciples' robes (people might get wrong ideas about the bride) but she was determined that the bridesmaids should be able to 'stand up' to the vivid stained glass by wearing, so she informed her nervous listeners, a really *powerful* gold. She eventually tracked down some shiny seersucker taffeta in a violent shade of mustard which fully met her requirements but was singularly unflattering. I doubt whether any of the wedding guests appreciated the significance of the choice of colour worn by my attendants. I thought it hideous at the time and doubtless said so in an undiplomatically bolshy way which cut no ice with my mother. Mum, a terrier when in pursuit of one of her idiosyncratic brainwaves, was running on a burning scent. I was not surprised to learn later that none of the bridesmaids' dresses were ever worn again.

There was one sad absence from my wedding: David, serving with the Coldstream Guards in the Suez Canal Zone, had just been appointed Staff Captain 1st Guards Brigade and could not get leave to come home. I was devastated that my beloved childhood companion, to whom I'd always been exceptionally close, could not be with me for my special day. After their wedding he and Louise had gone out to North Africa where he'd previously been stationed, and while on an extended honeymoon in Tripoli, he'd contracted typhus fever. He was rushed to the British Military Hospital to fight for his life while Louise had a miserably anxious time in a borrowed flat in a foreign city, with her new young husband on the danger list. She had no car or telephone and was only able to visit David—when allowed to do so—as a passenger in an army truck. On receiving a telegram with this alarming news, my parents had immediately looked up typhus in the medical dictionary to be greeted by the words 'usually fatal'. Due to the life-saving properties of Chloromycetin—the first time the drug had been used to treat typhus—he recovered, but when he was eventually well enough to be discharged from hospital he was only granted one week's sick leave before going to his new job in Egypt, where Louise could not accompany him. Louise had been flown back to England and was once again living with her parents in Windsor Castle. It was a difficult start for what was to be a long and extremely happy marriage.

Youth can be very self-centred. Looking back from the viewpoint of old age I wonder if I fully appreciated how difficult my mother must have found this period of her life. With her fiercely protective maternal instincts she must have struggled to cope with the fact of both her children flying the nest within six months of each other—let alone going through acute anxiety over the health of her adored son and her husband at the same time.

Instead of an address to the whole congregation, Charlie and I had opted for Cyril Alington to say a few private words to us as we knelt at the altar steps. I can't remember whose suggestion this was—not I think C.A.A's—but I now think it was a curious and rather selfish choice on our part, given that we had such an outstanding preacher to conduct the service, to deny our guests the opportunity of listening to him. It must also have been very boring for them, though I suppose it made it highly personal for us and I can still remember some of his excellent advice: never stop working to keep your marriage alive; never get out of the habit of kissing each other good morning and goodnight and always to try to resolve any disagreements, irritations or resentments that had built up during the day before going to sleep.

We came down the aisle to Henry Purcell's trumpet voluntary and this time I had wings on my feet and didn't even notice the length of the aisle or the uneven flagstones.

By 1953, the historic Upper School which adjoins the chapel at right angles and forms the west side of School Yard had just been restored and reopened after its partial destruction by the 1940's bomb. All the ancient woodwork had been shattered and the piecing together of millions of fragments of wood bearing the carved names of numerous old boys, some extremely famous, was a fantastic labour of love and skill—perhaps one of the most successful jigsaw puzzles ever completed. In Upper School, a long and beautifully proportioned room, one famous headmaster, Dr Keate, (1809- 4) taught a hundred and ninety boys at the same time. He was said to be a brilliant teacher but I fear his ability to keep order successfully enough to teach this number probably had much to do with his fearsome reputation for flogging the boys—but it makes an interesting comparison with our modern ideas of what constitutes a manageable size of class. Upper School had not previously been one of the places with which I was familiar. As a small child I don't suppose I was ever taken inside it, and after 1940 it was of course out of commission until shortly before my wedding. I was one of the first Eton brides to be allowed to have my wedding reception there and felt very privileged. Some fifty years later I was proud to hear one of my grandsons, William Shirley, take part in the traditional ceremony of Speeches given in Upper School by sixth form boys on the Fourth of June.

The day before the wedding my sister-in-law Louise and I had picked armloads of daffodils and blossom from the wonderful garden at Willowbrook where 'Bee' Mackinnon, the school bursar, and his wife Eva lived. I'd thought of making bridesmaids' wreaths for the marble busts of all the famous old Etonians round the room but my father had rightly vetoed this irreverent idea and we contented ourselves with huge vases of spring flowers in strategic corners. It was the perfect place for a reception and we only had to walk down the stone steps of the antechapel—which an hour before I'd had such anxiety and trouble getting my father up—and then walk up some more stairs a little further along.

Brides and grooms often seem to go through wedding receptions in a semi-anaesthetised state and I had no idea that during the lengthy process of shaking hands—a convention mercifully less popular nowadays than it was then—my mother realized there was something missing. In honour of my wedding she'd had a small plate with two teeth on it made to rectify an almost unnoticeable gap she'd had for years at the side of her mouth. We had laughed about this most uncharacteristic concern about her appearance, and my father had teased her that she was sure to forget to wear her little 'snapper', as he called it, when the great day dawned. He was right. Having discovered her lapse of memory, but typically undaunted, Mum dispatched her brother on foot to collect the missing bit of equipment from her bedroom in Common Lane House, the other side of what was then the main Windsor to Slough road. He returned with it in a handkerchief which he discreetly handed to my mother, who smiling widely, managed to pop it into her mouth with one hand while continuing to shake hands with a surprised guest with the other. Though she was standing so near me, I was luckily too busy greeting guests myself to be aware of this incident at the time.

Charlie was also unaware that his beloved mother, only in her late sixties, who we would now undoubtedly consider to have been suffering from Alzheimer's disease, had replied to a friend's polite comment that it was a lovely wedding, 'Yes isn't it? But I'm afraid I don't know either of the couple concerned!'

Until the war Olive Sheepshanks had lived in a house on the family estate at Arthington where her husband, the eldest son, acted as land agent to his father. Tragically he had died of pneumonia leaving her with two small boys aged four and two and a baby daughter of only two weeks old. She had brought her children up in the shadow of a dominating and interfering mother-in-law, but after the tragic death in 1938 in the Spanish Civil war of her brilliant firstborn, Dick, the estate had passed to her brother-in-law Charles Sheepshanks. Though The Sheep and Olive were extremely fond of each other and there was no question of her having to leave her house, after these two tragedies she could no longer bear to go on living at Arthington and had spent the duration of the war lodging with a married sister. Recently she had been living with Charlie in the cottage on the edge of the school grounds which he'd bought when he was demobbed, while she looked—in theory—for something more permanent for herself. The question of where she should live was a problem still to be sorted out, though it was becoming increasingly clear that she could not possibly live on her own. Charlie's sister Rosemary had offered to have her to stay when we first got back from our honeymoon but no one had much idea what to do in the longer term.

Soon after our engagement, at Charlie's suggestion, I had gone over to the cottage to have lunch with Olive Sheepshanks. Charlie was anxious that his mother and I should spend time together, optimistically convinced that because he loved us both so much, we would be bound to love each other too. Alas, time was not on our side. If we had met at some earlier stage of her life I am sure he would have been right. Photographs of her as a young woman show her not only to have been extremely beautiful but also, by many accounts, an enchanting person, but by the time I came along, dementia, that heartbreaking stealer of minds and personalities, already had her in its cruel grip. Charlie, who was on duty at the school that particular lunchtime, said he would come down and join us both later for coffee, and meanwhile Olive, though she clearly had no idea who I was, seemed friendly enough when I first arrived, if a little distraite. There was no sign at all of any lunch, however, and after an hour of sitting on the edge of the sofa in the drawing room trying to make conversation while she pottered around humming and muttering to herself I was getting increasingly nervous—and hungry. Eventually I followed her as she wandered off into the kitchen and when she opened a tin of dog food for Charlie's golden retriever, which had started barking persistently for his dinner, I wondered if I should start barking for mine too. When, to my fascinated horror, my hostess then proceeded to put a dollop of Pedigree Chum onto a dinner plate for herself and sat down at the table and started to eat it with a spoon I thought better of this idea and decided starvation was preferable.

On the eighth of April, however, the problem of my mother-in-law's increasingly bizarre behaviour was a matter for the future and meanwhile there had been an awkward hold-up in the queue waiting for us to greet them at the reception. The Sheep, now my uncle-in-law, had organized a coach to bring down a party from Arthington. Among this party was the wonderfully named Annie Annikin, my mother-in-law's old cook, resplendent in a battering-ram of a hat, shedding hairpins from her bun of white hair like the White Queen in *Alice*, and unlike my mother completely toothless. 'Ee, Mr Charlie, love! Whatever kind of scrape have you landed yourself in this time?' she demanded, with a cackle of laughter that momentarily silenced the astonished company, reducing my presence to the status of a passing peccadillo. She smothered Charlie with a hug, practically concussing him with the brim of her hat, and then caused a mammoth bottleneck in the queue while she embarked on a flood of reminiscences in which Charlie cheerfully joined, regardless of the fact that I had already exchanged greetings with a surge of guests, most of them friends of Charlie's whom I didn't know, before she could be persuaded to move on. Annie could single-handedly have removed the hind-legs off whole herds of donkeys, as I was later to discover during lengthy tea parties in her little cottage in the equally marvellously named village of Bedlam in Yorkshire.

Once we had finished our stint in the receiving line it was soon time to cut the wedding cake but as we attempted to do so, I was conscious of being tugged backwards from the head at an extremely awkward angle. Stout Mr Thomas, proprietor of the Eton hairdressing establishment down the High Street, not one to take a back seat, had pressed himself forward and was standing on the train of my veil, acting like a huge tent peg attached to a guy rope.

Jack Peterson, David's Eton housemaster, by this time headmaster of Shrewsbury, made our wedding speech. He was not only my father's oldest friend, but also a friend of Charlie's with whom he'd had a notable partnership at Eton Fives, together winning the Kinnaird cup a record three times. His nine year-old daughter Fiona was now one of my bridesmaids as, fifteen years earlier, and also in College Chapel, I had been one of a flock of little attendants—yellow silk-chiffon dresses and agonizingly prickly wreaths in our hair—to Jack's beautiful wife Rosemary McNeil, also the daughter of an Eton housemaster. The sun had shone that day too and they had made a golden couple but tragedy was to hit them soon. Rosemary developed multiple sclerosis and suffered a deadly deterioration that was agonizing for them both and was to leave Jack a desolate widower with three small children. We were all devoted to Jack and my mother had been a great support to him during Rosemary's heartrending illness when blindness and paralysis took a relentless hold of her life. As Rosemary's bright light faded, Jack's sadness cast a long shadow. I have painful memories of Rosemary, once so pretty and athletic, nearly blind and just managing to walk a very short distance with the aid of a stick on one of her 'good' days. Jack never remarried. Years later when he was staying with Charlie and me in Yorkshire, I asked him if he was very lonely. 'Yes,' he said simply, 'but then I've had years of practice at dealing with it.'

I don't remember much about Jack's speech except his reminder of my brother David's heartfelt complaint as a small boy that I was a very *igritating* little girl—a word that had gone into our family vocabulary.

In the late afternoon sunshine in School Yard, pigeons wheeled and swooped round the statue of King Henry the Sixth, Eton's founder, as Charlie and I left Upper School to go and change into our going-away clothes. Earlier, my father and I had been driven the few hundred yards to College Chapel by car, but after our reception Charlie and I walked back arm in arm to Common Lane House, my wedding veil, mercifully now released from under Mr Thomas's be-spatted feet, floating behind me in the breeze. Finally there was the release of much pent up post-wedding emotion as our families gathered to see us off: much laughter and a few tears; kisses and extra last minute hugs and wildly waving goodbyes as our best man, John Rickards, Charlie's Eton contemporary and long-time skiing companion, drove us up to Windsor where Charlie's enormous old Packard was secretly parked. At Sunningdale, Matron Wilson might have been astonished by our engagement but no one at Eton—with its super-effective bush telegraph—was at all surprised because during so many weekends for the last year this distinctive old tank of a car had so often been parked outside our house. So far my attempts to drive it had been hilarious but not very successful. In order to see out of the windscreen I had to be jacked up on so many cushions that my feet could barely touch the pedals.

From Windsor we set off to spend the first night of our honeymoon conveniently close to Heathrow airport at Great Fosters, an imposing Elizabethan mansion near Egham which had been turned into a luxury hotel. The following day we flew to Cyprus, which in those days involved landing at Rome and Athens to refuel the aircraft, for a fortnight of blazing sun and azure sea and the still snow-capped Troodos Mountains. I had never before had a hot holiday. This was partly due to post-war currency restrictions but more to the fact of the rest of my family's preference for inclement sporting holidays involving soggy biscuits, sodden sandwiches, clouds of midges—and for the women much trudging up vertical hills humping heavy picnic equipment while their men wielded rod or gun. Before mass tourism and the spoiling of so much of the Mediterranean coast with hideous, unregulated building programmes, it would be hard to imagine a more beautiful and romantic island than Cyprus. It was an island of contrasts: of fairy-tale crusaders' castles perched on impossible pinnacles of rock where golden eagles nested in the battlements and thrillingly dive-bombed unwelcome intruders; a place where great piles of ripe oranges, a rare treat in my childhood, were sold along the side of the primitive dirt-track roads all over the island—Cyprus was not then restricted or divided into Greek and Turkish sectors and the black-clad figure of Archbishop Makarios, leader of the Greek Cypriots' movement for *Enosis* (union with Greece), had not yet started to dominate our newspapers. It was an island of scarlet poppies under silver olive trees and drifts of wild cyclamen everywhere. I was amazed at the feast of colour and the constant wonderful warmth. I was entranced, I was bewitched, I was in love.

Those two weeks seemed like an oasis between two lives—a brilliant, irresponsible interlude before I had to face new challenges as a headmaster's wife.

11

SUNNINGDALE DÉBUT

CHARLIE was a born schoolmaster who never seriously contemplated any other career. He went straight from Cambridge to teach at Sunningdale where he immediately felt he'd found his niche in life. Part of his success as a schoolmaster was that he genuinely loved doing so many of the things that children enjoy. All his life he was a Pied Piper to the young. It wasn't only that he loved sport and was a superb athlete—a double 'blue' at Cambridge and a notable cricketer and tennis player—but he enjoyed playing almost any game from bridge to Happy Families, backgammon to Chase-the-Ace, and had numerous hobbies and interests which could be shared by those with no athletic ability—important for a schoolmaster. During his first term as a junior assistant master he took a party of boys on a bug-hunting expedition to the New Forest where they had a lovely time wielding nets, painting trees with honey and identifying moths and butterflies. Charlie was somewhat disconcerted however when a boy introduced him to his mother with the words 'Oh Mum you must meet our new master, Mr Sheepshanks—he's the most terrific bugger'.

1938 had been an unhappy year for Charlie. His beloved elder brother Dick—a star in the family firmament and his boon companion—was killed in Spain where he was the Reuters correspondent covering the Spanish Civil War. Not long afterwards, after much anguished heart-searching, Charlie who had recently become engaged, broke it off and the young woman in question was apparently devastated. In 1939 however his life was improving and he had just bought a share in Sunningdale and become a junior partner at the school when war broke out and everything changed. Aged twenty-eight he volunteered for the army and together with his old Eton contemporary and lifelong friend Brian Johnston, the cricket commentator, served with the Grenadiers throughout the war. It would be hard to imagine two less typical military men but though they must have made an unlikely pair of adjutants, they were apparently highly successful wartime soldiers. Many of their friends told me how much these two magically funny men helped to keep morale up during dark days. Brian and his wife Pauline sent all their three sons to us at Sunningdale. A school environment can be insular and I think Charlie's five years in the army gave him a much wider view of the outside world than he might otherwise have had, which consequently made him a better headmaster. Many of his contemporaries found it hard to settle into civilian life after the war, but Charlie said he just had a huge sense of relief at being back in his right milieu again, doing the thing he did best—teaching. Maths was his particular speciality but he got great satisfaction out of teaching almost anything, perhaps especially to those who found a subject difficult. Later on, our children used to tease: 'Give Dad two people and he's got a class' and there was some truth in it. Though he could be extremely efficient when he chose, he had little patience with red tape, pecking orders or unnecessary formality and as an administrator he occasionally drove his long-suffering staff crazy with his somewhat laissez-faire approach to organization—but most of them loved him all the same. Above all he was wonderfully good company and great fun to be with.

'I'll never marry a schoolmaster' I used to declare when I was growing up. This certainly wasn't because I was anti schoolmasters—but I'd seen too much of what was expected of their wives.

With the end of the war changes had come in the way boys' houses at Eton were financed and run. Before the war an assistant master's basic salary was poor, his income largely depending on how many pupils he could take on, but this situation improved dramatically if he became a housemaster because he then received the fees of the boys in his house—a legacy from the original system of the Dames' Boarding Houses (landladies in modern parlance) which had enabled the sons of fee-paying parents to benefit from the education offered to the original seventy King's Scholars of Henry VI. It was rather like running a hotel and some bachelor housemasters, who did not have the expense of supporting a wife and family, became very comfortably off. Given this system, there were always jokes about those who lined their own pockets rather than the boys' stomachs. On the other hand there were also those—Grizel and Hubert Hartley, that legendary Eton couple, for instance—who fed their boys so well and lavishly that they almost bankrupted themselves in the process.

Neither of my parents had private means when my father became a housemaster but they expected eventually to recover the money from the loan they'd taken out in order to build on to Common Lane House. The war put a stop to that. After the war my father was one of those who helped to change the system. Fees now became payable to the school and attempts were made to standardize expenditure. Pa became chairman of 'The House Fund Committee', the body which decided what each house could spend on food and maintenance and this became a source of friction in my parents' marriage. It was still permissible for the wife to do the catering—within the budgetary limits of the new rules—but the dames were better paid if they took on this responsibility and my father insisted that it was unfair to deny Miss Pearson, the charming and efficient dame who had succeeded the first two unsuccessful ladies, the chance to earn a higher salary. Having slaved away throughout the war to run the house in the most difficult circumstances, my mother was now furious at having this responsibility summarily removed. She saw the point, of course, but hated not being in command of her own household any more—married to the housemaster but no longer mistress of his house. It didn't help that she considered Pa—the least domesticated of men—quite unsuited to sit on any such committee in the first place.

Martin Forest, who took over the house when Pa retired in 1955, once told me that when he'd asked my father's advice about what pitfalls he should look out for, my father had gloomily replied 'It won't be to do with the boys. It'll be the women. The trouble is always caused by the women and you won't be able to do anything about it.'

During my childhood I'd observed the acrimonious power struggles between my mother and various dames and had no wish to be put in a similar situation. At Common Lane House we'd enjoyed a self-contained private side to the house, which Mum had succeeded in making into a delightful home. There was to be no such charm or seclusion in the quarters Charlie and I were about to inhabit at Sunningdale.

The original house, a Victorian building of virulent red brick surrounded by an unlovely (but useful) verandah, had once been an ordinary dwelling house onto which a vast three-storeyed institutional-looking block had been added by the worthy Canon Girdlestone who founded the school in 1874. Because of its location it came to be regarded as a feeder school for Eton, though it had always sent a certain number of boys to other schools; what it certainly had was a brilliant reputation for preparing boys for the Eton Scholarship exam. After the founder retired, the next headmaster was called Mr Crabtree so Sheepshanks seemed a suitably quirky name to add to the list of Dickensian-sounding principals. The school had grown in numbers since its inception and, though still quite small with only eighty boys, had long outgrown its original premises. The sizeable first floor rooms at the top of the main staircase, which had presumably once been the main bedrooms for the Girdlestones, were now classrooms and the Foxes had no cut-off private side of the house. They had a very public drawing room and dining room to the left of the front door which were mostly used for entertaining, and a bedroom in the attics over the classrooms, where other members of staff also lived. They took all their meals with either the boys or the rest of the staff unless they were entertaining privately, which usually involved bridge or poker.

When I accepted Charlie's proposal—in so far as I had thought of it at all—I had expected to live in Walter's Cottage, the house on the edge of the grounds which he had bought when he was demobbed and in which his mother was temporarily living until she found somewhere nearby for herself, but her rapidly deteriorating health was becoming a problem. We had another difficulty. With the Foxes' unexpectedly early retirement looming at the end of the summer, it was the general opinion that we ought to live in the school. Charlie was very apologetic about this, but clearly agreed with it.

My heart sank at the prospect of living there—it would not be too strong to say I dreaded it and came close to breaking off our engagement over this issue—but I agreed to try it on condition that if it proved too difficult we would review the situation of where we lived at the end of a year. I made one stipulation. I was very happy to have lunch with the boys every day—I could see that this could be a good way of me getting to know them all, but I refused to have breakfast in the boys' dining room and insisted that Charlie and I should be able to have our dinner on our own. As far as sleeping accommodation was concerned I had to accept the prospect of the Foxes' attic bedroom and bathroom at the top of the house because there was nowhere else for us to go. Next door to this bedroom on one side slept one of the three under-matrons and on the other side was the bed-sitting room of the alarming spinster Miss Paterson, Queen of Umbrage and form-mistress to the nine year-old boys in their second school year..

Miss Paterson, known as Patey, an ex-governess, was a brilliant teacher but given to huffs of such earth-shaking proportions that if scientifically measured they would have been completely off the Richter Scale. It wasn't so much a question of it being easy to hurt her feelings, as of it being quite impossible not to do so. For the year that they were under her special jurisdiction the little boys in her form certainly respected and largely enjoyed her. She ruled them with a rigid rod, never accepted second best, inspired them, championed their causes and stuck up for them to other members of staff—and then lost interest in them completely as soon as they were no longer in her form. Sadly, they quickly lost their affection for her too, and she became something of a figure of fun to the older boys—not very kind fun either. It was a recurring pattern, pitiful to watch and she was not a happy woman. In the years to come, I frequently ached for her isolated touchiness, sometimes seethed with irritation over her tiresomeness, often laughed about her ridiculous over-sensitivity and, saddest of all, never came to like her. She had no family and only one friend (My Friend from Lavenham) about whom we all knew a great deal but whom no one ever met. I sometimes wondered if she actually existed. I portrayed this invisible friend (though not Miss Paterson herself) in my second novel. The other occupant of our attic floor was nice, gentle, under-matron Wendy who had one of the worst stammers

I have ever come across. Matron Wilson, with her unerring aim for placing poisoned darts, took it upon herself to inform me that Wendy's stammer was always worse when I was present, a bit of information that did nothing to help either of us. Goodness knows what she may have felt impelled to tell Wendy about my supposed feelings.

When Charlie and I returned from Cyprus we went to Walter's Cottage and my sister-in-law kept her promise and had Charlie's mother to stay with her in Devon for most of the summer term. We had three happy months there before I was transplanted into a much less congenial environment. With hindsight I think it was probably the right decision. If I had been able to have the house of my own for which I longed, I don't think I would ever have become so integrated into, and involved with, the life of the school. But it wasn't easy.

The Cottage was an enchanting house around which Charlie was making a delightful garden. It had a pond full of wild yellow irises and when we got back from our honeymoon it was ablaze round the edges with azaleas and primulas. There were roses of many varieties including two spectacular half-moon beds of dark-red *Frenshams* and against a tall wooden fence were the delphiniums which Charlie grew from seed and which were his special pride. Wisteria scrambled round the old brick walls of the cottage, scenting the air on summer evenings; clematis swarmed over the garage that housed the old Packard and mesembryanthemums poked their bright faces between the flagstones outside the windows of the sitting room. Rows of sweet peas were trained up canes and it became my special task to tie them up each day and remove stray shoots and the little clutching, twiddley bits, so that all the growth could be channelled into flowering. Competitive Charlie intended to enter these for the Ascot Flower Show later in the summer. With this show in mind, he had also been disbudding a few of his hybrid tea roses to encourage perfect specimens of cabbage-like proportions. It seemed to me a curious thing to do, but I knew nothing of the technicalities of gardening and was sufficiently newly married to have a great desire to surprise and please the Beloved. I certainly succeeded in surprising him. I spent an entire day engaged in full scale infanticide.... unfortunately I didn't know the difference between one species of rose and another (*a rose is a rose is a rose*) and busily disbudded all the floribunda ones, leaving one pathetic little budlet on each cluster. It says much for Charlie that after one appalled look of shock he forgave me instantly and couldn't stop laughing about it for days. But I was never quite such a willing volunteer gardener again.

Brought up at Eton, where there was red-hatted, knife-wielding Miss Jackson to do the cooking and with all holidays spent at Cefn with Katie Jones to look after us, I had never cooked a meal in all my spoilt, protected life, but I fell enthusiastically on a cookery book of my mother-in-law's, a vast tome by an Edwardian lady called Florence Jack. Our meals varied from the gastronomic to the inedible. I produced some disgusting culinary disasters but we also consumed quantities of smoked salmon, strawberries and cream and lots of delicious roast duck. I became an ace at perfecting crispy skin and making apple sauce, but was stunned at how expensive our diet turned out to be when the bills came in after my first month of housekeeping. I experimented with such delicacies as crème brûlée and produced an inches-thick, tooth-breaking top like a skating rink at my first attempt, though I became a dab hand after a bit of practice; I mastered the art of making delicious summer pudding and really good cottage pie—still favourites in our family today. Years later, *Cotters* and *Summers* as he called them, together with his favourite champagne, became the chosen first-night menu of Brian Johnston, a regular visitor, whenever he came to stay with us at Arthington after we had retired to Yorkshire.

Unfortunately in those early married days Florence Jack had not indicated that you couldn't just shove the meaty remains of a cottage pie in the larder and expect the dish to be equally delicious a week later—even in an English summer. The resultant heaving mass of maggots was a horrible shock. I don't think Hickie can have taught us about the breeding habits of houseflies.

Charlie had a vast collection of records and in the evenings he introduced me to an eclectic mix of music from Wagner to The Inkspots, from Handel to Humphrey Lyttelton. When he had first arrived as a young master, fresh from Cambridge, Humph was in his last year at Sunningdale before going on to Eton. For the school concert Charlie organized a mock jazz band, the players blowing on combs through tissue paper, and in his autobiography *I Blow My Own Trumpet*, Humph credited Charlie with starting him off on his career as a jazz trumpeter. Later, after the war was over, they were to come across each other again as two rather unlikely Guards Officers sharing a room at Wellington Barracks while awaiting their demobilisation. They used to lie on their beds jazzing up *Eine Kleine Nachtmusik* on mouth organs.

On Saturdays in the summer term there were always cricket matches for Charlie to umpire, sometimes at Sunningdale, sometimes at whichever rival school the team was playing. I felt diffident at going up to the school to watch the cricket and didn't want to intrude on Nancy Fox's last term. I guessed she must be finding it as difficult to contemplate leaving the school as I was finding the prospect of taking it on. I was also wary of encounters with Matron Wilson.

Sports Day on the last Saturday in June was my first meeting with most of the parents—and theirs with me. I was conscious that they must consider me hopelessly inexperienced to follow in Nancy's footsteps. She may not have been someone in whose company I felt at ease, but she had been a notable headmaster's wife who had been genuinely devoted to the welfare of the boys.

People dressed much more formally for school functions in those days than they do now and most of the mothers looked wonderfully glamorous. To my over-awed eyes, they also looked awfully old— though I imagine their average age can't have been more than about thirty-five.

Amongst this elegance one parent, the mother of three scholarship-winning boys, stood out. In contrast to all the high-heeled shoes and immaculate sheer nylon clad legs on display, her somewhat hirsute shins were bare and she wore flat, toe-revealing, Jesus-type sandals. More surprisingly, since it was a glorious summer day, she also wore an Afghan-style coat of unbelievable shagginess which can't have been very expertly cured since it carried a distinct whiff of the old goat which must once have skipped about on the mountains before its hide came into her possession. She was a small earnest-looking woman with hair screwed up in a knot and anchored to her head by a tortoiseshell dagger. I was not to meet her again till the following term at the School Concert when, regardless of any seasonal change, she was identically clad. This time, on a chilly November day it was perhaps the bare legs that were more surprising, though not more memorable, than the unmistakable coat she still wore in all its embroidered, smelly, glory.

'Hello Mrs Brock, how nice to see you again,' I said, thrilled with myself for such social perspicacity. She looked at me in astonishment.

'How on earth did you manage to remember me?' she asked.

During that summer term, we usually went over one night a week to dine with my parents and it was a joy to find my father's health was steadily improving. Charlie and I often went up to Covent Garden to the ballet, still a passion with us both, though opera was later to take first place in our hearts. Because Charlie was always busy in the school at weekends he sometimes took a day off during the week. One day we drove to Hove for breakfast. Charlie had last been there in the war, waiting to cross the channel in a tank on D-Day for the invasion of Europe. Later in the morning we drove on to Brighton for lunch, ate delicious sea food, pottered round the antique shops in The Lanes— and played each other like a couple of children on the slot machines on the pier. In May we went to the Chelsea Flower Show. On a perfect June summer evening we attended a performance of *The Marriage* of *Figaro*—Sesto Bruscantini as Figaro, Irmgard Seefried as Susannah and Sena Jurinace, who we were later to see as the Countess, singing Cherubino—my first visit to Glyndebourne, of which Charlie was a member, and something which was to give us enormous pleasure in the years ahead.

For my birthday that summer, Charlie decided to give me a crocodile handbag. He gave me a £50 note—a serious sum of money in those days—drove me to Sunningdale station and sent me up to London to choose one for myself. When he met my train again at the end of the day he was surprised to discover that the crocodile bag had turned into an eight week old black and white Shih-tzu puppy. Ming had been sitting in a little gingham-covered armchair in the window of the shop in Hay Hill where the formidable Misses Ashton-Cross normally displayed the Pekingese puppies they bred. This tiny puppy was sole master of that chair, holding about five Peke puppies at bay with the power of his eye, and I was drawn into the shop as though by a magnet. When I discovered that he cost exactly £50 it seemed like fate. Shih-tzus, or Tibetan Lion Dogs, were little known in 1953 but I had met and been enchanted by one before—Choo-Choo the hairy charmer who belonged to the Royal Family, and whom I had liked much better than their trademark corgis. Ming was to become not only beloved by both Charlie and me but turned out to be the ideal prep school dog. He went everywhere with me and was adored by the boys. He learnt to do a spectacular Grand National gallop from bed to bed round and round the youngest boys' eight-bedded dormitory at incredible speed before finally leaping off the furthest bed and skidding back down the whole length of the room on his tummy, shooting along the slippery polished linoleum to wild applause—a stunt guaranteed to cheer up even the most homesick child.

I've never had a crocodile handbag but I've had Shih-tzus ever since. Two are lying on my feet as I write.

As the days of that summer term sped past I found myself increasingly dreading the thought of the Foxes' retirement. I was not only extremely nervous of the daunting responsibilities that lay ahead but anxious lest I would be unable to find a personal role that I felt capable of fulfilling—but worse, far worse, was the prospect of the loss of privacy and the fear of being under the constant scrutiny that the move to the school would inevitably mean.

Making Summer Pudding

Crouched on an upturned bucket, fingers stained,
I weigh the rival claims of summer fruit:
blackcurrants smell of old tom cat, but gleam
glossy as toe-caps on a soldier's boot;

delicious on their own, their forceful zest
can dominate a mix, and sometimes wreck
the subtle character of milder tastes
—would-be dictators should be kept in check.

Raspberries and redcurrants, paired in heaven
—the Romeos and Juliets of the punnet—
enhance each other to create a whole
as rhymes and metre make a perfect sonnet.

Strawberries, for me, are sovereigns of the clan:
Snow-capped with sugar, avalanched in cream
or gorged in secret underneath the net—
forbidden fruit of all our childhood dreams.

I'll blend my fruit together in a pan,
spoon it in bread-lined bowls and pack down tight;
add weights—heavy as age—to crush the juice
and hope for once I get life's balance right!

Interior Decoration

A floral chintz with a delicate air
I think, don't you, for my bedroom chair—
but dare I have the carpet mauve
like Lady Fresco's house at Hove?
Old bitch, though I could never stand her
I covet her trompe l'oeil verandah!
Now shall I have a Roman blind
or pleated curtains, interlined?

The bathroom's next—that must be done.
Bathrooms can give one endless fun—
there's even quite a lot of scope
in matching loo paper with soap.
And darling! How's this for an idée:
a goldfish swimming in my bidet?
But do you think gold cherub taps
a little OTT perhaps?

I always feel it's such a pity
to make a drawing room look too *pretty*....
sophistication is the rage
and nothing looks as smart as beige:
I think I've hit on just the thing
in seven different shades of string.
I flogged the Meissen to buy lots
of chic Victorian chamber pots.

Do come and see our gilded *Aga*
—obtaining that was quite a saga!
I died when Algie found the bill!
We haven't used the charcoal grill
since our *au pair*, the silly nut,
burnt the cork tiles—and then she shut
the budgie in the microwave....
Selina's being awfully brave.

Yes, darling, husbands are so funny
they seem to hate one spending money
and Algie's views are really quaint:
he says he doesn't like new paint!
That damp patch on his study ceiling
gives him a cosy, lived-in feeling;
he leaves his wellies in the hall—
the poor love has no taste at all.

This boring hall could take a mural:
something simple but wildly rural
with birds and bees and an urn or two
—I'm always mad about urns aren't you?
When I've done the house from hall to attic
life will really be dreadfully static;
I hate to feel I'm in a groove.
I must tell Algie...we'll have to move!

12

HEADMASTER'S WIFE

WE moved into the School during early September 1953. I much enjoyed choosing curtains and carpets for the so-called private side of the house. My architect godfather, Uncle Dick, who loved colour schemes as much as his mother had done—and especially loved spending other people's money—met me in London and whirled me round interior decorating establishments where he egged me on to select materials well beyond my budget. Outings with Uncle Dick tended to be expensive anyway as he invariably issued invitations to the most exclusive restaurants but never had any money to pay the bill.

For the curtains of the two big French windows in the drawing room I chose a toile de Jouy chintz with a design of exceptionally well-fed cherubs cavorting about and wielding garlands, which seemed to me an eminently suitable choice for a boys' prep school. Nancy Fox had cautioned me to select dark, patterned covers as little boys would inevitably be galumphing through the room but I'm ashamed to say this advice caused me to have the sofas and armchairs covered in off-white slubbed linen which I thought the acme of elegance but illustrates all too clearly my bolshy state of mind at the time. Nancy was right from a practical point of view but those ivory covers and the pale blue-grey carpet beneath them did much to reconcile me to the acres of dark green dados and awful margarine walls with which I felt surrounded.

Because we had to leave Walter's Cottage furnished for my mother-in-law, we needed to buy some furniture for ourselves and this introduced me to the lifelong delight of haunting antique shops and attending auctions. So carried away did I become by the excitement of bidding that had it not been for the fact that the local auctioneer, Timothy Tufnell, had been a fellow Grenadier with Charlie, I might have found myself with some huge bills to pay. 'There's only your wife against you now,' he announced, highly amused but poker-faced, to Charlie at one particularly tempting house clearance sale as I waved my hand excitedly to up the bidding, unaware that the lots in question were about to be knocked down to my husband.

One of the decisions to be taken was the role I was to play in the school. For the last thirty years Nancy Fox had run practically everything, something I was singularly unfitted to do. The consensus of opinion was that though I might need help with the catering, I ought to take at least titular responsibility for the matrons and the domestic staff. My heart sank at this prospect—as no doubt did several other hearts. The thought of me being in charge of Matron Wilson was farcical.

My biggest bugbear was the weekly pay day for the domestic staff which took place on Thursdays. Nancy Fox, a shrewd business woman who had a brain like a calculator under her blue rinsed waves, impressed on me that it was most important for me to pay the staff myself. It would demonstrate to them, she said, that I had a *grip* on things. Unfortunately grip wasn't my forte. As she explained the mysteries of the threatening-looking ledger marked WAGES with its columns of figures, and took me on a whistle-stop tour of deductions, insurance and different hourly rates of pay, I felt a shutter come down over my mind as I nodded and smiled like a bemused traveller listening to complicated route instructions in a foreign language and not taking any of them in. Thursday mornings became my dread.

Though I'm all for having a go at most things, once you have discovered that you are really bad at a particular job, it seems wiser to let someone more competent do it and concentrate on your own, different, strengths; but it took me a year to realize that my relationships with the staff did not have to depend on my prowess, or lack of it, with a column of figures and to have the courage to refuse to go on doing it. The first year of marriage can be a testing time for any couple, but if played out in conditions of goldfish-bowl exposure before many—not all benevolent—spectators, it is truly difficult. I fluctuated between secret bouts of tears when I thought life in the school was so awful I couldn't stand it, or fits of laughter because I thought all the pecking orders, petty feuds and bizarre eccentricities that flourish in small residential communities were hilariously funny. Charlie must have wondered if he'd been mad to introduce such a volatile element into his hitherto smooth bachelor existence—but if so he hid it well. I seldom felt the big age gap between us on a personal level but I sometimes found it difficult in the company of some of his friends, charming though most of them were to me.

There was no question of continuing with my newly acquired—if not always successful—cooking skills, which I would have loved to do, because there was only the one, huge school kitchen and it certainly would not have been welcome if I'd started pottering about in there, knocking up little dishes just for us. Domestic staff were hard to come by in the 1950s, especially in such an affluent neighbourhood as Ascot and Sunningdale where the demand for help was high and many people could afford to pay much better wages than we could offer. As a result most of the staff I inherited from Nancy Fox seemed to have some special drawback guaranteed to make them less enticing to other, wealthier employers.

Mrs Davis, in charge of the kitchen, for instance, though quite a good cook, had the misfortune not only to be completely bald but to have no outer ears. To cover this lack of lobes and hair, she wore an ill-fitting, bouffant wig which had a disconcerting tendency to slip sideways, giving her a spuriously rakish air and revealing neat little holes in the side of her head. Her real disadvantage, however, was that she was always accompanied by her grumpy lesbian companion, Ellen, whose sole duty, apart from answering the school telephone for one hour between seven and eight in the evenings, was to act as handmaid to Mrs Davis. Nancy had warned me that it was unwise to upset Mrs Davis and I was terrified of her. One evening Ellen answered the telephone to Sir Derek Vestey—of beef baron lineage—the peppery father of one of the boys. He asked to speak to Charlie but Ellen said that he was out. One of the matrons, coming down the stairs at that moment and overhearing this conversation, announced that Charlie was only on the lawn just outside the dining room window. 'Well I'm bloody well not fetching him,' said Ellen without putting her hand over the receiver, and then reiterated: 'I said he's *OUT*.' Unfortunately both conversations were clearly audible to Sir Derek, who was far from amused and rang me up later to demand that the perpetrator of this rudeness should be instantly dismissed. I apologised profusely and assured him I would deal with the situation, but I knew I couldn't sack Ellen, since, although she lived free in return for her one hour of dubious service on the telephone, the school didn't actually employ her. However, I remonstrated with her, took her permanently off telephone duty and felt I'd dealt adequately with the situation—which up to this point I'd privately thought extremely funny. Not so entertainingly, however, next morning Ellen and Mrs Davis had completely vanished—my first taste of suddenly being without a cook with a household of a hundred to cater for.

Red-haired Molly, who was nominally in charge of the boys' dining room, was always accompanied by snivelling two year-old Darren who clung round her legs like an ankle shackle, much impeding progress when she was carrying a tray. The crash of cascading crockery was an all too familiar sound. I felt very sorry for Molly, a natural victim, who brought out bullying tendencies in everyone she worked with. Battered-looking Mrs Tedder's drawback was VEINS. Mrs Tedder, in theory, came in daily from the village to wash up (no dishwashers in 1953) and stood in the stone-floored scullery in bedroom slippers, her stockings rolled down to her ankles to disclose a sort of viper's nest crawling up each leg, as awful to behold as a depiction of torment by Hieronymus Bosch. When, not infrequently, she didn't turn up for work the excuse was always 'It was me VEINS'—all too believable, poor woman. Jolly, rotund Mrs Kettle's personal drawback was the equally rotund Mr Kettle, though he was sometimes an advantage as far as I was concerned, because when he had one of his little disagreements with the law, Mrs Kettle became keen for extra work. The Kettles had three large, jolly children and Mrs Kettle could usually be heard humming happily as she worked. Needless to say she was known as the Singing Kettle.

An early domestic drama occurred when Mrs Davis's successor, a dazzlingly blonde Czechoslovakian lady of huge appetite and

Wagnerian proportions—came to complain to me that large amounts of cheese kept disappearing from the larder. I had no idea how to deal with this emergency but I didn't have to play at being Miss Marple for long. A few days later one of the daily helpers, a large and ponderous lady given to wearing voluminous clothes, was seen waddling off down the drive when her knicker elastic suddenly broke with a loud snap and out fell a whole catering pack of mature Cheddar cheese. We didn't use it.

I was to learn that getting enough domestic help would always be difficult and over the years tried various methods of finding staff. At one time, in answer to an advertisement I placed in a northern paper I found three splendid Geordie lasses from Sunderland, Helen, Olive and Kathleen who came to me aged seventeen and remained for a surprisingly long time. They were feisty, funny, hardworking and outspoken and I loved them—but they were not without drawbacks. Soon after they arrived I heard tremendous cheering coming from the boys' dining room after tea one afternoon and thinking someone must have been awarded their football colours poked my nose round the door to offer congratulations. But the applause had nothing to do with soccer. My three handmaidens were having a no holds barred fight involving punches, hair-pulling, scratching, spitting and blood-letting while an enthusiastic crowd of onlookers had gathered to cheer for their favourites with cries of 'Get her Helen! Come on Olive!' and 'Well done Kathleen! '

'It was an awful pity you had to come in just then. It was getting really exciting,' one of the boys complained to me later. As for the participants, they seemed to bear each other no malice after the event, and expressed themselves penitent but puzzled by my disapprobation at what, to them, seemed a routine way of settling a tiff. 'We allus fight. Both me Grannies were great fighters' Helen told me proudly. 'Did your Nans never fight each other?'

I had a sudden irresistible vision of my two grandmothers, bejewelled, be-hatted and be-furred slugging it out in one of their drawing rooms. It gave a whole new meaning to the idea of pearl chokers. Later, other difficulties, including alcohol and boyfriend troubles occasionally cropped up with Helen, Olive and Kathleen and not all members of the teaching and matron staff enjoyed the trio as much as I did. As they all three lived in, my role often seemed more that of nightclub bouncer then respectable headmaster's wife.

These were some of the characters in the domestic army of which I now found myself supposedly in charge and I sometimes felt I had fallen into the pages of a novel by Dickens. There was one brilliant exception for me in the form of Val, wife of the somewhat unreliable school handyman Bill, for whose shortcomings she usually managed to cover up. Val had originally come to work for Nancy Fox as a house parlourmaid on the school side but when we took over from the Foxes she switched to working personally for Charlie and me. Val was exceptional and I owe her more than I can say. She must have been in her early thirties, about ten years older than me, and she became my great support. She was fiercely loyal to what she perceived were my interests and helped me to come to terms with my new life and even become reasonably competent at running a large establishment. Val had a zany sense of humour, a sardonic view of the other members of our varied household—whether on the teaching or domestic staff—and great personal stoicism. She laughed with me, stiffened my spine and in the years ahead was to help us through some years of difficulty and sadness, about which I have written in *The Bird of My Loving*, the book on grief I was commissioned to write for Penguin Books. Tragically Val died unexpectedly of skin cancer, leaving a distraught husband and two young daughters. We were in the process of building a house for her and Bill in the school grounds when she died—the home of her own she had always longed for but was never able to live in. Oh that Dame Cecily Saunders had started the Hospice movement before Val died, but that was not to be till 1967. We kept her at home as long as we could but eventually she had to go into hospital. The day before she died I sat beside her bed holding her hand in a huge, hectic and impersonal ward in Hammersmith Hospital. 'No one will ever know how bad I feel. No one,' were her last whispered words to me. I shall never forget her.

One of the tasks I had agreed to take on was the correspondence with parents about the health and welfare of the boys. There was no school secretary, Matron Wilson had no wish to do it herself and it seemed a good way for me to get to learn about both the boys and the parents. Even I thought this job was within my capabilities—though as it turned out I didn't make a very auspicious start.

From the beginning I loved and enjoyed the boys. I had got to know a few of the senior boys during the winter term when Charlie and I were engaged and I'd come over to teach them to dance reels, which was huge fun. Now I had new boys aged eight to cope with and have never changed my original opinion that, except for reasons of special home difficulties, eight year-olds are not old enough to be sent to boarding school. This is not to say that some children are not perfectly happy at school, nor that there are no benefits at all to the system—but in my view eight is simply too young.

One of the new boys my first term was Miles Templer, son of the distinguished soldier General Sir Gerald Templer, later to become a Field Marshal and CIGS, but then serving in Malaya as British High Commissioner, appointed by Churchill to deal with the Emergency there. He became known as the 'Tiger of Malaya' and was famous for remarking that 'The answer lies not in pouring more troops into the jungle, but in capturing the hearts and minds of the people', words which seem as relevant today as when he first said them. Gerald's wife Peggy was out in Malaya with him, so Miles was indeed a case of a child for whom early boarding school was helpful and it was six months before I met either of his parents. Presumably they had met and approved the Foxes but it must have been an awful anxiety for Peggy Templer to entrust her treasured only son to such an unknown quantity as me. Acting *in loco parentis* for Miles were David Lloyd Owen, later to become a general himself, and his wife Ursie who had three small boys themselves and both became good friends of ours.

My first health letter to Peggy Templer must have caused her to wonder if a complete imbecile now had charge of her little boy. *Dear Lady Templer*, I wrote, *I thought you would like to know that the School Doctor reports that Miles has vulgar ankles and Matron tells me he is also suffering from Faroukas.*

'WHAT DO YOU MEAN?' she telegraphed back.

I had hesitated about the scribbled word on the medical report: vulgar did not seem a tactful adjective to apply to anyone's child, even if only to his ankles—somehow conjuring up the expression 'hairy-heeled'. However I blithely presumed that the doctor (whose handwriting I rightly never trusted again) must know best, so I went along with what I thought he'd put. What he'd actually written was Valgus Ankles, the medical term for flat feet. Nor had I yet become familiar with the foot complaints to which schoolboys are so prone, though after my years at Sunningdale I imagine the word verruca may well be imprinted on my person like Calais on Queen Mary Tudor's heart. This was the era of the notorious King Farouk, grossly obese ruler of Egypt whose name was constantly in the papers—and spelling has never been my strong point. After that I was careful to check up on medical conditions before informing parents and had a dictionary to hand before I wrote to anxious mothers.

When I finally met Peggy Templer for the first time, she swept into the drawing room looking alarmingly formal in a cartwheel hat. After about ten minutes she suddenly said 'Oh good—now I can take my hat off', unpinned the hat, hurled it to the other end of the sofa, kicked off her shoes and put her feet up. I took this unexpected behaviour to mean that I had managed to pass some esoteric test known only to her and felt deeply relieved. I also thought it was very forgiving of her considering my ludicrous letter—something I was never allowed to live down—and I became very fond of her. You never knew what to expect. She once parked her car backed up to the grassy bank that fell sharply away from the sweep of gravel in front of the house and took the brake off while absorbed in chatting to a friend out of the window. She was blissfully unaware of the shouts and wild gesticulations of horrified spectators as she and the car disappeared slowly backwards from view. Why the car didn't turn over I don't know but luckily it finally came to rest against a rhododendron bush and Peggy stepped out unruffled and still chatting. A breakdown team had to be summoned to winch the car uphill again. For the duration of Miles' years at Sunningdale Peggy always addressed Charlie as Henry.

I also have a memory of Gerald Templer giving a hilarious imitation round my drawing room of the dancing display he'd had to sit through at his daughter Jane's school. He may have missed his vocation.

Three weeks into my first term we had a terrible tragedy to cope with. One of the other new boys was Clement Franckenstein, the eight year-old only child of elderly parents. His retired diplomat father, Sir George Franckenstein had been the strongly anti-Nazi Austrian Ambassador to England from 1920-1938 who had been forced to remain in England during the war, was knighted by King George VI and had married an English wife late in life. I had only met them once, on the day they brought Clement to school for his first term, though I had spoken to his mother several times on the telephone and was expecting them to come and take Clement out on the first exeat. This was not to be: they were in a plane crash and were both killed instantly. On top of this disaster, it was soon discovered that neither of them had made a will or appointed any guardian for their son. Distant and unsuitable elderly relatives, half of them Protestant and half Roman Catholic, started to materialize, all demanding custody of this little boy whom none of them knew. Shockingly, their motives seemed to be either a supposed financial advantage or religious sectarianism but had little to do with the child's welfare, and they proceeded to fight each other over him in the most unedifying way. Eventually, in order to protect him, he had to be made a ward of court. I can still visualise this bewildered small boy, who had suddenly lost his whole world, sitting between Charlie and me on our drawing room sofa being interviewed by two Chancery lawyers. Eventually, after one traumatic false start, there was an unexpectedly good outcome to this dilemma. A couple, not actually related, but who'd had connections with Clement's parents in the past, heard something about the problems and offered to welcome him into their family as a thanksgiving gesture for the blessing of their own children who were around his age. Of course, after such a trauma, there were occasional difficulties, but on the whole this arrangement was a real success and they provided Clement with the normal, loving background he so badly needed and my admiration for them was unbounded. Clement eventually became a successful film actor in the U.S.

This episode impressed on me the importance of appointing legal guardians for one's children, something that had never occurred to me before.

The school concert always took place at the end of November in a wooden building known as The Army Hut, which normally comprised two classrooms but could be opened up to form one big room and had a stage at one end. The first half of the performance was mainly musical, with a good deal of singing and the occasional excruciating violin solo and the second half concentrated on drama and the spoken word. The aim of the concert was to get as many boys as possible to take part and perform *something*, no matter how insignificant. I loved helping with rehearsals and organizing the dressing-up and that year Charlie and I produced a series of tableaux with boys reciting from Eleanor Farjeon's delightful book of poems on Kings and Queens. I was somewhat taken aback when one little boy, whom I was kitting out in one of my evening dresses to be a wife of Henry VIII said speculatively 'I suppose these are the clothes you wore when you were still quite young?'

I also remember Matron Wilson, all starched and bustling, crackling in to check on what I was up to, as I experimented with cross gartering the football-stockinged legs of a would-be Alfred the Great with scarlet bias binding tape.

'What on earth are you doing to Hill-Walker's leg?' she asked suspiciously.

'Oh, just concocting a red warning sign to stop anyone bumping into him since he broke it playing football this afternoon,' I said.

'Why wasn't I told about this at once?' she demanded furiously and was then, not surprisingly, very put out at my teasing and her own gullibility—Alfred the Great could hardly have been bouncing around rehearsing for the concert if he'd just broken his leg. I was rather ashamed of my facetiousness—but felt I'd evened the score a little between myself and Mrs Wilson all the same.

I decorated the school with huge arrangements of flowers for the concert—a self-appointed task I really enjoyed. At my first school concert, though very apprehensive beforehand, I discovered to my surprise that I also enjoyed playing the role of hostess—another experience that was new to me.

It's possible that I could lay claim to being the first person to have produced the actor Ian Ogilvy in a play—I remember him looking very fetching in a red wig as the princess in a mime play called *The Tall, Tall Castle*. He was a natural and years later when he became famous as *The Saint*, I was not at all surprised.

Despite times of enjoyment, I had a strong sense of relief when my first term at Sunningdale came to an end. I still felt an angular peg in a rigidly round hole, as though I had spent twelve long weeks trying to play a part for which I was totally miscast and which was well beyond my acting capabilities. I have no doubt that I must have seemed ill-equipped for the job despite the kindness and encouragement I received from most of the parents.

My own parents delayed going to Cefn and stayed at Eton that Christmas so that we were able to be with them and in the New Year Charlie and I went off skiing to Lenzerheide. We had a blissful fortnight enjoying the occupation that, together with music, was to give us both so much shared pleasure over the years, but when we returned to Sunningdale I felt so alarmingly miserable that I could hardly get through the first two days of term. I was ashamed of my overwhelming feeling of malaise and tried to snap out of it. It seemed unwelcome proof of my unsuitability to school life but it never occurred to me that I might be sickening for something, so it was almost a relief when I suddenly became seriously ill. The specialist, whom the school doctor immediately called in, took one look at my by now bright yellow face and said he hadn't seen anything like it since Burma in the war. I had caught infective hepatitis. At the height of my sickness I was visited again by my old childhood affliction of feeling I was about to burst out of my body. I had forgotten what a terrifying sensation it was.

We discovered that there was an epidemic in the Grisons area of Switzerland and hotels were being commandeered as hospitals by the Swiss army which had been badly hit by the virus. Out of our large skiing party only two people escaped. Naturally there was huge concern lest the boys become infected. I was isolated in our attic bedroom, disinfectant-soaked sheets were hung over the door, the wonderful Val volunteered to nurse me and no one else was allowed anywhere near me. A few days later however I was joined in my segregation by Charlie. He wasn't as violently affected as I was but he felt dreadfully ill all the same and it took us both a long time to recover. It was strange to be trapped, incommunicado, in the heart of such a busy environment. For weeks we lay side by side in solitary confinement, like a pair of wilting daffodils and saw no one except Val—who uncomplainingly carried trays up two steep flights of stairs,—and the school doctor, Charles Duncan, a wonderful physician and a highly entertaining eccentric who gave us his own slanted view of what was going on in the school, made us laugh and was to become a much loved friend. After days of this proximity to each other, with neither of us feeling well enough even to read, Charlie had the bright idea of hiring a television. As we convalesced. we got hooked on *Emergency Ward 10*, the first of television's medical soap operas to obsess the nation, and various quiz shows such as *What's my Line* and *Animal, Vegetable or Mineral;* Charlie also became glued to all the sporting programmes. Television is such an accepted part of everyday life nowadays that it is hard to convey its novelty to us in the early nineteen fifties and it was a great aid to convalescence. We were surprised to find that a nine month ban on drinking alcohol was no hardship to either of us. Luckily no one else succumbed to the infection.

From my point of view one good thing came out of this period of marital overexposure and the literally jaundiced view we had been forced to take of each other. Next door to our bedroom was a small attic which had long been used as a box room and was filled with ancient trunks, battered suitcases and boxes of discarded clobber dating back for goodness knows how many years, though not, alas, secreting any valuable old masterpieces. The walls sloped so sharply under the eaves that it was only possible to stand upright in the middle of the room, but it had a serviceable fireplace, a window that could be made to open and a view over the garden. We decided to turn it into a room in which, unlike the very public drawing room two floors down, we could enjoy some privacy. Val's husband Bill disposed of the rubbish, put up some bookshelves and gave it a coat of paint. I ordered inexpensive curtains and carpet and within a matter of days it was useable. I was thrilled. This small sitting room was to make all the difference to my acceptance of the school as our home. It probably saved our marriage.

At the end of March my mother-in-law died. She had been getting progressively sadder and more disorientated and we were very bothered as to what the next move should be. Living at Walter's Cottage was no longer an option for her unless she had a resident carer, something to which she did not take kindly and during the autumn term there had been one or two dramas with carers walking out because she was so tricky. We had tried having her to stay with us in the school but that had proved extremely difficult. We would find her wandering round the passages completely lost and she found my presence in her son's life very disturbing. *'When* is this girl going to *go?'* she demanded plaintively to Charlie. 'I found her *in your bedroom.'* His patient explanation that I was his wife, meant nothing to her. I knew from other people that she'd been a great charmer in her day, both beautiful and beloved and that she had once longed for Charlie to marry—but by the time I came along it was hard for either of us to see the best in the other. We had managed to get her into an excellent local nursing home while we went skiing, and the Matron had kindly agreed to keep her for a bit longer after we went down with jaundice, but we would have had to make a new arrangement soon. Charlie, who had been deluding himself that a cure could be found for her condition and that she might recover her memory and her personality, was very sad at her loss. I felt extremely sorry for him but I couldn't help being relieved for both my mother-in-law and myself. Olive had in many ways had a tragic life—widowed with three little children when my sister-in-law was only a fortnight old, she had also lost her adored eldest son, Dick, a brilliant Reuters Correspondent, when the car in which he was travelling was blown up in the Spanish Civil War. It was thought at the time to have been hit by a stray shell, though it transpired years later that he may well have been murdered by the spy, Kim Philby, whom he had just accused of passing secrets to the Russians. We shall never know for certain.

After our turbulent first year of marriage, during which we'd both made some major adjustments, we celebrated our first wedding anniversary by taking the car to Holland with my parents to look at pictures and bulb fields and to retrace Charlie's war, driving across northern France, to Brussels and on to Amsterdam. We had a wonderfully happy week. I have a treasured memory of my mother, never one to doubt her opinions, sitting in the front seat of Charlie's car, endeavouring to map read him round Amsterdam but refusing to admit that what she took to be roads were actually canals.

When we returned to Sunningdale for the summer term we both felt restored to health and I felt more grown-up, perhaps a little wiser, and determined to cope better with my new life.

13

PERSONALITIES

SUNNINGDALE was run as a company and after Charlie bought out the Foxes he owned about two thirds of the shares, while his partners owned the remaining third between them. They were three very different characters.

J. B. Burrows was the most senior, the most difficult and the least likeable of them. A tall, military-looking bachelor, he had a fierce little clipped moustache above a thin inflexible little mouth and had already been a partner and minor shareholder at the school for years by the time I came along. The boys called him Budgie but he was always known to the staff as 'J.B'. though never addressed as such to his face and in all the years that I knew him I never heard anyone call him by his Christian name. Those colleagues he considered to be his equals—male naturally—were permitted to call him Burrows and the rest of us addressed him as Mr Burrows. When, after a decent interval—a couple of years, at least—I tentatively suggested that I might call him Jack his response was to shrug and say: 'I can't stop you.' He was wrong in this as he effectively stopped me calling him anything! He prided himself on being a disciplinarian and his teaching methods produced excellent examination results, but they were based on fear—not a good way of achieving success. My husband's relaxed approach to schoolmastering drove him mad and I suspect he deeply envied the ease with which Charlie could keep order without having to exploit anxiety, and also resented the fun and laughter he shared with the boys. Another cause for resentment was that Charlie was lucky enough to have some private means and Mr Burrows would like to have been able to afford a greater share in the school. I fear poor Jack Burrows was an embittered and lonely man but it was difficult to feel real affection for him. I tried hard, but failed. The next partner, Michael Tupholme, was different in every way. He had no private means either but oozed the milk of human kindness. He was capable of being obstinate about small matters but could usually be talked round to almost any viewpoint if you knew how to go about it—and most of us did: it was just a question of who had seen him last. Unlike dapper Mr Burrows, Mike always looked as if he had picked up his clothes at a jumble sale and was about to report for duty in a newly planted field of cabbages. He came from a clerical family, one of six brothers and sisters none of whom ever married, and on the rather flimsy grounds that his father had been a vicar, he was in charge of chapel services. I loved to watch him hurrying across the lawn every morning at five to nine, struggling to get his arms and head through the right holes of his crumpled old surplice as he scurried along in the ancient sneakers he habitually wore. He never wore a cassock so why he bothered with the surplice I never knew, but perhaps this partial attempt to don priestly garb gave him the idea that if he made some concession to dressing the part, God might pay more attention. The boys laughed at him but loved him—and so did I. He had an endearing habit of chatting to himself and as I sat at my desk in the drawing room every morning, writing letters to the boys' mothers, I would hear him muttering away in the hall as he sorted the post. He and Charlie had partnered each other in county tennis tournaments before the war and become good friends. Phil Squarey, the other partner was a friend too—a breezy extrovert with a fine command of the English language and splendidly unconventional views on a variety of unlikely subjects. He always wore a rose in his buttonhole and never did his shoe laces up. Because he lived in his own delightful house at Winkfield Row, where he gardened brilliantly and had a private life away from the school, he brought a welcome whiff of outside air to the sometimes claustrophobic atmosphere of a community in which most of the staff lived—so much behaviour in residential institutions seems to be caused by perceptions of territory. His wife Veronica was a tiny, forthright lady, usually weighed down with enormously chunky pieces of costume jewellery and never afraid of treading on anyone's toes. Years later, after we had retired up to Yorkshire, my family were highly amused to read Phil's unusual choice of words for the announcement of his wife's death in *The Times*: 'Veronica, ' it read, 'sturdy wife of Philip Squarey...' It started my children on a craze for thinking of suitable adjectives for me, should I suffer an unexpectedly early demise. I rather hope they have forgotten about this parlour game now!

When I first married, a notable member of the staff was ancient Mr Ling, to whose remarkable teaching of Classics many old Sunningdalians owed the scholarships they won. He was much missed when he retired. There was also a transitory assortment of youthful assistant masters, and young under matrons with whom I felt much more at home than with the old stagers. An important early appointment made by Charlie—anything but transitory as it turned out—was of Nick Dawson as a junior master, to be joined a few years later by his identical twin, Tim. Their father Andy, a Yorkshire and cricketing friend of the Sheepshanks family, had asked Charlie's advice when the twins expressed a desire to become schoolmasters. Charlie jumped at the chance of taking one of them on at Sunningdale but advised that having so far always done everything together, including prep school and Eton followed by National Service with the Rifle Brigade, it was important that they should separate for a while, so Tim served his schoolmastering apprenticeship at Cothill, while Nick came to us. In due course after Tim joined us too, they became partners in the school and eventually took on from us as joint headmasters. It was to become a wonderfully family affair as Tim and Prue Dawson's son Tom is now the headmaster.

For my first few terms my childhood friend Margaret Horton-Fawkes, fresh from music college and hoping to become a professional singer, was the resident music mistress. We hadn't seen much of each other since her father inherited Farnley Hall in Wharfedale before the war and the family left Eton for Yorkshire, though we were to become neighbours again later in our lives. It was a great bonus for me to have a friend of my own age on the staff and I missed her when she left to get married. Because I found Charlie's tank-like old Packard so difficult to drive he bought me a small Austin car—one size up from the famous Baby Austin model. It had belonged for many years to the headmistress of Windsor County Girls' School but on retirement she had dashingly decided to buy herself a new one. We called the car Miss Curtis after its previous owner because it looked so staid and dependable like her, and it gave me much welcome independence. The only snag was the problem of getting any use out of it for myself. None of the young members of staff had cars of their own, so there was always a queue of would-be drivers longing to borrow it and I found it hard to refuse them. Eventually Miss Curtis literally fell to pieces after too much heavy-footed use of the accelerator by too many over-enthusiastic users, myself included—but she was my first car and I have fond memories of her.

At the end of our first year, Matron Wilson decided to retire to live near her married daughter and grandchildren and she and I parted company with mutual relief. After much discussion with Dr Duncan and consultations with a cross section of the parents, Charlie and I decided to appoint the senior assistant matron, Pauline Doyle, in her place. This was a difficult decision because though Pauline had done three years' nursing training at the renowned Radcliffe Infirmary in Oxford, she'd had to give up her career to look after her sick father at the crucial moment when she was due to qualify, so she could never put the important letters SRN after her name. It hadn't taken me long to discover that though the highly qualified Mrs Wilson was the figurehead, it was actually Pauline who ran the matrons' department and Charles Duncan had the highest opinion of her medical capabilities. We wondered if we were laying ourselves open to criticism by appointing someone who wasn't State Registered but decided to take the risk. She was to continue in the position for over forty years.

Pauline was a complex character and there were areas of her life that were shrouded in mystery—her age, a closely guarded secret, being one of them. When I arrived at Sunningdale aged twenty-one, Pauline was said to be thirty; but when fourteen years later Charlie and I retired to Yorkshire she had miraculously become exactly the same age as me. To match this achievement she remained for years extraordinarily unchanged in appearance (except that her clothes grew smarter and her once very dark hair turned prematurely orange, like President Reagan's), and she appeared more youthful in her long extended middle age than she had when I first met her. She was reticent about her background and, apart from a cousin who provided her with a base during the holidays and whose daughter was a much loved godchild, claimed to have no living relations—which when she died, was discovered to be far from true. It transpired that she not only had brothers living but a sister unexpectedly turned up to her memorial service, having seen the announcement in the paper, and looking so spookily like her that for a moment as I walked into the chapel at Sunningdale I thought I'd seen a ghost. I couldn't help thinking it would have been typical of Pauline to manage to materialize at her own service just to make sure it was properly organized. Apparently the two sisters had for years been at a boarding school together in Llandudno, but though Pauline was well aware of my connection with that part of the world and knew how often I took the children to North Wales to visit my parents, I never heard her admit to any knowledge of the area. Another mystery. What the teaching was like at this school I can't imagine because though Pauline was highly intelligent and a great reader, communications from her were bordering on the illiterate and any idea of using punctuation or capital letters seemed to have been entirely omitted from her education. Her letters were always written in 'lower case' like an email address or a poem by the American poet ee cummings.

Pauline's devotion to the school and the boys was absolute; her willingness for self-sacrifice could be astonishing; her competence and organizational abilities were unquestionable—but her tendency to jealousy and her dangerous tongue could have troubling consequences. She was passionately interested in all the boys' doings, their successes or disappointments, and had an invaluable ability to spot trouble brewing if anything were amiss with any of them. She stood at the bottom of the stairs, unobtrusively watching the boys as they went in and out of all meals and maintained that she learnt more from this observation than from anything that was ever reported to her. If any of the boys were really ill she would nurse them with unstinting dedication, sitting up by their bedside all night if need be, but she showed scant patience to malingerers and a few boys were frightened of her.

Pauline had a good sense of humour and could be great fun, but she was indeed a force to be reckoned with. She adored my husband and later my children and became genuinely fond of me too, but this affection brought with it the drawback that she also became jealous of my relationship with other members of staff, though never, to her credit, over my relationships with the boys. If she had chosen to withhold her information or concerns about the boys from me, she could have made my position very difficult but, surprisingly, she was always good about this. We worked closely together for many years, she often sought my opinion and I learnt a great deal from her about the health and welfare of small boys. I also learnt, though it took me a little time, how to stand up to her, how to keep my own counsel and the absolute necessity of facing up to the occasional difficult confrontation with her—something I hate.

Twenty-five years later, I drew on the experience of my Sunningdale years for my second novel *Facing the Music* which I set in a boys' prep school. The story is entirely fictitious, none of the characters are portraits and nor are the make-believe headmaster and his young musician wife at all like Charlie and me, but as the advice given to aspiring novelists is to write about what you know, I tried to paint a picture of a world with which I was very familiar. I was thrilled to get letters from readers who had taught or worked in all sorts of different schools saying they recognized the atmosphere and even felt they knew some of the staff in my imaginary establishment!

A school year, divided so neatly into three terms, each with their own particular flavour, has a structured rhythm to it and our lives soon fell into a regular pattern. The summer term brought cricket matches with neighbouring schools every Wednesday and Saturday afternoon: deck chairs and seats were put out for watching adults to sit on, benches and rugs for the boys to loll about on and tea was laid out for visiting spectators in the Pavilion. Nancy Fox had prided herself on her cricket teas and this was one of her traditions I tried to continue. Parents who lived close enough often came to watch and there was always a fathers' match at some stage in the term, an informal occasion but not without its anxieties for the participants as fathers and sons desperately wanted to do each other credit. The last Saturday in June was sacred to Sports Day and in the fourteen years I was there, though we had some anxious moments, we only had one day when the events had to be called off for rain and tea taken indoors. Traditionally there had always been parents' races though after a few years Charlie and I put a stop to these as being too hazardous—competitive but sometimes overweight fathers suddenly bursting their lungs and ligaments to do their child credit is not a wise idea and I've never forgotten the mothers' race on my first Sports Day as Headmaster's Wife. One set of parents comprised the gravely imposing Cecil Boyd-Rochfort, racing trainer to the Queen, and his fey, glamorous but not always sober wife Rohays. Cecil had just been in much publicised trouble with the Jockey Club for supposedly having a horse pulled at Ascot when Rohays decided to run in the mothers' race at Sunningdale. She had lunched well but unwisely and was in garrulous good form but as the starting pistol went off and she immediately measured her length on the track a loud voice from amongst the spectators boomed over the microphone 'Poor old Cecil—up before the Stewards *again!*' It brought the house down, but Rohays had to be escorted off to go and sleep it off in the sick room for the rest of the afternoon. Their son, an engaging, bullet-headed little boy who looked like the baby in the Giles cartoons, was called Arthur, a name of which at that stage he was deeply ashamed. When he was taken out one Sunday by the parents of a friend, they enquired cosily what his Christian name was, 'Because we can't possibly keep calling you Boyd-Rochfort all day can we?'

'But you can call me *Mr* Boyd-Rochfort if you like,' said Arthur graciously.

For years I treasured a wonderfully succinct literary effort by Arthur Boyd-Rochfort on the subject of Moses. It was titled 'MOUSE AND THE BUGEING BUS: *Once upon a time there was a man called Mouse who met a bus and it started bugeing.*' Another little boy answered the exam question: *What do you know about Moses?* with the intriguing answer *I know a great deal about Moses.* Of course we collected our share of genuine schoolboy howlers over the years, of which my favourite concerned Jericho. *Jericho was circumcised six times and the seventh time the walls fell down.* Ouch! Aladdin bringing Christianity to Britain was also a nice thought.

One year we had the idea of seating a row of boys at one end of the field with pillowcases on their heads and volunteer mothers had to identify the right child who was not allowed to speak and lead him, hooded, to the finish. Since most mothers are convinced that they could pick out their own offspring from any crowd by his big toe alone, there was a confident supply of entrants. Their confidence was misplaced. Frantic cries of 'Jeremy, Jeremy—*speak* to me! It's Mummy, darling,' echoed round the field and doting mothers were not pleased to find they had dragged someone else's little treasure to the winning post only to be disqualified.

There was also swimming in the summer term. With the help of an Appeal, we managed to replace the disgusting indoor swimming pool in a gloomy tin shack in the back yard in which all boys were supposed to learn to swim—though not all did—with a much more salubrious outdoor one. I never braved the old pool myself which may have been an innovative amenity in its Edwardian heyday but was well past its shelf life and distinctly uninviting by the time I got married. Fierce arguments took place about what temperature the pool should be kept at and, more crucially, how often the water should be changed, with Mr Burrows, who was in charge of this sport, though he certainly never entered the water himself, grumpily maintaining it was perfectly all right while Pauline and I furiously compared it to iced pea soup. Health & Safety would have had a field day at Sunningdale.

No one could have called the school buildings either charming or cosy but the grounds and gardens were lovely and the honeyed smell of azaleas immediately takes me back to summer days at Sunningdale. I used to pick great armfuls of the yellow, flame and apricot ones which rampaged like a forest fire in the surrounding woods and scented the whole house in May—preferable to the distinctive background aroma of blackboard chalk, old socks, floor polish and the faint whiff of cooked cabbage, which tends to hang about the passages of boys' schools.

'Would you like to sniff the tassel of my dressing gown cord?' an eight year-old boy once asked me. Realizing this was intended as an honour, I said I would and he held it out to me like a nosegay. He explained that when he'd first arrived, he had noticed the distinctive smell of school but now that he was used to it he couldn't smell it any more. 'But,' he informed me solemnly 'Now it's all gone into my dressing gown cord so I can always take a sniff if I want to be reminded.' As I cautiously inhaled I understood what he meant— relieved it hadn't had the same effect on my own dressing gown.

The autumn term brought muddy knees, football matches, fireworks and the school concert. The boys did well on November 5th because Charlie was a sucker for fireworks and adored letting them off. He was usually aided by an assistant master and the school carpenter would have spent the afternoon setting everything up on the football field. One memorable year the rather gormless young man who had volunteered to help accidentally dropped a lighted taper into a cardboard box full of fireworks with sensational results. Luckily no one was hurt but the display of pyrotechnics was too thrilling for comfort and a rocket passed clean through the chapel, leaving a tiny hole in each of the stained-glass windows on either side of the altar. When visiting a grandson at Sunningdale a few years ago he and I checked to see if the holes were still there. They are.

My writing ambitions went into cold storage at this stage in my life, but almost since I was first able to string words together I've possessed the knack of being able to produce doggerel and the school concert provided a great excuse to write new words to old music. For a few years Ian Harland, then a junior master—later to become a much loved Bishop of Carlisle—and I collaborated happily in producing topical songs and sketches for the concerts which amused the two of us enormously—if no one else—but any aptitude I'd had to write more serious poetry seemed to have vanished and was not to surface again till after we left Sunningdale. Creative processes are very odd and you don't know what may be yeasting away inside during these fallow periods. I may have hoped that what my father used to call my 'Muse' would return one day, but I certainly made no efforts to foster this, which now seems to me to have been pretty feeble. I have learnt that muses are unreliable friends who need to be goaded into activity: waiting patiently for them to drop in is not good policy.

The autumn term always ended with the Carol Service. There is nothing like the soaring treble of a boy's solo voice singing 'Once in Royal David's City' to tug the heartstrings and put one in the right frame of mind for Christmas. We may not have been quite on a par with King's College, Cambridge, at Sunningdale—but we weren't bad either.

The spring term was most people's least favourite, but was also the shortest. It tended to be the term when epidemics might occur, though this was by no means always the case. Sunningdale had one big advantage concerning health. When Canon Girdlestone built the main block of the school in 1874 he instigated an unusual feature in the design of the sleeping quarters. There were two dormitories for the youngest boys but all the others were housed in individual cubicles, each with their own door, the wooden partitions stopping about a foot short of the ceiling like racing stables or public lavatories. Though they were a nightmare from a cleaning point of view there is no doubt that they were a huge advantage in helping to prevent the spread of infection. The boys' favourite dare—strictly forbidden of course—was to snake their way along the top of the partitions on one side of the cubicles, crawl across at the end, return down the other side and get back to their own bed undetected. Most of the boys loved the cubicles and relished the privacy their small individual space gave them, though they would not have been so good for the eight and nine year-olds who might have found them isolating. With that age group you need to be able to see at a glance what everyone is up to and if everyone is all right. There was certainly no privacy about the boys' bathroom—this was before showers became customary—which contained ten claw-footed baths round the edge of one big room, so bathing was a noisy and convivial affair. 'Oh good, beans for supper - bubbles in the bath tonight!' a boy once remarked to me. As far as I was concerned the boys' bathroom had an alternative use: it was a brilliant place for washing small dogs. You filled up several baths with tepid water, shampooed the dog in the first one, rinsed it by dunking in the next ones, turned on the overhead ceiling fan and allowed the hairy hearthrugs that shih-tzus resemble to roar round until they were dry. I always had an eager band of volunteer helpers to assist me in this wild and watery performance. We disinfected the baths afterwards.

Weekends were a busy time for Charlie and me as we usually had prospective parents to take round the school. Once I had gained a little confidence in my new role, I enjoyed doing this. We were in the happy position that if we really didn't like someone—rare—we didn't need to accept them and I learnt the curious quirk of human nature, that if you actively try to put people off something, it nearly always makes them keener to have it. Occasionally tours round the school didn't go quite as expected. Taking a distinctly prim couple on a tour round the grounds one day Charlie opened his mouth to reply to the question— not one we were usually asked—'Do you have any problems with bad language?' when a voice from under a rhododendron bush where two boys were playing scorebook cricket said : 'Oh for God's sake keep your f...ing feet still'. It didn't usually fall to my lot to expound on education so Charlie must have been unexpectedly absent, but I was disconcerted once on entering the Sixth Form classroom, burbling happily on about the school's record of classical scholarships. On the blackboard was written: *Royal Flush, Straight Flush, Four of a kind, Full House, Flush, Straight, Three of a kind, Two pairs, Pair.*

'Very impressive,' said the visiting father dryly.

On Sunday mornings there was chapel. Sometimes we had a visiting preacher, sometimes Charlie spoke himself or read something, often using one of Cyril Alington's *Eton Fables* which the boys loved. Occasionally Charlie stood in for the music mistress and played the organ. He liked the hymns to zip along smartly and always played at a rollicking tempo when he was at the pedals, but became infuriated by one particular music mistress's constantly dirge-like pace, despite repeated requests for her to speed things up a bit. One Sunday, as she dragged out the notes of *God is working his purpose out,* Charlie couldn't resist bellowing out its chorus line *WHAT can we do to hasten the time* in his extremely carrying baritone. The choir were convulsed with laughter but there were angry tears and much flouncing from the young woman in question after the service and I was called in to smooth her down. I was cross with Charlie at the time—but she never played quite so slowly again.

Music was important and a place in the choir was coveted by the boys and taken very seriously. The chapel itself—an unpretentious white-painted 'tin tabernacle' from the outside, but charming in its wood-panelled simplicity inside—was separate from the house, something that I liked, making it more special than if it had been part of the main house with all its attendant noise and bustle. If it was an exeat Sunday, parents would arrive after the service to take their children out for the day and we would be available morning and evening to see them if they wanted to discuss anything, as would Pauline and whichever masters were on weekend duty. Before the war, during a particularly hard winter when the football fields had been out of action for weeks, Charlie had invented a game called Convoys—the rules of which I never fully mastered because they always seemed to be changing—which involved hunting or being hunted throughout the twenty-eight acres of grounds, with ambushes in rhododendron bushes and much happy tearing about. It could incorporate any number of participants and it became traditional to play this on Sundays. I believe it's still played. Most of the boys adored it, but there is always the problem, in any school, of the few children who really dislike group activities. As a bit of a non-conformer myself they had my sympathy but it is not easy to accommodate individualists at all times and there is no doubt that schooldays are easier for those who like team efforts and enjoy games.

On Sunday evenings I read to the youngest boys who came down to the drawing room after supper in their dressing gowns and sprawled about on sofas and floor. They were always full of chat and I loved this special time with them. Sharing a love of books with children is a particular pleasure and in those less sophisticated times it was perhaps more appreciated than it would be now, though it wasn't always easy

227

to find books of the right length that they would all like but none of them had read before. They loved C.S. Lewis's Narnia books and though most of them were already familiar with the first one, *The Lion The Witch and the Wardrobe*, there was great excitement when a new one in the series came out—as a recent generation of children have found with the publication of each successive new *Harry Potter* saga. Tolkien's *The Hobbit* was popular but *The Lord of the Rings* when it appeared was too long and involved for my purpose. There were certain top favourites from my own childhood to fall back on, such as *Hildebrand*, which never failed to make them roll about with laughter, or A. W. Dunn's *An Experiment with St George*, with its irresistible account of a dragon drive when an escaped witch called Howling Harriet unexpectedly flies over the line of butts, is fruitlessly fired at by St George with a bow and arrow—who doesn't realize that witches can only be killed by silver arrows—and turns the elephant-riding line of beaters to marble. A belief in magic is a strong instinct in children as I witnessed when a small boy burst into the drawing room one day in torrents of tears, waving a piece of paper at me and announcing that he thought he was going to die. 'I hate Cookson minor,' he informed me between sobs, 'and I thought if I crossed his name off the school list it might kill him…. but I made a bosh shot and crossed my own name off instead!' I managed to assure him that I thought he'd survive and hope I convinced him that attempted murder is not a good idea.

When I arrived at Sunningdale, a good many of the boys' parents were friends of Charlie's from his Eton or Army days which was great fun for us, but the majority of the parents anyway were extremely appreciative and nice to deal with and some of them became new, lifelong friends of ours; there were always a few ultra fussy mothers but I greatly preferred the over-anxious approach to the unconcerned—which was mercifully rare, but disturbing when it happened. One mother I remember painfully for her consistent failure to turn up. Pauline and I used to take it in turns to be the one to break it to her wretched child that his mother—yet again—was not going to keep her promise to take him out, watch him play in a match or attend the school sports or concert. His unrealistic hopes, followed by disappointment and distress were always agonizing to cope with. If she remembered to communicate with us at all, her excuses were endless and lame in the extreme and no compensatory treat we ever managed to concoct for her son ever made up for her absences.

There was one mother whose approach to the school was unlike that of any other parent with whom I ever had dealings. Lady P.B., a well-known socialite and political hostess could certainly not have been labelled a neglectful parent; it couldn't be said that she ignored her son's welfare, failed to take him out on appropriate Sundays or attend school functions, but during the two and a half years after we had taken over from the Foxes and I had arrived as an unknown, although she entrusted her boy to our care—I never actually met her. Charlie and I were always available on the exeat Sundays, not to mention concerts and sports days, but though she rang up to make particular requests—once because she wanted me to undertake the personal task of breaking it to her child that his grandfather had died—she never bothered to make my acquaintance. At the end of her son's last term, one of the mothers, Gracia Howard, decided to invite the other leaving parents to subscribe towards robing the chapel choir as a farewell present. The response was immediate and generous from all except Lady P.B. She wrote to Gracia to say that as they had paid the school fees regularly for four and a half years she could see no reason why they should be expected to contribute to dressing the choir. Gracia wrote back: *Dear Lady P.B., if you have friends to stay, do you expect them to tip your butler?* She received a £10 note by return. Before her son's last school concert, after which we always gave all the parents tea, I remember saying to Charlie that I couldn't help hoping that Lady P.B. wouldn't spoil her record by suddenly deciding to come and say a first hello or last goodbye to me. I needn't have worried.

This disinterest was in contrast to another celebrity parent we had at the same time—the widowed Princess Marina, Duchess of Kent, mother of Prince Michael of Kent. No one could have been easier, friendlier or less formal to deal with. Princess Marina had a delightful Polish friend Madame Poklewska who often came down to Sunningdale with her and acted as her unofficial Lady-in-Waiting.

Unlike the glamorous Princess Marina, Madame Poklewska was neither a beauty nor a fashion plate but she had great charm and was full of amazing stories about pre-war European high life. As a young bride she had contracted smallpox on her honeymoon and to save her from being compulsorily incarcerated in the grim Isolation Hospital her distraught husband had purchased the local lunatic asylum and had it turned into a private hospital just for her. I don't know what happened to the previous inmates, but she survived—though not unscarred—to tell the tale. Prince Michael was a delightful, unassuming boy with a very good sense of humour. Later he sent his own son to Sunningdale.

Inevitably it is sometimes the unenviable lot of headmasters and occasionally their wives to break tragic news to children of death, divorce or difficult and life-changing circumstances and it is always an awful thing to do. There may be wrong ways of doing this but there is no one right way, no blueprint to follow and children can be highly unpredictable in the way they react—or appear not to react at all—to devastating shock. We never had to do what our successor did, which was to tell a child that instead of having a mummy and a daddy he would now effectively have two mummies because his father had just had a change of sex. I can't help feeling that in such circumstances it should be up to the parents to break this news themselves.

Neither Charlie nor I had to break the news of his parents' impending divorce to Carey Harrison, son of Rex Harrison and Lilli Palmer, because they forgot to mention it and we read about it in the papers after it had taken place. Charlie and I made a very wrong assessment about Carey when he left Sunningdale. 'Now there's a boy we'll never see again,' we said to each other—rather sadly, because we liked clever Carey—basing this opinion on his cosmopolitan Hollywood and New York upbringing and jet set lifestyle. We could not have been more wrong. Carey not only made the effort to come over to Sunningdale for Sports Days and old boy events from Harrow—far more difficult than from the much closer Eton—but came to see us several times in Yorkshire after we retired and wrote me the star letter when Charlie died. Carey, a prolific, international award-winning novelist, playwright and journalist is Professor of English at

Brooklyn College, New York City University. He is still in touch and I hugely look forward to his entertaining Christmas letters. Such was his father, 'Sexy Rexy's', reputation as a ladykiller, that when we first met the Harrisons I fully expected to feel an electric shock run up my right arm when I shook hands with him—but was disappointed! My hand was not unaffected by shaking the hand of Lilli Palmer however because an echo of whatever powerful scent she was wearing must have rubbed off so that I too smelt delicious for the rest of the day and was loathe to wash it off—the opposite of Lady Macbeth's problem.

Two parents whose dignity under impossible conditions I admired were Jack and Valerie Profumo. Their eight year-old son David came to us at the height of the publicity over what has universally come to be called The Profumo Affair. They had not intended to send him to a boarding school at this age but with the explosion of press intrusion into their lives, urgently wanted to get him out of the limelight. Charlie was approached by a fellow MP of Jack Profumo's, the father of three boys in the school, and asked if we could fit David in at very short notice. Charlie was prepared to discuss it and the Profumos came to see us. I shall never forget their distress at how their son's future might be affected by what had happened. We didn't really have a place for him but Charlie agreed to make an exception and to fit David in at the beginning of the next term. We thought it might be easier for Jack and Valerie if they skipped the dreaded tea party for new boys and their parents—never a good occasion anyway—but they insisted they must do exactly what the other parents did. It was enormously courageous of them both but I remember the occasion as being agonizingly difficult for everyone concerned. Our anxiety was whether we could protect David, a very bright and perspicacious child, from the continually recurring headlines and from the tongues of other boys. Charlie made it clear to the whole school that if there was ever any teasing or unkindness on the subject he would take it extremely seriously and it would under no circumstances be tolerated. I think this was successful for a while, but there was an incident after about two years when the whole topic blew up again in the press and despite having managed to suppress the papers over a weekend, one boy who'd been home for a family reason deliberately smuggled the Sunday papers back into school, showed them to other boys and something was said to David who was distressed. Charlie was very angry and upset that this had happened. In his own beautifully written book, *Bringing the House Down*, David does not refer to this incident but recalls that he went to Eton woefully unprepared and mostly in ignorance about the sexual scandals surrounding his father's name, with painful results. We had retired to Yorkshire the year before he left Sunningdale so I don't have first-hand knowledge of what went wrong over this. Perhaps despite the best of intentions we all overdid the protection, but knowing children's involuntary ability to reject or blank out information for which they are not ready, it is possible that his parents did try to tell him some version of the truth which he did not fully take in. At any rate his cruel enlightenment out of the mouth of an oafish bully on arrival at Eton must have been shattering.

We were lucky to have in Charles Duncan a remarkable school doctor, an unconventional character who wasn't everybody's ideal GP but was certainly ours. He was not only a brilliant diagnostician himself but was also good at knowing when a specialist opinion might be required—and there were no lengths to which he wouldn't go for the patients he loved. We were lucky too that antibiotics had been discovered by the time we had charge of other people's precious children. I would not have liked that huge responsibility in an earlier medical era. The Foxes had endured a tragedy before the war when there was an outbreak of the dreaded mastoiditis caused by middle ear infection and a boy had died. In these days when antibiotics have sometimes been over-prescribed for lesser ailments, it is easy to forget what a miracle they were when they first became available— literally lifesaving. Charles, at six foot seven was a larger than life personality—an eccentric with a heart as big as his frame, an offbeat sense of humour and varied interests which included ballet, racing and breeding Pekingese. He roared around in an ancient green Jaguar sports car in which, when he lowered himself into it, he drove in a horizontal position and was usually accompanied by several unbelievably bad tempered small dogs of whom we were all justifiably terrified. To be asked to go and fetch his stethoscope or some other vital bit of medical paraphernalia from his car was to risk losing your fingers. I was puzzled in my early Sunningdale days by the number of medical check-ups which certain apparently healthy boys seemed to require and for which they had to be got out of school, until I cottoned on to the fact that all their fathers belonged to the racing fraternity— of whom there were a number—and, far from having their tonsils inspected by the doctor, they were being consulted by him about hot tips for Ascot or Goodwood. I would go upstairs with my notebook to enquire about the boys' health to be provided with such riveting bits of information as 'Tell Mrs Snooks her son's got an undescended testicle—and put your last pair of knickers on Goldilocks in the two-thirty.'

Jumping on Shadows

An afternoon
of raucous sun, unruly clouds:
I watch my children
playing tig with shadows,
steering bright boats of laughter
to race their stretched black sails
across cut grass;
they chase and try to capture
fleeting messages
with plimsolled feet.

If poems flicker memories
through your brain
jump on their shadows quick
. . . before the sun goes down.

14

FAMILY LIFE

O UR life settled into a routine pattern of terms and holidays.

To our great delight, on May 12th 1955, after we had been married for two years, our first child, a baby daughter was born. I was surprised to find how fascinated the boys were by Belinda. They were always hanging round the pram wanting to push it round the lawn and play with her. 'How many babies do you think you're going to have?' one of them had asked me, looking me over in a knowledgeably appraising way shortly before she was born. I said I thought only one. He was clearly disappointed in me. 'Our spaniel had ten,' he said.

We had nowhere to put a baby so we built on a small nursery wing overlooking the lawn at the side of the existing house. It was to give us the private quarters which made all the difference to me. The advent of Belinda, along with all the joy she brought us, also brought a remarkable woman into our lives. Marian Stewart, a nanny of the old-fashioned school, was, despite her Scottish sounding name, a Cornish woman who loomed into my life, all six foot two of her, with her hair scraped back in a bun under a squashy navy blue felt hat, a vast uniform grey coat, a deaf aid, a whiskery chin and the best blue eyes I've ever seen. Bar the whiskers and the deaf aid, she might have stepped from the frame of a portrait by Fran Hals or Rembrandt. When she came for an interview I had very little idea of how to conduct such an occasion but no hesitation whatever in offering her the job. Nan was a real countrywoman who knew about birds and wild flowers and could cook and knit and sew and do beautiful smocking. She was a fund of ancient weather lore but also something of a Mrs Malaprop who often got words slightly wrong. If you greeted her with a non-specific meteorological observation such as 'Lovely morning, Nan,' she was likely to straighten you up by saying, 'Ah but they've got bad floods in East Angela, Mummy,' or 'London Hairport has just been closed by fog.' Belinda, who had an ear for words and spoke almost as soon as she breathed, had a rubber duck called London Hairport. My classical scholar father became very excited when he discovered that she also had a pink teddy bear called Ambrosia but was disappointed when he discovered its name derived from a tin of creamed rice pudding. Along with these quirky attributes, Nan was also a saint: one of the loveliest women I have ever been privileged to meet. She taught me the meaning of an unselfish, unconditional, unpossessive love which I could bask in and admire but never hope to live up to. She had started in service as an under nursery maid aged fourteen (apparently they used to wash the nursery floors with milk in order to feed the linoleum) and risen through the nursery ranks to become Nanny to the Bolitho family in Cornwall—about whom we were to learn a great many intimate details in the following years. She had been betrothed to a local schoolmaster but after a three year engagement her possessive and dictatorial old father still refused to allow them to marry and after war broke out and he was called up, she never saw her one great love again. He was taken prisoner by the Japanese and like many other young British soldiers in their prime, died of sickness and starvation on the notorious Burma Road. 'If we'd only been married for a very short time, I might have had a little one of my very own,' she once said wistfully to me and I found it humbling that she could long for her own children and still give such unstinting devotion to mine.

The advent of a family gave me a life of my own as well as the school life into which I had gradually became integrated and I made good friends locally. In the April before Belinda was born, my father, now recovered from his mystery illness, retired from Eton to join my Uncle Jack in the family business—a brilliant schoolmaster, Pa was not a natural tycoon and never looked quite as at home in a bowler hat as he had in his mortarboard. He and my mother went to live at Cefn Isaf, the second Nickson house, just below Cefn, where my mother made a wonderfully happy and welcoming home which all future grandchildren loved to visit and where I think she was happier than she had been since our early days at Baldwin's End Cottage.

We never stayed at Sunningdale for more than a few days at each end of the holidays but went either to North Wales to my parents or to stay at Arthington with Charlie's family. I had already formed a close bond with his bachelor Uncle Charles, 'The Sheep', but I soon became devoted to his formidable Aunt Evelyn too. I had initially regarded her with some trepidation because she was notoriously acerbic and I knew that over the years my mother had found her a very alarming hostess at the shooting house parties she and my father attended at Arthington, with a disconcerting flair for wrong-footing her guests. She could be wonderfully good company however, was much travelled, with widely varied interests and a very good brain. She had been one of the early students at Lady Margaret Hall in the days when women were still barred from qualifying for a degree at the end of their studies. She played hockey for her college and was a wily tennis player with a demon underarm serve. It was a golden period in her life, but after university, until she was well into her fifties, she had then led a life of enforced leisure as the unmarried daughter at home, under the velvet-gloved thumb of her diminutive, straight-laced, iron-willed mother. Had she been born a generation later she would almost certainly have had a distinguished career of some sort and I think her bouts of unkindness were the result of deep frustrations. By the time I knew her, in her late seventies, she was very smart and well dressed but as a young woman she had cruelly been considered frumpy and plain and had probably frightened off any potential suitors with her often funny but usually withering character assessments of other people, relying on her considerable intellectual acuteness and verbal dexterity to gain attention, even if unfavourable, rather than making efforts to please which might have been rejected. Sadly an appalling number of young men, potential husband material for her generation of women, had been killed in the trenches of the First World War—at any rate she neither married nor had any particular occupation until she came to act as hostess and keep house for her much younger brother. She had been corrodingly jealous of Charlie's mother, Olive, the sister-in-law married to her favourite brother, who lived in a house across the park, very much in the shadow of 'The Big House', with her three young children, whose pretty looks and easy charm, despite all the tragedies that befell her, were always painful thorns of envy in Aunt Evelyn's flesh, causing her sharp tongue to become even sharper. The two of them had apparently inflicted awful psychological wounds on each other, but by the time I appeared on the scene Aunt Evelyn had mellowed, my mother-in-law was no longer a challenge, and she gave me the most generous of welcomes.

She became a book-swapping friend and the most stimulating of companions, and whenever we went to stay at Arthington she and I used to jaunt off to the cinema together in Harrogate or Leeds to see the latest films, kangaroo jumping along in her dashing little souped up Mini Minor de luxe in a series of violent surges because she adored the feeling of power which bursts of sudden pressure on the accelerator gave her. She always wore special leather gauntlets for driving but had a disconcerting habit of taking her hands off the steering wheel when she had something specially interesting to say. I loved her dearly.

Sheepshanks is a trade name like Smith, Fletcher or Carpenter. The family were originally hill farmers in the Yorkshire Dales—there are sixteenth century graves in the beautiful old churchyard of Linton-in-Craven in Upper Wharfedale—who came down to sell their wool in Leeds market with cries of 'Sheeps' hanks for sale!'. The nautical figure-of-eight sheepshank knot is based on a hank or skein of wool. The family prospered and by the eighteenth century were wealthy woollen merchants. When I was first married there was still a Sheepshanks' Yard in the middle of Leeds (Aunt Evelyn loved to park there illicitly on our cinema trips) but it has long since disappeared under a shopping centre. In 1800 Richard Sheepshanks made a runaway marriage with Lady Mary Lascelles, eldest daughter of The Earl of Harewood and family legend has it that he told the young couple he wasn't having any daughter of his called a damn silly name like Sheepshanks. 'Call yourselves Leeds or Bradford or anything else you like!' he is reputed to have said—so they changed their name to York. The portrait of Lady Mary York by Reynolds in Harewood House shows a plump, pleasant looking woman but according to George Harewood she was so grossly obese by the time she died that she burst her lead-lined coffin. Obviously a lady who enjoyed the pleasures of the flesh—perhaps she had a secret supply of junk food. Other colourful family members include The Rev. Richard Sheepshanks, a renowned astronomer equally famous in his lifetime for his quarrels and litigious exploits. Despite being a bachelor in Holy Orders he fathered six children from a relationship with an Irish dancer, one of whom was the father of the painter Walter Sickert. His brother John Sheepshanks, friend of many British artists and a great patron of the arts, collected pictures from every Royal Academician exhibited during his lifetime and gave his collection, which includes wonderful Constables and Turners, to the Nation in 1857. They now hang in the V. & A. His nephew, another John Sheepshanks, became Bishop of Norwich. He wrote an unreadably dull book with the promising title of *A Bishop in the Rough* and had seventeen children, the eldest of whom, my namesake Mary Sheepshanks, became a well-known suffragette. She was also an atheist and when her parents entertained King Edward VII and Queen Alexandra to a garden party at the Bishop's Palace, stationed herself at the gates with a placard which read THERE IS NO GOD. Tricky! Thomas Sheepshanks, Charlie's great-grandfather, lived the life of a sporting parson—or 'Squarson'—at Arthington, running his estate while holding the living of two parishes, assisted by several curates. He chose his tenant farmers for their vocal chords rather than their agricultural knowhow as they were expected to sing in the choir on Sundays and all the children at Arthington School had compulsory music lessons for which he paid. An energetic little man, he muddled up the generations on the family tree by marrying again aged seventy-five, saying to Charlie's grandfather 'Don't worry about the inheritance, I'm unlikely to have any more children at my age'—and then produced three.

The two stable cottages into which Charles and Evelyn Sheepshanks had moved at the outbreak of war had only been partially converted into one house so that there was a way through on the ground floor but no access from one to the other upstairs, which suited their particular ménage perfectly. Their devoted and long-standing cook and parlourmaid, Elizabeth Maud and Cissie Jackson, lived in the left-hand house over the kitchen, the scullery and their little sitting room, and the larger, right hand cottage contained Uncle Charles's bedroom, the dining room, a pantry and a cloakroom downstairs, while the drawing room, Aunt Evelyn's bedroom and a small spare room were upstairs. Separate from the house, across the stable yard and over the old saddle rooms was a bigger spare room with its own bathroom which was used for visiting married couples in the summer months— it was far too cold to be used in the winter. Life for this bachelor and spinster pair was normally lived to a very set pattern and during our early married years a three week visit was a delight, but it was not a very easy household to visit once we had children and a nanny in tow. We must have disrupted everyone's tranquillity dreadfully, but they were touchingly insistent that we must still come for three weeks every summer, to coincide with the opening of the grouse shooting season on the famous Twelfth of August. Despite the disruption our presence must have caused they always gave us a tremendous welcome and a lovely time. Elizabeth was a superb plain cook and the food was always traditional English fare at its very best, with wonderful vegetables and fruit from the extensive kitchen gardens, including Muscat grapes and hothouse peaches and nectarines. Meals were taken on the dot of the appointed hour and we always changed for dinner even if there were only the four of us present. Jackson would ring a five minute warning gong before banging out the final booming announcement that dinner was ready. No one was ever late. I adored going there, and The Sheep and Aunt Evelyn both spoilt me rotten in their very different ways, but it says much for Nan's sweetness and tact, and the kindness and forbearance of Jackson and Elizabeth, that harmony was also maintained behind the scenes in this very *Upstairs, Downstairs* existence. It was always a relief to Nan when we moved on to my parents' infinitely more child-friendly household at Cefn Isaf.

Uncle Charles who regularly had to come south on Red Cross business often used to stay with us at Sunningdale too. He loved to boast that our attic spare room was the only room in which he'd ever managed to bump his head on the ceiling. I used to go up to London (always wearing, to the astonishment of my grandchildren today, a hat and three quarter length suede gloves) to lunch with him at his favourite restaurant, L'Apéritif in Jermyn Street, where we drank White Lady cocktails and made each other laugh inordinately. He was always the best company.

When Belinda was two and a half I gave birth to a second daughter, Amanda. I had felt very unwell during the pregnancy but no one, including myself, had been at all worried about the outcome. It soon became apparent however that there was plenty to worry about and this little daughter, had she lived, would have been profoundly handicapped in many ways. She was a diagnostic enigma—a source of burning interest and curiosity to the medical profession which I found very difficult to bear—but after much agonising uncertainty, I was eventually diagnosed as having picked up the Toxoplasmosis virus (now a well known medical condition, but only recently discovered and still little understood then) early in my pregnancy with disastrous results.

I have written extensively about the effect this and other dramas had on our lives in *The Bird of My Loving*, the book I was commissioned to write on grief, and I don't propose to dwell in detail on it now. Amanda died when she was six months old but her birth marked the start of a spell of other troubles for us—a time that was not without its joyful highlights such as the arrival two years later of a healthy baby to join Belinda. The doctors could give us no idea at the time if it would be safe for me to try for another child or whether subsequent children might still be affected by the virus, but though extremely anxious about the outcome, Charlie and I both felt we had to take the risk and try. Our wonderful reward was our daughter Susannah but despite the delight our two little girls now gave us, we seldom seemed to be free from some new drama at this time and nearly lost Susannah too when she was a year old. She picked up a severe gastroenteritis bug which was going round the neighbourhood and was on the danger list in King Edward VII Hospital in Windsor for a terrifying three days while doctors fought for her life and I sat by the cot feeling dreadfully helpless but passionately willing her to recover.

Four days after Amanda was born, a horrendous accident occurred on Pockstones, the small but prolific grouse moor which had been bought by Charlie's great grandfather and has been enjoyed by the Sheepshanks family and their friends ever since. Like many expanses of wild countryside throughout Britain, the Yorkshire Moors had been used in the war as practice sites for firing live ammunition and though they had all been officially cleared by mine sweeping after the war, unexploded shells still occasionally worked their way up through the deep peat many years later. More than ten years after the war had ended there were still warning signs on the moors instructing anyone who found a shell not to touch it. Despite this, however, during a shoot on the third of October 1957 one of the beaters saw a metal object in the heather, picked it up and carried it to Leslie Myers, Uncle Charles's head keeper. This was at the end of a drive when the Guns were still picking up birds, but all the beaters were gathered together round one of the butts. Leslie (whose father and grandfather had been head keepers on Pockstones before him) warned everyone not to touch it when one of the beaters, a young local lad, known to most people present, picked it up, saying that it couldn't possibly still be live after all this time, tossed it in the air like a tennis ball and took a swipe at it with his stick. He lost both legs in the colossal explosion that followed, three other young men were killed outright, another man was blinded and there were numerous other, if less devastating, injuries. Leslie himself who was walking on down the line of butts was lifted off his feet and blown about thirty yards with the force of the blast. Nowadays there would have been mobile telephones and vehicles on the spot to summon help but in 1957 there was only Leslie's ancient tractor and trailer, some way off by the lunch hut and the nearest telephone was over half an hour's walk away at a farm. No ambulance could get to the scene and it was over three hours before two helicopters arrived and got the seriously wounded to hospital. It was a dreadful tragedy and devastated several local families. Perhaps not entirely surprisingly— given human beings' inclination to apportion blame after any major disaster—there were a few people in the neighbourhood who most unfairly held Leslie Myers responsible for this awful episode and he suffered some distressing hostility in the ensuing months—though not from any of the actual eyewitnesses who knew exactly what had happened. It was a long time before he could go to the local pub for a drink unless accompanied by friends in case of an actual attack. He bore this with great stoicism but it was a terrible time for the Myers family as well as for the agonised families of the victims. Neither Uncle Charles nor Leslie Myers were seriously wounded themselves but neither of them were ever quite the same again.

I was still in hospital in Windsor with my very sick new baby, desperately trying to come to terms with her disabilities and the autumn term was underway at Sunningdale when The Sheep rang Charlie late at night, after he'd finally got back home from accompanying the wounded to hospital, to tell him the devastating news. Charlie's instinct was to go straight up to Yorkshire to support his uncle, but the 1957 pandemic of Asian flu that was sweeping the country had already hit the school and by the next day Charlie had not only gone down with it himself, but was seriously ill with pneumonia so we were neither of us any help to Uncle Charles at all. I desperately longed to be at home but was not allowed back to the school for fear that Amanda or I would catch the flu.

Looking back at this time after more than fifty years I still feel my throat constrict when I think about it. I wondered what else could go wrong and it was just as well that I did not know because there was plenty more to follow. That bout of pneumonia was the precursor of much serious ill health for Charlie. He was soon to wage a gallant and ultimately triumphant battle against cancer, which burst on us as yet another complete shock. Our devoted supporter Val succumbed to the malignant melanoma which I have already mentioned, and Charles and Evelyn Sheepshanks died within a week of each other, at the same time as Charlie was in the Middlesex hospital having just undergone another major cancer operation. Hospitals had become part of our lives and I felt my world to be a very precarious place: it was hard to keep optimism, that potent, vital drug, alive and I had to divide my time between a very ill husband in London and the sad task, for which I felt myself quite unqualified, of arranging two big funerals in quick succession at Arthington while rushing back to Sunningdale to see my two little girls whenever possible. I had only been to two funerals in my life: my Nickson grandfather's at the church at Caerhûn when I was twelve, and Amanda's sad little service with only me and Charlie present and I had no yardstick of what was expected. I was greatly helped over the order of service by Canon Charles Ellison, the Archdeacon of Leeds, a friend and great admirer of The Sheep's, but he omitted to make one important suggestion. Arthington church— one of two built by Charlie's great-great-grandfather, William Sheepshanks, so that his son Thomas, could be the vicar ('You want to be a parson, my boy? I'll build a couple of churches for you!')— seats over three hundred. It was packed—but I'd slipped up badly on one thing. I hadn't thought of asking anyone to give a eulogy simply because I had no idea that this would be expected, and everyone on the Estate was very disappointed. 'Ee Mrs Charlie—you didn't give Colonel a right proper send off, did you?' an old man said to me reproachfully after the service. I was mortified. My sister-in-law Rosemary who now lived in Ireland with her ex-naval husband and two small children managed to come over the day before the service and I was very thankful for her presence. My parents both came from Wales even though my poor mother was feeling terrible with a bad attack of shingles; it was wonderful to have them with me, but it seemed terribly sad that Charlie, who had always been so devoted to his uncle, could not be there too. Dennis Wilkinson, my father's old Eton friend and also a friend of the Sheepshanks family, suddenly collapsed with a heart attack and died during the service which must have been ghastly for Gillian, his wife. It was an awful day.

A week later, Aunt Evelyn died and there was a terrible feeling of déjà vu as Rosemary and I arranged and attended another funeral. Two very special people had gone out of our lives.

Far Cry
Remembering Amanda

A small blue flower lives inside my head.
It did not flourish in the flowerbed
where I first tried to plant it out,
but in tight bud, still wrapped in early dew,
put down its trembling roots and then withdrew.

Though hidden in my skull for twenty years
this ghostly plant blows echoes through my ear.
I may not hear its thirsty cry for months
or rake about its weedy patch, and yet
I can still water it—shall not forget.

15

DECISIONS

On the death of his uncle in April 1961, Charlie inherited the Arthington estate of about a thousand acres which then included four farms, Arthington Hall with its six acres of gardens, and also Pockstones Moor—which had not yet been shot over since the disaster of 1957. The Hall itself is a large stone house, imposing rather than beautiful since its classical proportions were ruined by 'Squarson' Thomas Sheepshanks, who with typical Victorian meddling altered and enlarged it in 1865. Luckily Thomas could not interfere with its spectacular position It stands on a high ridge of land with an incomparable view up the River Wharfe and over the Arthington viaduct to the legendary local landmark and famous climbing location of Almscliffe Crag, with the rolling North Yorkshire moors dissolving into the skyline beyond.

While our personal lives had often been in turmoil for the last four years, I had been constantly supported by Nan. I don't know how I would have got through without her, but she was always devotedly looking after the children for me if I could not be with them— loving, sympathetic but totally practical: a rock. Sunningdale had continued to thrive. Except when he was actually in hospital Charlie never relinquished either the running of the school or his teaching, occasionally conducting Maths classes from his bed which I found very trying. I would rush upstairs to change for some event only to find twelve boys sprawled around on our bedroom floor with all their clobber of exercise books, pencils and rubbers strewn about, while crabby old Mr Burrows and Mike Tupholme tended to wander in unannounced and seem surprised and put out to find me there.

Charlie's operations were public knowledge, but the fact that his surgery had been for cancer was not. The attitude of secrecy surrounding cancer was very different then to what it is now, but even so it had come as a surprise to me when the doctors first told me the diagnosis and indicated that, provided I agreed, they did not propose to tell Charlie himself. The degree of malignancy was serious and I was left in no doubt that the outlook was poor, but the surgeons felt any possible chance of recovery would be better if he were presented with an optimistic view. His particular condition could have been non-malignant so it was a plausible evasion of the truth but even so I wasn't sure that this pretence was something I could sustain—or even if it was right. It was a lonely choice, but I eventually decided that if Charlie was not to know the truth himself, then neither should anyone at or connected with the school be told either, and Charles Duncan supported me. If I had to act a lie, then it must be convincing—a brilliant lie—and I determined that I would put on a great show of outward confidence. Had Charlie ever asked me a direct question, I would have told him the truth. He never did. Years later, after a major coronary, a heart specialist said to him 'I see you've already made one amazing recovery from cancer,' and this was the first time we'd ever discussed it together. I asked him if, deep down, he'd always known and he said yes, but that he had not at all wanted to have his suspicions confirmed—so I felt vindicated for what had occasionally felt like my duplicitous behaviour. He could hardly not have suspected because for the next five years he had to go up to the Middlesex every few months for internal examinations under anaesthetic, blood and urine tests not being so sophisticated then, and of course there were no scans. He was surprised to discover that I'd always known the truth because he didn't think I'd have been capable of keeping it to myself. Not very flattering! Because I badly needed some personal support I told my parents, my brother David, and Charlie's sister Rosemary, but not Uncle Charles or Aunt Evelyn and I'm glad I spared them that anxiety just before the end of their lives. Two friends whom I did tell were Gordon and Peggie Richardson. Their son Simon was already at Sunningdale when I first arrived and they had become great personal friends of ours; we had holidayed together and shared a lot of outings and fun. When Charlie, after a recurrence of the original cancer, was moved from our local hospital to London to be under the care of the brilliant Sir Eric Riches at the Middlesex Hospital—to whom we undoubtedly owed his life—Gordon and Peggie insisted on keeping a room permanently free for me for weeks in their house in Chelsea Square so that I could have a London base whenever I needed it. They were wonderful to me and I shall never forget their friendship. Gordon, later Lord Richardson, was a rising Chancery barrister when we first met but had moved into the world of finance and was to become a distinguished Governor of the Bank of England. Peggie was godmother to our daughter Susannah.

After the deaths of my in-laws we spent that first long summer holidays with Nan and the children in the Cottage at Arthington, and Elizabeth Maud and Cissie Jackson postponed their overdue and richly deserved retirement to come and look after us. So devoted were they to Charles and Evelyn Sheepshanks that they had refused even to consider retiring before, but as both were well into in their seventies they were more than ready for an easier life. I wondered if they might resent my new position and our much less formal way of life, but they gave me huge encouragement to make any changes I wanted. I adored feeling that I had my own house for the first time, after spending eight years in the school. I understood why my mother had always loved being at Cefn so much.

Shortly before Uncle Charles's death, The West Riding County Council, which had taken over the Hall from the Military after the war as a men's convalescent hospital, decided—most unexpectedly—not to renew their lease. Coming so soon after the Pockstones disaster, this development was a major anxiety to Uncle Charles. He had been negotiating with the Deaf and Dumb Society to lease the house as a school when he had died so suddenly of a heart attack. We reopened the negotiations but there were too many complications and the deal fell through. By this time the house, already in a state of disrepair, had stood empty for a year and was deteriorating fast. Our first thought was to convert the Cottage into a more convenient family house but we hadn't the faintest idea what to do with the Hall—or rather there were plenty of wild ideas flying round, none of which proved practical. We tried and failed to re-let it as an institution; we tried to sell it, but because we didn't want to part with the surrounding land, the only offer we received was ludicrously low; we got an estimate for pulling it down which would have cost a fortune and discovered from Peter Chance, an Eton contemporary of Charlie's and by then chairman of Christie's, that there might be a market for selling separately the unique flying staircase, that is the house's claim to fame. Peter seemed to think eccentric American billionaires sometimes bought staircases as other people might buy sofas and chairs, and would then transport the whole thing to the States and build a new house round it. This seemed a marvellously Alice Through the Looking Glass sort of notion but we were ready to consider anything. No mad millionaire crazy enough to offer for the stairs turned up however, and the option we finally fell for was even crazier.

Charlie's health was noticeably beginning to improve. He suddenly looked different—and even to my anxious eyes he seemed better than he'd been for ages. I was beginning to dare to hope that we might yet have a future. Privately, the few people who knew just how gloomy his prognosis was had begged me not to encourage him to take any risks over property. 'You are likely to be left a widow with two young children—for God's sake don't do anything foolish' was the counsel from loving and concerned family and advisers, but doing something foolish began to seem to me a way of putting two fingers up at fate—a gesture of faith, folly and defiance that might, just might, pay off. I could not explain, still less justify, this hunch but the more everyone told me what a colossal white elephant our large, decaying house was, the more fond of elephants I became. I knew how much Charlie had always loved this house which had been in his family since 1840, in which his grandparents had lived during his childhood and where he'd spent much time when growing up. In particular I knew how much the gardens would mean to him, the enjoyment he would get from having fresh ideas about planting and layout, and I thought a new challenge might give him the extra will to go on living.

One September evening, just before we were due to return to Sunningdale for the autumn term Charlie and I went over to the Hall together and made our way out onto the roof. We ducked our way through the attics where footmen had once slept under the ancient beams and came across fifteen tin hats hanging on pegs—a legacy of ARP wardens with fire-watching duties in the war—they were to come in useful for charades in the years to come. We looked down through the glass dome in the centre of the house to where the famous staircase was still boarded in, jacked up with the wooded props which had been installed as a safety measure in 1939. You can't carry stretcher cases up and down an unsupported flight of stairs, comprising sixteen treads, which bounce up and down with every step. Charlie remembered that when his grandfather died, his lead-lined coffin had to be taken down the back stairs. We squeezed our way out through the lead trapdoor that leads to the parapet round the outer edge of the house. Arms round each other we stood side by side, leaning on the stone balustrade and gazing down on the Wharfe as it wound its way through the farmland below; stubble fields were a pinkish gold in the evening light and the Friesian cows in the meadows by the river seemed like toys from a child's model farm. We looked up to the blue hills of the moors beyond—a view that has to be one of the great views of Yorkshire.

We decided to move back into the house ourselves.

Kingfisher Days

An electric flash of unexplained delight
—a kingfisher moment—streaked across my day,
a blue-green rocket torched on bonfire night.
Where did it come from? Why? I cannot say.

When Turner dreamed of painting storms at sea
or mixed his palette for The Téméraire
did he recall a Yorkshire memory
of walking by the Washburn valley, where

he must have seen a feathered shaft of light
explode above dark waters, felt the thrill
of unexpected colour flood his sight,
and held his breath, heart-stopped, on heathered hill?

Kingfisher days grow scarce. I watch and wait:
send me one more—before it is too late.

Shall we go Alternative?

I used to find it too much rush
with Church and Sunday Lunch,
but now I go with New Age Friends
to Meditation Brunch:
while we contemplate our navels
and eat Veggie kedgeree
I pine for Bloody Marys
— but there's only Herbal Tea.

We're learning Paneurythmy;
we go dancing every dawn
— in our Barbours and green wellies —
on a sacred stretch of lawn.
Next week we're starting classes
to 'heal the child within'
where you learn that guilty feelings
are a kind of New Age sin.

We can energise a chakra
and see an aura flicker -
which is certainly more thrilling
than a sermon from the Vicar!
We clank with Celtic crosses,
draped in bangles, beads and serapes;
we're blessed with many ailments
— and we're loving all the therapies.

I go for weekly channelling
— Burnt Feathers is my guide.
In a previous incarnation
he says he was my bride.
He is very wise and holy
but it's well within his range
to give me helpful little hints
about the Stock Exchange.

Reflexology's as easy
as falling off a ladder:
you press the sole of someone's foot
  — and activate their bladder!
I'm trying Crystal Healing,
and find that Acupressure
has done wonders for my sex life
  — makes my husband so much fresher.

I subscribe to lots of Healing mags
and gobble up each issue,
and I never leave the house without
a charged up Kleenex tissue;
I book on every Shrine crawl
—I've got hooked on Holy Water—
when I've learnt to travel astrally
the journeys may seem shorter.

BUT in Metamorphic Massage
as I toned my special note,
I suddenly got smitten
with a streptococcal throat.
I MUST HAVE PENICILLIN!
Though it means committing perjury
I'll say I'm at the Yoga class
  — and sneak off to the surgery!

16

ARTHINGTON

As soon as we went south, Charlie had to go in to the Middlesex for a check-up before the start of the term. The test results were all clear which was enormously encouraging—but there was to be one more bombshell to explode in our family life.

In October we took a three day break away from the school and went down to Suffolk to stay with Robin and Lilias Sheepshanks. As well as being cousins they were great friends, we were in celebratory mood and we had a lovely weekend—a most unusual absence for us during the term time. We were about to set off for home after breakfast on the Monday morning when Lilias, looking distraught, came to tell us there was an urgent telephone message from Sunningdale. Nan, aged only fifty-three, had suffered a massive heart attack in the night and had been found dead in bed by six year-old Belinda in the morning. Belinda was eventually discovered by one of the friends with whom I shared a school run, who came round to the nursery wing to investigate why she and Nanny were not ready at the front door waiting to be picked up. Having tried pummelling Nan and jumping on her to no avail for what must have been well over an hour, Belinda was desperately trying to shove Nan's deaf aid into her unresponsive ear while the nearly two year-old Susannah was screaming the house down in her cot in the next door bedroom. The horror of this is still a vivid memory for Belinda. A very bright, highly strung little girl, not surprisingly she became extremely difficult for a time.

If the birth of Amanda had heralded the start of a four year period of trouble for us, it seemed as if the death of Nan was to bring our spell of misfortune to a close. It may sound whimsical but I came to feel that someone very special had come to help me through a testing time and when she had accomplished her mission, she departed—as angels do. But we missed her dreadfully. Despite our grieving for those who had gone and the inevitable continuing sadness for the might-have-beens of Amanda's short life, our fortunes turned at this point. Our resolve to reclaim Arthington and turn the crumbling house back from being an institution into being a family home again was to prove a wonderfully happy, if financially disastrous, decision. It brought us plenty of headaches but no regrets. A halcyon period in our lives was about to begin.

For the next five years we lived a double life between Sunningdale and Yorkshire. We spent the school holidays at Arthington and during the term I went north for a few days each month, while Charlie tried to go up for one or two weekends a term. His health continued to improve and if I had private anxieties, I tried not to show them. It was an enormous relief when the results of his check-ups continued to be clear.

In November 1962, a year after Nan's death, when Susannah was three and Belinda seven and a half, our son William was born. His arrival set a seal on our happiness and I could hardly believe our good fortune.

Josephine Featherstone came to help me with the children. She was very different from Nan: round, jolly and usually great fun though occasionally given to black moods which luckily didn't last long but could temporarily cast a cloud over us. I specially appreciated the big-heartedness that made her love all three children equally and not just William, who was 'her' baby—by no means always the case with nannies taking on older children as well as a new baby. She was a sociable and robust character who stood up well to living in a school and could give as good as she got if there was any infighting going on. She and Pauline treated each other with a degree of circumspection that was a great relief to me. They reminded me of two dogs, walking round each other stiff-legged, both itching for a scrap but each unwilling to be seen to deliver the first bite. Having my own home during the holidays enormously helped me to tolerate the difficulties, which I had found so irksome to start with, of combining a private family life with living in a residential community. In my early thirties I had grown into my role as a headmaster's wife and was much better able to cope with—and enjoy—the responsibilities that had seemed so burdensome aged twenty-one.

In Yorkshire we were lucky to have the help and advice of Neville Ussher, a remarkable man of rare charm—temperamentally the driest of blankets—whose wild enthusiasms and fondness for mad enterprises made him, if not the canniest of financial advisers, then certainly the most enjoyable of supporters for our project of reclaiming the house. Neville was the land agent at Harewood and a year earlier Lord Harewood and Princess Mary had kindly agreed to a suggestion of Charlie's that Neville might also take on the running of the Arthington estate for Uncle Charles. Neville and George Harewood had struck up an enduring friendship at the end of the war when they were both ADCs to the Governor General of Canada, George's great-uncle, the Earl of Athlone. Neville had subsequently accepted George's invitation to come to Harewood. They had many shared interests, Harewood House being one of them, but music, George's ruling passion, most certainly was not amongst them. Neville might help organize, but seldom actually attended any of the many musical events at Harewood House but I once sat next to him when he was surprisingly present at a performance of Walton's *Façade* in the Long Gallery. Half way through he hissed in my ear 'I'd sooner hear a pig being stuck any day!'

Neville had already been an invaluable help to me over coping with the deaths of my in-laws and he and his pretty French wife Marguerite were to become great friends of ours with whom we shared all sorts of family, social and sporting occasions over the years. Without his involvement in our affairs at Arthington we could never have gone on running two such geographically separate and very different lives for so long.

We had endless discussions with Neville about how we might convert the house, let part of it and adapt the rest for family life again, but it wasn't long before the enormity of what I'd taken on started to hit home. Most of the rooms were in a lamentable state of dilapidation—far worse than I'd realised while blinkered by the rose-tinted spectacles of my determined optimism. I was once more surrounded by the acres of margarine walls and the dark green dados that I had so disliked in my early Sunningdale years—standard hospital décor, pre-war, when the idea that bright paintwork might be beneficial to patients' health had not yet come in. In the bedroom that we decided to have for our ourselves—it had to be on the west side of the house so that we could enjoy the stunning view—there were three doors all painted in different shades of bilious green and in its adjoining bathroom, another hospital legacy, there were four baths but no loo. Despite the proven advantages I'd discovered at Sunningdale of multiple baths for dog-washing I didn't feel drawn to starting a fashion for communal bathing with our future guests! Inevitably the house had got damp while standing empty for so long and there was a particularly nasty moment when we turned on the ancient central heating to try to dry the house out and great splodges of mould, like a measles rash only black, erupted all over the walls. An architect's proposal for converting the house was so horrendously costly that we decided to do without professional advice. Luckily Neville with his usual encouragement said that the Harewood Estate could carry out any alterations and suggested that he and I, together with Johnny Lister, the wonderful Harewood clerk of works, could come up with all the ideas ourselves.

In the end we simply divided the house down the middle, which required no structural alterations, and made two apartments in the east side of the house while keeping the principal rooms for ourselves. Out of a wing which Charlie's grandmother had converted for staff bedrooms in 1908, and where nurses had slept during the hospital occupation, we made a small two bedroomed flat for a bachelor friend of ours whose firm had just moved him to Leeds. He rented this flat from us for several years and after he left to get married we were always able to re-let it with great ease, but the other, two-storeyed apartment—a sizeable dwelling by any standards—was another matter and I made a mistake over this. We were lucky enough to start with to have a delightful family with two teenage boys living in this side of the house but when they eventually bought a place of their own we had difficulty in finding anyone suitable who wanted to live in such a large chunk of someone else's house, no matter how pleasant the surroundings, which had huge rooms and no private garden. I eventually hit on the solution of making a spacious, self-contained upstairs flat and derating the ground floor rooms and leaving them empty, and this worked perfectly. It was to this flat that, much later, my parents finally moved.

We converted the old butler's pantry opposite the original dining room into a new kitchen for ourselves, and turned Charlie's grandmother's morning room into a playroom for the children. We also had a billiard room which became hugely popular with the young and their visiting friends as they grew up. Our side of the house included the oval hall with its glass dome above, and the two graceful flights of stairs which curve up each side to a small half landing before sweeping back overhead in one spectacular unsupported straight flight of sixteen treads to the oval landing on the first floor—a triumph of innovative design by the Yorkshire architect John Carr. In 1801 Carr had revamped a much older, grander house which had been partially burned down a few years earlier. The existing house is a hotchpotch of different dates. The Victorian architect Alfred Waterhouse altered it again in 1865 for the meddling Thomas Sheepshanks, sadly removing the classical pediment and putting a huge and hideous—though extremely useful—conservatory on the front and adding a gimmicky wing down the west side of the house. I came to think of Waterhouse as being exceptionally well-named— perhaps a perspicacious but malevolent fairy godmother had attended his christening—because anything he designed seemed especially prone to leaks, and an unreliable roof became part of my life. One particular trouble spot was the moulded ceiling of the bay window in the drawing room, where an elegant nymph stands coyly inside a garland of leaves. I shall never forget the surprise of a visiting architectural group to whom I was giving a conducted tour of the house. I had just got nicely into my guide book speak stride and they were admiring the stairs, when Susannah rushed up to say 'Mummy, Mummy, come *quickly*! That naked lady in the drawing room is leaking all over the carpet again!'

It was a thrilling moment when the protective boarding was taken off the banisters and the struts were removed from underneath the stairs. I volunteered to be the human sacrifice and do a trial run. With Charlie and Neville holding their breath at the bottom, I raced up to the top landing and, as Charlie had promised, the unsupported stretch bounced up and down like a trampoline. Over the ensuing years the staircase has taken some terrific punishment as our children and grandchildren have thundered up and down it—though deliberate bouncing is not encouraged and sitting out on the stairs during teenage parties has to be banned. In answer to the question sometimes posed by nervous visitors: 'How do you know it's safe?' the answer has to be … 'we don't'.

We renovated rooms gradually. Harry Pennington, or Pen, as everyone called him, who had worked as handyman for the family for more years than anyone could remember, became my ally and teacher. Under his instruction I eventually became a dab hand at wallpapering and wielding a paint brush. I wasn't very good at the boring preparation but I loved the quick fix of slapping on paper, though my first attempt was a disaster as I became wound round and round with a sixteen foot length of soggy paper on which I'd sloshed far too much glue and was in danger of turning myself into a papier mâché statue, patterned by Colefax and Fowler, when Pen rescued me. Pen, who loved the house as much as I did, was thrilled at our decision to move back into it. If ever my optimism started to wobble as much as I frequently wobbled physically up scarily tall stepladders, Pen would inspire me all over again. His daughter, Mary Pennington came to help me in the house and was to be my great friend and support for over forty years.

There were three full time gardeners when we inherited Arthington but luckily one of them was on the point of retirement anyway so we didn't have to make anyone redundant. Harry Ward, the head-gardener had started work there aged fourteen as a garden boy and had specially loved to weed the flowerbeds outside the drawing room windows so that he could hear Charlie's grandfather playing the splendid organ that used to be in there. It was a source of regret to Charlie, who played the organ too, that it had been dismantled and removed by the hospital to make room for more beds, and had then been given to a Youth Club in York by his uncle after the war. Harry had the greenest fingers and one of the most charming personalities of anyone I've ever met. He and Charlie had played much village cricket together as boys and were to garden together in perfect amity in the years ahead. They admired and amused each other in equal proportions but they couldn't have been more different: Harry highly organized, methodical, conventional and pin-neat; Charlie eccentric, inspired but often shambolic. They might have driven each other mad—but they didn't. We opened the gardens every summer for various gardening societies and also for the National Gardens Scheme. The first time we did this it poured with rain all afternoon and we only got seven visitors. The following year we got seven hundred! In a book on private gardens sometimes open to the public, a well known gardening writer once described our garden at Arthington as being wonderfully colourful and full of interest but somewhat idiosyncratic and commented that its eclectic mix of styles was perhaps not for the faint-hearted—not a bad description of its owner too! During the war, the two big walled gardens at Arthington, like so many other similar ones, had been turned into a market garden to produce food for the war effort and afterwards my in-laws went on to sell tomatoes and soft fruit, a practice we continued. There was also a vinery with hothouse Muscat grapes more delicious than any I have ever tasted, a peach and nectarine house, a melon house and a Victorian fernery. There was a long herbaceous border which ran along a beautiful old brick wall, a dahlia border and a rockery but nothing had been changed by way of layout for years. Charlie was to revolutionize the border which became a mass of colour with wonderful shrub roses and spectacular delphiniums grown from seed he took himself. He did away with the rockery to make room for azaleas and species rhododendrons, though after gardening in the Sunningdale area where these flourish so easily, their growth in Yorkshire seemed disappointingly slow to us. Other projects included a heather garden on the west side of the house and a rose garden in one of the sheltered walled gardens. Over the years, trees became Charlie's greatest interest; he built up a wonderful collection of acers and planted a notable arboretum beyond the tennis court—but really he loved growing almost anything. If he could get a plant or tree to flourish that was not supposed to do well so far north he would be well pleased and his enthusiasm for experimenting with new ideas never waned.

We knew we couldn't go on juggling the rival demands of both the Arthington Estate and the school indefinitely but it was difficult to know when to retire from Sunningdale. We anguished about the decision but in the end I think we got the timing about right. Nick and Tim Dawson were ready and keen to take on the school and after so much ill health, Charlie's doctors felt he should move up to his beloved Yorkshire and enjoy a less demanding lifestyle before our present frenetic existence became too much for him. We also thought that the uncertainly of not knowing how long the present regime might continue could prove difficult for prospective parents. We weighed the pros and cons endlessly but eventually decided to leave at the end of the summer term 1967 when Charlie would be fifty-five and I would be thirty-five. I was afraid that Charlie, a truly vocational schoolmaster, might miss the school dreadfully but the five interim years of combining the two lives made the final break easier and though our farewells were very emotional and there was much about the school which we were very sad to leave, I think we both felt ready for the change.

We took to Yorkshire life immediately and soon got embroiled with local affairs; Charlie, the expert gardener, was quickly involved with various horticultural ploys and committees and both of us became governors of local schools. I became a magistrate with a particular interest in the juvenile bench.

Belinda had already started at boarding school when we moved north and was happily established at St Mary's, Wantage, but Susannah, a more reserved character, took time to settle into a new school and found the move difficult to start with. She adored Arthington, as they all three did, but had been particularly happy at her day school in Sunningdale which specialised in dancing and where she had excelled at ballet. William, at four and a half, had the luck to start his school career at the small but brilliant Arthington village school—sadly no longer in existence—under its eccentric but beloved headmistress Jane Handley. He was soon joined there by Mark Lascelles, my godson, son of our great friends George and Patricia Harewood with whom we were to enjoy much music, sport, laughter and hospitality in the years ahead and who were both to be a notable support to me when ill health eventually caught up with Charlie again some years later.

The highlight of the Arthington School year was the Nativity Play which the whole village attended. It roughly followed the traditional story but as Jane Handley encouraged creative initiative in the children, it was only semi-scripted with plenty of scope for some surprising variations and it always took place 'in the round' amongst the audience, rather then on a stage. William only had a minor role as a shepherd's boy his first term. Apart from the statutory Nativity garb of a winter dressing gown with a checked tea towel round the head to indicate Biblical dress, I had been instructed to produce a real snack—a packet of potato crisps—wrapped up in a red spotted handkerchief on the end of a stick. William looked like a cross between Yasser Arafat and Dick Whittington, but the crisps, intended by Jane for consumption round the shepherds' campfire—possibly to be offered to the Heavenly Host, sharing being much encouraged by Jane as good for the character—proved a mistake because William immediately sat down and started munching. Jane, crouched agonizingly behind the upright piano with her huge bust squashed against it so that she could hardly breathe, could be heard gasping urgently: 'William Sheepshanks—it's not *time* for the picnic yet. Leave those crisps alone and GO TO BETHLEHEM.' *Leave the crisps alone and go to Bethlehem* became a family catch phrase.

'Aw, look! God's baby's been born' announced a surprised Mary, yanking a rag doll Jesus from beneath her. ''E's just come out of me bum!' When the Magi finally put in an appearance, galumphing round the room on invisible camels before dismounting to tether and water their mounts (coming from rural stock, they were savvy about animal husbandry) we were surprised to see only two of them.

'I've brought gift of GOLD' bellowed the first King producing a *Kitkat* wrapped in crumpled gilt foil.

'I've brought gift of frankincense,' said the second one brandishing a small, round bottle of his mother's 4711 *eau de cologne*. Then in unison they announced: 'T'oother king, 'e would have brought the myrrh but 'e's poorly with the measles.'

There were more Biblical dramas to be enjoyed on the first Monday of each month when we gathered for *Our Mummies' Monthly Assembly*. I particularly remember a suitably diminutive Zachaeus, peering out through the back of the Windsor chair which represented a sycamore tree while a jovial Jesus exhorted him: 'If you come along down from there I'll come over to yours to have me dinner with you,' to which Zachaeus, suffering an identity crisis, wailed: 'I can't! I'm 'aving me tea today with Kevin Mitchell'.

When the school, perhaps predictably, but none the less sadly, was closed a few years later because the attending children fell for one term below the arbitrary number of twenty-seven, a unifying bond was lost to the village and our small, scattered, community was never the same again.

Jane Handley was endlessly good to William and Mark, frequently having them to stay and taking then on expeditions. I have unforgettable memories of collecting them both from swimming sessions with her in Aireborough Baths. To watch Jane launch herself horizontally off the high diving board was an experience not to be missed. She would hit the water, bosom first, with such a tremendous thwack it practically emptied the pool—not so much bellyflops as bustflops. They were unique. She had many talents but technology was not amongst them and anything electrical had her flummoxed. She once called me in to diagnose problems with her deep freeze, surprised that having knocked off one of the pins from a three pin plug it wouldn't work with only two. 'How clever of you to know that!' she said admiringly and was tremendously impressed that I could change a plug. We had the freezer purring away again in no time, but I stupidly omitted to ask her for how long it had been out of order. She called me in again a few days later—all the contents, she said, now looked 'a bit funny'. They did indeed. The entire deep-freeze was filled with little iced fairy cakes decorated with cute angelica and cherry faces, which, having first thawed and then re-frozen, all looked as if they were suffering from a severe case of Bell's Palsy.

Jane was the worst driver I have ever known. Because she could never master the art of turning right across oncoming traffic, she frequently drove miles out of her way in order to avoid having to do so. Planning routes that only involved left turns eventually became too taxing and when her long-suffering husband Jack retired from teaching in Leeds and was free to become her full time chauffeur, to everyone's relief she gave up driving.

It was a delight to feel the old house springing to life again. We made wonderful new friends and Charlie was able to resume some old friendships from his youth. I enormously enjoyed having people to stay—something we hadn't easily been able to do at Sunningdale.

Arthington may not be the most convenient house to run, but it lends itself to being filled with family and friends. We played a lot of tennis and many needle games of croquet—always the Sheepshanks family's preferred golf croquet rather than association croquet. Wild games of 'sardines' were played all over the house when the children were young, and later we often had informal parties for all ages with charades—always of the non-speaking *Nebuchadnezzar* variety—as the entertainment after supper. The most unlikely people turned out to have histrionic talents but acting games can be an agony to some people, so anyone with inhibitions was always allowed to opt out and watch, or have a non-extrovert part: as a tree perhaps, Birnam Wood marching on Macbeth for instance—not a taxing dramatic role— or as a tidal wave, anonymously hidden under a rug while creeping up on King Canute. Some memorable individual performances stay in my mind however: Neville Ussher leaping the drawing room sofa as Nijinsky; artist Graham Rust as Lady Docker, mincing defiantly onto an aeroplane after banishment from Monaco; the enigmatic Peter Diamand, Director of the Edinburgh Festival who had been brought to dinner by the Harewoods, writhing about on the carpet with an apple as a saucily seductive serpent in the Garden of Eden; my father wielding a wallpaper brush and stumping about on his knees as Toulouse Lautrec while a lumbering chorus line danced the Cancan; the children and their friends in a huge variety of roles. Things occasionally got a bit out of hand and I almost threatened divorce when Charlie in the guise of footballer Nobby Stiles, kicked a football through the drawing room window, narrowly missing a Meissen vase en route. Clearing up after these occasions, when every room in the house had been ransacked for 'props' could be chaotic.

As they grew older, our children, three equally strong but very different characters who have remained exceptionally close, started to ask their own contemporaries to stay and Charlie and I loved their company. Belinda in particular invited droves of friends to Arthington and Susannah and William hugely enjoyed it when she did. We had many happy family shooting days on Pockstones—starting again four years after the accident. The first time was a difficult exercise in laying ghosts, but it was a relief to discover that everyone locally was keen to have the moor operational again. It always gave Charlie special pleasure if any young visitor shot his—or her—first grouse there. We had many memorable shooting lunches in the little stone lunch hut, built by Charlie's great-grandfather, overlooking the Washburn where Turner had walked and painted over a hundred years earlier. It belongs to William now who still makes it a special place to us all.

Because it was always such an anxiety getting and keeping domestic staff at Sunningdale, I had sworn that I would never let myself be in a position again of not being able to manage on my own if I needed to, but the perfect solution cropped up. Apart from wonderful Mary Pen, we now heard through friends that Dorothy Sykes, the younger sister of Dick, Charlie and Rosemary's childhood nanny, had recently been widowed and would like occasional part time work. When she was a young girl, Doffy—as she had been known to the Sheepshanks children—had gone to work for my mother-in-law as a parlourmaid, and later had married from Arthington. She had always adored my husband and was thrilled to see him again. She now divided her time between her cottage at Bugthorpe on the Garrowby Estate where her husband had been head keeper to Lord Halifax, with occasional work for a café in Stamford Bridge ... and us. It was to be a wonderful arrangement. Darling Doffy, of the bandy legs, cackling laugh, sparkling repartee and huge heart, how we all loved her! Though I sometimes draw on different aspects of real people and mix them with the purely imaginary in my fiction, I normally avoid doing portraits (far too dangerous!) but I made an exception for Doffy and tried to immortalise her in my first novel, *A Price for Everything*, a tale about a crumbling house partly inspired by our efforts to reclaim Arthington. I hope I caught something of her wonderfully astringent flavour. I am not naturally very domesticated—and my school upbringing didn't help—but Doffy could turn her hand to anything and under her tutelage I learnt much about running a house and cooking. I loved having my own kitchen and my culinary efforts became much more reliable than in my hit or miss days at Walter's Cottage.

David and Louise also had three children, my darling nieces Felicity, Lucy and Rosie, who matched our children in age. We often stayed with them in Scotland and they came to us in Yorkshire and we had a lot of fun together. David had come out of the army to join the business side of William Collins in Glasgow and he and Louise made their home in Scotland. His business career was meteoric and we were— and are—intensely proud of his many and varied achievements. Public recognition came as he was first knighted in 1987 and made a Life Peer in 1994, but to me he has always remained the boon companion of my childhood and a very special brother.

Once Charlie was sufficiently recovered we continued to have spectacular skiing holidays, initially in Lenzerheide, and later in Meribel, and took our children too. We joined up each January with Rickards, Campbell-Prestons, Gordons and McGrigors—I think other hotel guests must have loathed our large, noisy, mixed ages party—and Charlie was in his element leading a party down the mountain in soft snow. A bonus of the big age gap between Charlie and me was that we often enjoyed the friendship of varied generations. An example would be Frances Campbell-Preston, between us in age herself, who became a special friend, as later, did her son Robert and his wife Rosie, who like me had enjoyed an Eton childhood and whose father Martin Forest had taken over my father's house before becoming Lower Master. Apart from the skiing holidays, Robert and Rosie became favourite guests at Arthington after they started their highly successful mail order business Inverawe Smokehouses from their home near Oban. They used to arrive in an enormous white van (which invariably broke down at some stage) with a varied retinue of family helpers whenever they were selling their delectable smoked salmon products at game fairs or agricultural shows in the vicinity. They were hugely good company and despite some nail-biting dramas in the early days over deep freezes containing fish or punctures en route to shows, their visits were greatly looked forward to by all of us. Later, after I was widowed and had embarked on a writing career, they still used to come and stay with me in my cottage at Leathley. In the evenings Rosie and I would be glued to our respective laptops, she writing mouth-watering descriptions of new products for the next season's Inverawe catalogue ('Does this sound really yummy?') and me endeavouring to think up plausible plots ('Would this be too far-fetched?')

In the summer there were shooting and tennis parties and frequent picnics to Brimham Rocks—that spectacular fifty acres of rocky outcrop on the moors near Pateley Bridge, where vast millstone-grit rock formations, sculpted over thousands of years by wind and weather, resemble weird animal shapes. It belongs to the National Trust now and though inevitably that means it has to have rules and restrictions, it is still a paradise for children. When our family were young it was wilder and much less frequented and there were no set opening or closing hours. To go there at night was considered a tremendous treat, when the light of a full moon turned the great rocks into pleasurably terrifying monsters which cast sinister shadows across a silver landscape. Eating hot fish pie and sausage rolls under a spookily crouching dinosaur was a memorable experience.

Leeds, only eight miles from Arthington has always been a great musical centre, and music continued to be a shared enjoyment for Charlie and me. It was a wonderful bonus when Opera North, which started as an offshoot of English National Opera, came to be based at

Leeds Grand Theatre. Patrick Libby, the company's first Director of Productions, lived in one of our flats, so we always felt very involved.

Life at Arthington was busy and fulfilling and I hadn't given my poetic ambitions a thought for ages when, soon after we left Sunningdale, the writing bug suddenly returned in a curious way. I woke up in the middle of one night with a pounding migraine and three verses of a fully fledged poem about Amanda hammering away inside my brain. All I had to do was write it down—it was like taking dictation. It was ten years since her short life had ended and I have no idea what suddenly flipped this particular switch in my brain, but it removed whatever poetic block had been there and started me writing again. I believe this process is called *vers donné*. It has happened to me a few times, though never quite so dramatically or completely, and if I occasionally 'receive' a stanza or part of a poem, I usually have to work very hard to match or complete it. This poem, *'Why Were you Born?'* arrived ready made. I'm certainly not claiming that it's especially good, but where did it come from? I've no idea. The subconscious mind is very odd. From then on I started to have occasional poems published, mostly countryside ones, in magazines such as *The Field, Country Life* or *The Countryman*, which delighted me, but when rejection slips also started to come in I feebly lost confidence again. I didn't stop writing poems but I gave up sending them out for ages. I didn't realise that rejection slips are the lot of most embryonic writers and you continually have to cut, revise, improve… and above all persist. I seldom showed my efforts to anyone, except occasionally to my brother David who has always been my great supporter. That I eventually mustered up enough perseverance to start sending work out again and getting it published was in no small way due to his enthusiasm. I owe a debt of gratitude to the late Laurence Cotterell, a life vice president of the Poetry Society, for his faith in me and his insistence that I should persevere. I started to receive welcome encouragement and criticism from the editors of various poetry magazines and also from fellow Yorkshire poets, in particular the Pennine Poets and the Aireings group of poets. Pauline Kirk, herself an acclaimed poet who is now my editor and publisher at Fighting Cock Press, was a fellow member of both these groups. I value her judgement and am hugely grateful for her support. Charlie was always keen for me to follow my own star and was delighted when I met with any success—so long as he didn't have to read my poetic attempts! He claimed to be tone deaf to the music of words and usually thought my ideas were most peculiar anyway.

I have written in *The Bird of My Loving* about my growing interest in healing, the effects of mind and spirit on physical health—and vice versa—and the bringing together of orthodox medicine with complementary therapies. I started to go each spring with a party of fellow 'seekers' ('Mum's cranky friends' to my children!) to the island of Iona and got involved in a doctors' and healers' network. At a meeting of the latter someone once remarked that though there are always lots of doctor and nurse jokes, plenty of send-ups of vicars, monks and nuns, there didn't seem to be many jokes about healers— so I thought I'd write one. I have included the result at the end of the last chapter. It first appeared on the cover of *Network*, the magazine of the Mystics and Scientists Association, together with a brilliant cartoon by Robin Chapman Campbell, and it has been requested and read on *Poetry Please* on Radio Four. If one is going to dabble in the ever-fascinating occult, or the esoteric world of the healing arts, then I think a sense of humour and a healthy sense of scepticism are good accompaniments—and laughter is always wonderful medicine.

Of course there were normal family ups and downs during this period, but we had some years of great happiness before health problems loomed again. Charlie's cancer—miraculously, considering the degree of malignancy and the dire warnings I'd been given— never recurred, but two weeks before our silver wedding he had his first major coronary and this issued in another period of drama and anxiety. Charlie's final years were dogged by illness—including a stroke, a degenerative neuropathy and several major, though not malignant, abdominal operations. We lurched from crisis to crisis. Charlie, the most athletic and active of men, bore his increasing incapacity with extraordinary fortitude, dignity and humour and I was enormously proud of him—but watching someone you love suffer over a long period is tough and it was often hard for both of us. An electric buggy, which became his garden legs, enabled him to get around his beloved garden and the making of an amazing needlepoint screen—the Arthington Tapestry—designed by artist and muralist Graham Rust helped to keep his life productive and fulfilling. Our children called it 'Dad's indoor gardening'. Graham had painted spectacular murals in the house for us in 1973 and remains a special family friend. I shall always be grateful to him for his part in helping to transform the frustrations of Charlie's last years into something so creative. Soon after it was finished the screen was borrowed for an exhibition in London called *The Glory of the Garden*, jointly sponsored by Sotheby's and the RHS. We glowed with pride when it got a special mention in a review on Radio 4 by Roy Strong. If anyone had told me in our early married days that Charlie would become an expert and dedicated stitcher, I would have thought they were completely mad. The screen is now my most treasured possession.

The support of our three children was constant and we gained two very beloved sons-in-law, Charles Cox and Robert Tamworth, and our first six grandchildren who all gave Charlie enormous pleasure and interest. Belinda and Susannah frequently brought their families to stay and the house once more came alive to racing feet and the shrieks of children's laughter—and occasionally their tantrums too! Skiing was no longer an option but we had some memorable family holidays in Corfu before travel became impossible for Charlie. It became a special place to us all and some years later I set my fifth novel, *The Venetian House*, mainly in Corfu and loved writing about the island, with its long history of occupation by the Venetians, its magical scenery, changing light and kingfisher colours. Sadly Charlie died shortly before William got engaged to my now much loved daughter-in-law Alice Robertson—though he met her several times not long before his death when Will invited her to stay for weekends. Charlie took to her at once and had shrewdly asked me if I thought this new girlfriend might turn out to be *'the* one'—but alas he never knew about their marriage or their two delightful children, who have brought our quota of grandchildren up to eight. I so much wish they could have known him too.

My parents had eventually left North Wales. Cefn became too isolated once my father's health started to fail, so they moved into the larger of our two flats at Arthington. They missed the Conwy Valley very much but on the whole the arrangement worked extremely well. They both ended their days with us in Yorkshire, though my mother outlived my father by several years and reached an indomitable ninety-one, still firing on all cylinders. She was still driving—not much more dangerously than she had ever done—till five weeks before her death. At just short of ninety she was prosecuted for reckless driving in Harrogate. When a police officer turned up at Arthington to interview her about the incident—of which she had been blissfully unaware—and inspect her car for dents and scratches (no shortage of either) Mum floored him by her reply: 'Don't be ridiculous Officer!' she said. 'There isn't enough room in Harrogate to *be* reckless!' I have a treasured recording of her on tape telling me how she was originally taught to drive by my great-grandfather's old coachman-turned-chauffeur, who greatly preferred horses to engines, and how he had advised her never to allow herself to be pushed off the crown of the road. 'And I never have' said my mother triumphantly—which was wonderfully true of her in more ways than one.

At Needlepoint
For C.E.W.S.

You hold your life
together with stitches,
force frayed thread
through the narrowing eye
of each day's sharp needle
And ward off death
with a bodkin.

Once you climbed mountains
hit boundaries, served aces;
planted avenues of poplars,
nurtured *Loderi St. George*
and grew exotic fruit.
You pruned vines from the top
of a tall ladder.

Now with great effort
you dig embroidered gardens
and labour in herbaceous
needlepoint. Each vanquished row
is the end of a tournament
and you ski down your precipice
on a strand of wool.

They are very beautiful
these new flowers you grow:
you still use green fingers
but cultivate strange plants
in an unlikely climate—
and nothing can unravel
the tapestry of our love.

Arthington Viaduct

An ectoplasm of a morning . . .

. . . and the viaduct looms
above the River Wharfe
to hump its arches over the haze
unsettling as a sighting
of the Loch Ness monster.

A banshee wail echoes eerily
as a ghost train rattles
over slippery rails to be
swallowed by the tunnel's mouth
—and lost to view.

Mist is a rising sea of doubt;
questions swirl and hover;
hide hopes; veil ancient beliefs.
When will the sun rise again
to dispel uncertainty?

17

NEW BEGINNINGS

CHARLIE died in April 1991. After many false alarms and amazing recoveries—each of which left him a little weaker than the last—I knew for certain that the end was really approaching when he suddenly said to me 'This one's got me. I'm not getting better,' Against all the doctors' predictions, he had never admitted such a possibility before, but he'd endured so many terrifying emergency dashes to hospital in the last few years that it was a great relief to me that when he finally died he was at home with me, in his beloved Arthington and having seen each of his adored three children during his last week. I could not have wanted him to battle on any longer but I missed him dreadfully.

We took comfort in planning Charlie's funeral service, helped by our vicar, Denys de la Hoyde. Some previous vicars of Arthington, of which Charlie was the patron, had occasionally felt terrorised by Charlie, but Denys was different. Though they had only known each other in Charlie's last years as an invalid, they had come to love and respect each other. Charlie had always enjoyed organizing services himself, so although he left no list of specific wishes we had a clear idea of his likes and dislikes. Belinda, Susannah and I went wild doing the flowers for the church, determined to have a riot of the colours Charlie loved. Perhaps it looked more suitable for a wedding than a funeral but it seemed right to us. The Church was packed and we felt wonderfully supported by neighbours and friends. William read the lesson from St John, 'In the beginning was the Word' which we had so often heard Charlie read at Christmas, and read it so clearly and beautifully we were all deeply moved, but when Brian Johnson, that veteran broadcaster, read the passage on death by Canon Henry Scott-Holland, he nearly came unstuck—and that was moving too.

Later that summer Nick and Tim Dawson kindly let us have a memorial service at Sunningdale. We wore our brightest clothes in

Charlie's honour and chose more of his favourite hymns; Nick gave a wonderful address and the school choir excelled themselves. We had wanted it to be as joyful an occasion as possible—there were so many happy times for which to be thankful—and I think we succeeded, but I had not taken account of the flood of memories it would release in me of our early married days and I found myself struggling. Some weeks previously, Bamber Gascoigne, who read a lesson at the service, had invited me to go with him and Christina to a performance of Tosca at Covent Garden with Placido Domingo and Maria Ewing. After the service, I wasn't sure that I was going to make it but it turned out to be a catharsis to attend such an unforgettable performance and to go, vicariously, through such passionate feelings unconnected with my own private emotions. It was a wonderful evening.

Change can be hard to face but decay is even harder. After our happy halcyon years both house and garden had started to deteriorate again and we no longer had the resources to deal with this. Following Charlie's death we discovered we had serious financial difficulties to cope with. It looked as though we were would have to part with the family home, but perhaps rash and impractical decisions run in the blood because though the only remaining farm out of the original four now had to be sold as well, William and Alice are still living in the house with their children—as happily, and as crazily as we did. Alice once said to me 'You had a love affair with this house. I've got an arranged marriage!' I think she loves it too now but who can tell what the future will bring?

Will was working for Sotheby's in London when Charlie died but with wonderful timing was moved up to Yorkshire the following January to run their Harrogate office. He and Alice took over the big house eighteen months after Charlie's death. I bought an old stone cottage five miles away on a hill above the Washburn Valley, where Turner tramped the moors when staying at nearby Farnley Hall with his patron, Walter Fawkes, and where he painted so many of his Yorkshire watercolours. I moved there with three beloved dogs—and enough misgivings about starting a new life on my own to sink a battleship. It was here that I intended to try to keep the promise I mentioned at the beginning of this book: the promise which I had made to Charlie just before he died, to try to take my writing seriously when I was living on my own.

To begin with I felt horribly disenchanted with myself. I got up each morning full of good intentions—and went to bed in a state of misery not having written a word. Then I saw an advertisement for a correspondence course in journalism and as a way of putting jump-leads on my flat batteries I signed on—and had a colossal stroke of luck. The luck was that my tutor on the course was Dr Hilary Johnson, to whom I owe the start of my professional writing career. Hilary, herself a good poet, was a creative writing tutor as well as a scout for a literary agency and a publishing house. She was—and is—a marvellously shrewd and helpful critic who now runs her own Authors' Advisory Service. After I'd completed the first four lessons Hilary wrote to say she thought I should show her the 'dud' novel which I'd mentioned that I'd written a few years earlier, spurred on by the encouragement I'd received during a five day writing course at the Arvon Foundation at Lumb Bank near Hebden Bridge. I had submitted the finished manuscript to three different publishers, but after three rejections in quick succession had decided that though it had been enormous fun writing it, it obviously wasn't good enough for publication. Now, with no great optimism, I dug the dog-eared manuscript out of a drawer and sent it off to Hilary. When she rang me up to ask if I'd mind if she showed it to a friend of hers who was a literary agent, I was rendered speechless for several moments— something my son would say is very unusual. MIND??!

My next bit of luck was that the agent in question was Sarah Molloy at A. M. Heath to whom I also owe so much. She in her turn sent my novel to Century, where Lizzie Buchan, then one of their commissioning editors, though soon to give up editing to concentrate on her own brilliant novels, sent me a lot of extremely perspicacious criticism—but she also said the book was funny and she thought I could write. Was I prepared to change the improbable plot and rewrite the whole book, bearing her criticisms in mind? If so, Century would make no promise to publish it, but they would guarantee to read it again. Of course I said yes. When I eventually heard that my new version of *A Price for Everything* had been accepted, I first of all felt totally euphoric … and then I cried and cried because Charlie was not there to share the moment with me. In an interview for The Times after its publication I said I hoped my late-flowering success might give hope to other widows or widowers facing change and got quite a spate of letters from people saying that my story had given them encouragement.

When Kate Parkin, then managing director of Century, took me out to lunch to celebrate her acceptance of my book, she asked what my second novel was going to be about. *Second novel?* I hadn't dared to give such a possibility any serious thought, but intercepting a meaningful look from my agent, Sarah Molloy, I announced that I might set it in a boys' prep school as I felt this was a world I could portray with confidence. 'Fine,' said Kate. 'Let me have a synopsis next week.' So I did.

My first novel had been about family life and the efforts to save a crumbling house and a crumbling marriage. As far as the house—though not the marriage—was concerned I was drawing on first-hand experience. After years of living at Arthington there wasn't much I didn't know about leaking roofs, decaying plasterwork, dry rot and burst pipes. My two sons-in-law nicknamed me *Mumma-the-plumber* and invented the theory that I have missed my true vocation. They couldn't be more wrong though I admit to owning a blowtorch which I have found equally useful for thawing frozen pipes or making crème brûlée. Writing fiction is a bit like making soup—you never quite know how it's going to end up: you throw a whole lot of ingredients into a blender, using whatever is to hand, season the mixture highly, whizz it all together and transform it into something different. In my sixth novel, *Secrets and Shadows*, one of my characters, an author who is giving a lecture at a writing course, tells his audience: '*Most of us who write fiction have never outgrown the childish ability to live in a fantasy world and have imaginary companions unseen by anyone else.*' This is certainly true of me. Perhaps novelists are mentally retarded!

My second novel introduced me to the pleasures of research, of a non-academic nature. Because it was so long since I'd actually lived in a school I felt I needed to bring myself up to date with various changes and by this time I not only had two grandsons, William Shirley and Geordie Cox, at Sunningdale, eager to give me colourful—though not always reliable—updated information, but the Dawsons bravely agreed to have me to stay and let me loose to talk to anyone I chose. 'Oh do put that *awful* tape recorder away!' said Nick nervously when I picked his brains. My heroine in this book was a young flautist and I loved researching her career and was amazed at how helpful various professional musicians were. One of my new neighbours, Stina Bisengaliev, was principal flute with The Northern Philharmonia— the orchestra of Opera North—and was endlessly kind in checking anything I'd written for possible mistakes, talking to me about performing and organizing for me to sit in on rehearsals. I dedicated this book to George and Patricia Harewood with whom Charlie and I enjoyed so much music and their advice was invaluable too. When I was writing *The Venetian House*, George also generously agreed to talk to me about his experiences in the war of being badly wounded and taken prisoner. Other friends I consulted had overwhelmed me with technical details about tanks and guns but George provided me with just the sort of personal snippets an author wants. 'What was the worst thing you remember about being wounded?' I asked him and he immediately answered: 'The over–inflated tyres of the ambulance over fifty miles of appallingly rutted roads to the nearest field hospital when I'd just been shot up the backside,' a bit of information that made my toes curl in my shoes.

In my third novel, *Picking Up the Pieces*, there is a character who is a monk and I needed to know what the Roman Catholic Church's attitude might be under certain circumstances. I was given an introduction to a well known Benedictine boys' school where I was lucky enough to spend a happy and hilarious afternoon with the Father Prior who completely entered into the spirit of my project, seemed much amused by my questions and was wonderfully helpful. When the book came out I sent him a copy saying he did not need to plough through the whole book but might just like to glance at the relevant chapter. I was touched and delighted to get a card back from him saying: 'You got your monk exactly right'.

It was while I was writing my second novel that I was unexpectedly approached through Sarah Molloy to write a book on bereavement. I was stunned and initially said no. However when I had finished *Facing the Music* I agreed to meet Susan Watt, then managing director of Michael Joseph, whose idea it was to publish a book about coming to terms with loss, not written as a 'how to' book by professional counsellors but from an ordinary person's own experience. She had herself suffered a terrible tragedy when her husband, David, a well known political journalist, had picked up a live electric cable and been instantly killed, leaving her with four young boys to bring up. I went to London to meet Susan and liked and trusted her immediately but was very doubtful as to whether I could write such a book. However I agreed to try to put my own feelings on paper provided I could also draw on other people's stories—including hers—and not limit it to my own experience. I shall always be grateful to the friends who were brave and generous enough to share their own journeys through loss and sadness with me. They made the book. The result was *The Bird of my Loving—a personal response to loss and grief,* which became a Penguin paperback. This book has brought me a large postbag from all sorts of people many of whose traumas have been infinitely worse than anything I've had to face but who say they have been comforted to read about shared difficulties and emotions. I have found their response both humbling and uplifting.

During this period another surprising new venture also came my way which was to prove both challenging and hugely enjoyable. I'd attended a concert on Iona given by singer and classical guitarist Caroline McCausland and the following evening was persuaded to read a few of my poems in the St Columba Hotel where I was staying with my Network of 'seekers' whom my son William had christened *The Crusties* (Cranky Upwardly Spiritual Tryers). As well as her solo performances Caroline had given several joint concerts of words and music with broadcaster Richard Baker and now unexpectedly asked me if I would consider collaborating with her to give a concert combining music and my own poetry. I was very surprised but also flattered and despite being extremely dubious about my capabilities, I rashly agreed. Caroline is one of those people who manage to persuade you that you can do almost anything—while you are with her. It's after you have agreed to do whatever she has suggested and she's whisked off to some other enterprise that the doubts set in! However, our first joint performance in Cirencester in aid of a hospice was a great success. It was the beginning of an enormously happy partnership and for the next ten years we did several concerts a year and helped to raise considerable amounts of money in aid of various charities in many very different locations. We loved working together and trying to arrange programmes to suit the audiences and the particular causes for whom we were appearing. Writing is inevitably a solitary pursuit and this collaboration with someone else was a marvellous contrast and greatly enriched my life. Caroline taught me everything I know about performing.

Another new experience was giving talks, arranged by the publishers, in various venues to promote my books. On the first such occasion, in Leeds City Library, I had felt very nervous beforehand but allowed myself to be quite pleased with how it had gone. When I was signing books afterwards, an elderly lady came up to make herself known. 'You've really done something for me this afternoon,' she said. 'You've changed my life.' I felt myself start to glow with pride. 'My doctor's been on at me for months to get a hearing aid but I've never fancied the idea,' she went on, 'but I came in late and sat at the back and we'll never know if I'd have enjoyed your little talk because I couldn't hear a word you said.' She beamed at me. 'The doctor's going to be ever so pleased with me because it's finally decided me to try a deaf aid and I thought you'd like to know.' I expressed myself delighted for her and laughed at myself for my deflated ego all the way home. On another occasion I was asked to give a talk at the delightful little theatre in Chipping Norton where Graham Rust had been commissioned to paint pantomime murals when it was renovated with Lottery funding. The audience were surprised to learn that I had modelled for him as both the Ugly Sisters in *Cinderella*—one fat, one thin! I was relieved that my listeners had not immediately recognized me from the caricatures on the wall.

Poetry was—still is—my first love and I was thrilled to have four small volumes of poetry published as well as having verse accepted by various magazines. It was a particular pleasure to have occasional poems in *The Spectator* and I felt very honoured when John Julius Norwich asked if he could include one of my poems in his Millennium anthology of *Christmas Crackers*.

I love writing about places and children and family relationships. My grandchildren and their friends help to keep me up to date with changing lifestyles and the jargon of a younger generation. This can be a tightrope for a novelist, because fashions in words change so quickly: to use slang too freely is to risk your work dating very quickly but if you set your story in contemporary times and fail to keep abreast of current trends, then dialogue can seem stuffy and unconvincing. Knowingly or unknowingly my grandchildren have all helped me enormously with my writing. One grandchild, James, who has special needs, has not only been a considerable catalyst for my poetry but provided me with the inspiration for a character in my fourth novel *Off Balance*. It was Charlie and Belinda's suggestion that I should write about a child not only with learning difficulties but some physical disabilities too. Belinda, who has fought many battles for James with remarkable results, said to me 'There are important things that might be said—but in a light sort of way—not just about the pains and heartache but about the joys and triumphs of bringing up a child like James. Why don't you include one in your next novel, Mum?' So I did. The character of Edward in my book does not present an exact picture of James, but draws on experiences gained from him and the other young people I've met through him. We have all been enriched by what we have learned from James who is a very beloved member of our family. I ended *The Bird of my Loving* with my favourite quotation from Callisthenes; '*Laughter is Man's declaration of freedom. It is his refusal to go into bondage to his troubles.*' It seems especially relevant to James. There have been many occasions for either laughter or tears, but as well as a highly original mind, he has a marvellous sense of humour himself and laughter has usually prevailed. When James's younger brother Geordie Cox was seven it was suggested to his form at school that they should ask their grandmothers to write a letter about what it was like growing up during the war. When my letter was read out to the class, Geordie apparently leapt to his feet and said: 'I *told* you I had a wild writing Granny!'... hence the title of this book.

It has been a wonderful change from writing novels to take this trip into my past because all the material was already in existence and I have not had to try and conjure anything out of my imagination—which may be the excitement but is also the terror of writing fiction. To have found a career so late in life has been a tremendous bonus; it has been a huge surprise and pleasure to have my novels translated into seven languages; I have gained new friends and new experiences—and above all it has given me some self-respect because I do believe that if you have a talent, however small it may be, you should try to use it—though it certainly took me a long time to do so.

My time at West Winds, the aptly named little house built up the side of a hill where I started my writing career, turned out to be unexpectedly fruitful and I had twelve happy years there, but just before the Millennium I had a very bad fall and fractured my right leg in several places which put me in a wheelchair for three months and on crutches for five. Though the surgeon did an amazing job of pinning me together and I made an almost complete recovery, it made me realise that West Winds, with all its different levels, steep stairs and many stone steps—which up to then had not bothered me at all—would not make an ideal house for my declining years. I was in no hurry to move and particularly wanted to stay near my Yorkshire grandchildren while they were growing up, but realised it might be a clever idea to move while I was still comparatively hale and hearty and in a position to make a choice. When a charming old croft, all on one level and situated on the edge of my son-in-law Charlie Cox's farm in Perthshire, unexpectedly came up for sale, it seemed too good a chance to be missed, and with all my family's approval I moved up to Scotland. I am lucky to have yet another house with lovely views; to be surrounded by stunning countryside with fascinating wildlife and best of all, still to have family near at hand.

I have been blessed in so many ways. I can't express how much my writing career helped me to come to terms with loss after Charlie died and to move forwards with my life. Of course I missed him—even after all these years, I often still do; of course there have been times of loneliness and private sadness but friends have been wonderfully hospitable and I still have a lot of fun. Above all I've loved the companionship of my three grown-up children—and their spouses— and the fun of sharing in their family lives. It is wonderful indeed when not only children, but also grandchildren, become one's best friends. I hope my grandparents got even half as much pleasure and interest out of us as I get from my eight grandchildren. They couldn't possibly have got more.

Old age brings many changes but I still love storytelling and since starting this memoir I have embarked on a seventh novel, had a fifth small volume of poetry published—and have turned eighty. My wonderful family took me to Corfu to celebrate this big birthday, where we had a magical week of sun and sea and laughter to add to my treasure-store of happy memories. Inevitably the greatest change of all cannot lie so very far ahead for me now so the future is even more shrouded in mystery than usual. But if consciousness survives death, then I expect the unexpected—and I have always believed in travelling hopefully.

I hope I may continue to be 'a wild writing Granny' for a few more years yet.

James's Song

Oh did you volunteer to come
and how long will you stay
and can we learn enough of love
before you slip away?

We greeted you with fear and grief
you seemed beyond our reach
but now we know a child of light
who has so much to teach.

Sometimes you look with baffled eyes
which fills our hearts with pain.
oh is it that we are obtuse
and you cannot explain?

We march our roads with hustled tread
you step a different pace
but your path may be more direct
to reach your special place.

Oh did you volunteer to come
and how long will you stay
to teach us unconditional love
before you go away?

ACKNOWLEDGEMENTS

I owe a huge debt of gratitude to Caroline Knox for her generous help and constructive criticism during the writing of this book: without her wonderful encouragement I might well not have persevered with it.

My thanks and much appreciation go to my editor and publisher, George Ramsden, for the trouble he has taken. I should like to thank Hilary Johnson, who was so instrumental in launching my career as a published writer, for her continued enthusiasm over the years, and a thank you, as always, goes to my agent Sarah Molloy.

I have been lucky to have many wonderful friends over the years who have enhanced my life and would like to thank them all—whether their names appear in these pages or not.

Above all I would like to pay a heartfelt tribute to my family who have shared so much fun and laughter with me and been an unfailing source of love and support through many ups and downs. Special thanks go to my brother David for his faith in my writing and to my invaluable team of home-grown editors: my daughters Belinda Cox and Susannah Tamworth and especially my daughter-in-law Alice Sheepshanks for all her patient proofreading.

*

Some of the poems in this book first appeared in The Spectator, The Countryman, Outposts, Pennine Platform and Aireings.